C000264665

AUTOETHNOGRAPHY

SERIES IN UNDERSTANDING STATISTICS

S. NATASHA BERETVAS   Series Editor

SERIES IN UNDERSTANDING MEASUREMENT

S. NATASHA BERETVAS   Series Editor

SERIES IN UNDERSTANDING QUALITATIVE RESEARCH

PATRICIA LEAVY   Series Editor

TONY E. ADAMS
STACY HOLMAN JONES
CAROLYN ELLIS

AUTOETHNOGRAPHY

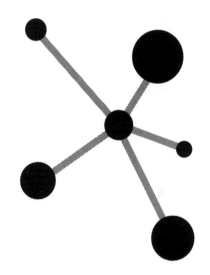

OXFORD
UNIVERSITY PRESS

OXFORD
UNIVERSITY PRESS

Oxford University Press is a department of the University of Oxford.
It furthers the University's objective of excellence in research, scholarship,
and education by publishing worldwide.

Oxford   New York
Auckland   Cape Town   Dar es Salaam   Hong Kong   Karachi
Kuala Lumpur   Madrid   Melbourne   Mexico City   Nairobi
New Delhi   Shanghai   Taipei   Toronto

With offices in
Argentina   Austria   Brazil   Chile   Czech Republic   France   Greece
Guatemala   Hungary   Italy   Japan   Poland   Portugal   Singapore
South Korea   Switzerland   Thailand   Turkey   Ukraine   Vietnam

Oxford is a registered trademark of Oxford University Press
in the UK and certain other countries.

Published in the United States of America by
Oxford University Press
198 Madison Avenue, New York, NY 10016

© Oxford University Press 2015

All rights reserved. No part of this publication may be reproduced, stored in
a retrieval system, or transmitted, in any form or by any means, without the prior
permission in writing of Oxford University Press, or as expressly permitted by law,
by license, or under terms agreed with the appropriate reproduction rights
organization. Inquiries concerning reproduction outside the scope of the above should
be sent to the Rights Department, Oxford University Press, at the address above.

You must not circulate this work in any other form
and you must impose this same condition on any acquirer.

Library of Congress Cataloging-in-Publication Data
Adams, Tony E.
Autoethnography / Tony E. Adams, Stacy Holman Jones, Carolyn Ellis.
   pages cm
Includes bibliographical references and index.
ISBN 978-0-19-997209-8
1. Ethnology—Authorship.   I. Holman Jones, Stacy Linn, 1966–   II. Ellis, Carolyn,
1950–   III. Title.
GN307.7.A33 2015
305.8'00723—dc23
2014012167

9 8 7 6 5 4 3 2 1
Printed in the United States of America
on acid-free paper

CONTENTS

ACKNOWLEDGMENTS

Writing this book has been a challenge and a joy. Translating our knowledge about and experience with autoethnography into an interesting story and a useful resource challenged us to make our values, approaches to research, and writing practices manifest on the page. Sharing the ways our autoethnographic work has enriched and deepened our research practices and everyday lives has left us feeling humble, grateful, and full of optimism about the future of autoethnography and qualitative scholarship.

Of course, writing a book doesn't happen in isolation. Here, we would like to thank the people who have supported our work on this project and throughout our research and writing lives. We especially thank Patricia Leavy for making this book possible; it is an honor to work with you and to publish in your book series. Your support and editorship have been invaluable.

Tony

I am grateful to many others for their support of my life and work, including Brett Aldridge, Mitch Allen, Nilanjana Bardhan, Christopher Birdsong, Derek Bolen, Robin Boylorn, Jay Brower, Marcy Chvasta, Ken Cissna, Norman Denzin, Rachel

Dubrofsky, Craig Engstrom, Brian Flowers, Brad Gangnon, Craig Gingrich-Philbrook, Jonny Gray, Andrew Herrmann, Kim Kline, Lenore Langsdorf, Michael LeVan, Jimmie Manning, Michaela Meyer, Nicole Neuman, Mark Neumann, Ron Pelias, Sandy Pensoneau-Conway, Carl Ratner, Jillian Tullis, John Warren, Jules Wight, Jonathan Wyatt, and Stephanie Young. I appreciate my students and colleagues at Northeastern Illinois University, including Wilfredo Alvarez, Anna Antaramian, Katrina Bell-Jordan, Bernard Brommel, Rodney Higginbotham, Kristen Hunt, Alan Mace, Nancy McVittie, Cyndi Moran, Seung-Hwan Mun, Shayne Pepper, Nanette Potee, Edie Rubinowitz, and Angie Sweigart-Gallagher.

I thank Keith Berry for the everyday, meaningful, and loving banter, and I thank Art Bochner for his continued care, love, encouragement, mentorship, and support. I thank my stepfather, Michael Rome, and my parents, Phil Adams and Sheri Rome, for cultivating my strong work ethic and my compassion for others, and I thank Gerardo (Jerry) Moreno for loving me through many days of reading, writing, and editing.

I also thank Stacy for taking a risk to write with me many years ago; I love us and I look forward to our future collaborations. And I thank Carolyn for working with me on another project; I am grateful for the many personal and professional opportunities you've made available to me as well as your staunch support of me/my work. It is an honor and a blessing to work with you both.

Stacy

I'll begin by thanking Tony and Carolyn for making this work so rewarding and enjoyable. You are wonderful coauthors, editors, friends, and mentors. Carolyn, I am grateful that you and Art Bochner encouraged me to write autoethnography all those years ago and for creating opportunities for me to do my best research and writing ever since. Tony, I thank you for always being willing to take on projects, to talk and write, and to laugh with me. Our research and writing collaborations energize and sustain me. I hope we will always find the time and opportunity to work together.

I also thank all of my wonderful colleagues and students at California State University Northridge and at the University of South Florida, especially Ben Attias, Ashley Beard, Sakilé Camara, Aimee Carillo Rowe, Ken Cissna, Eric Eisenberg, Sara Dykins Callahan, Elizabeth Edgecomb, John Kephart, Adolfo Lagomasino, Michael LeVan, Kathryn Sorrells, Jillian Tullis, Lori Roscoe, and Rachel Silverman. I am grateful to the people who've taught me all I know about writing and performance: Art Bochner, Tessa Carr, Norman Denzin, Craig Gingrich-Philbrook, Bud Goodall, Paul Gray, Chris McRae, Lynn Miller, Jeanine Mingé, Omi Osun, Ron Pelias, Deanna Shoemaker, Kathleen Stewart, and Nick Trujillo. And I thank my longtime reading and writing friends Brenna Curtis, Georgine Hodgkinson, and Linda Yakle for their talents and good humor.

My research and writing life isn't possible without the love and support of my family. I thank my grandparents, William Blackburn and Bernice Holman, for encouraging the writer in me. I thank my parents, Dean and Mary Holman, for their love and support. And I thank my beautiful child for making our life together so meaningful and so much fun.

Carolyn

What an honor and privilege to work with Tony and Stacy again, the best dream team imaginable. They work hard and efficiently, challengingly and lovingly, with imagination and rigor, loving kindness and compassion. It is a scholar's greatest hope—that those who work beside and follow afterwards will surpass and enhance what already has been done. These two scholars exemplify that hope fulfilled. I have smiled the entire time we have worked on this project as I read their thoughtful prose and observed how they both always volunteer for whatever task needs to be done. That's not quite right—they don't volunteer, they just do it. Most impressive is that they led the way in modeling how three authors might write together. They said to me, "It's not necessary to use Microsoft Word Editing. Just make the changes that are needed." At first hesitant, I joined in, and we all freely edited each other's words time and time again. The result, I think, is a thoroughly integrated text composed of three voices where our words and thoughts blend together yet our individual voices still twinkle through.

Thanks to all of you who have contributed to autoethnography by writing your and others' vulnerable selves, supporting and assisting those who need to write, reading and valuing this work, and adding your voices in myriad ways to the growing movement. What a wonderful time to be qualitative researchers who care about vulnerable selves and about contributing to the kind of world we hope to live in. I acknowledge my partner Art Bochner, along with Buddha and Zen, and colleagues and students—all who remind me to approach each day mindfully, open to wonder and surprise, filled with passion and love, and ready to embrace the new day with gusto.

AUTOETHNOGRAPHY

INTRODUCTION TO AUTOETHNOGRAPHY

What Is Autoethnography?

Writer Joan Didion notes simply and powerfully, "we tell stories in order to live."[1] In this book, we embrace Didion's call, believing the stories we tell enable us to live and to live *better*; stories allow us to lead more reflective, more meaningful, and more just lives. The stories we discuss in this book—*autoethnographic stories*—are stories of/about the self told through the lens of culture. Autoethnographic stories are artistic and analytic demonstrations of how we come to know, name, and interpret personal and cultural experience. With autoethnography, we use our experience to engage ourselves, others, culture(s), politics, and social research.[2] In doing autoethnography, we confront "the tension between insider and outsider perspectives, between social practice and social constraint."[3] Hence, autoethnography is a research method that:

- Uses a researcher's personal experience to describe and critique cultural beliefs, practices, and experiences.[4]
- Acknowledges and values a researcher's relationships with others.[5]

- Uses deep and careful self-reflection—typically referred to as "reflexivity"—to name and interrogate the intersections between self and society, the particular and the general, the personal and the political.[6]
- Shows "people in the process of figuring out what to do, how to live, and the meaning of their struggles."[7]
- Balances intellectual and methodological rigor, emotion, and creativity.[8]
- Strives for social justice and to make life better.[9]

The goal of this book is to demonstrate how qualitative researchers can use autoethnography as a research method. In this chapter, we tell our stories of coming to autoethnography, discuss the concerns and considerations that led to the development of autoethnographic methodologies, provide a brief history of autoethnography, and describe our plan for this volume. We hope this book will inspire you to use autoethnographic methods and provide you with ideas to explore and guidelines for researching and writing your autoethnographies.

A note on our writing and citation choices: As you may have noticed, we use endnotes to document our sources and/or elaborate our ideas. We do this for two reasons. First, we want to keep the primary text as readable as possible; an abundance of citations can interrupt and clutter the narrative. Second, while the primary text tells *one* story about autoethnography, the endnotes provide an additional, and perhaps more nuanced, account of the method. This secondary text also offers you additional resources for doing and thinking about autoethnography. You can decide how to read the text—for example, you might read the primary text all the way through and then turn your attention to the endnotes; other readers might move from primary text to endnotes and back, while still others might turn first to the endnotes. Choose whatever reading method is most comfortable and helpful to you.

Coming to Autoethnography

Carolyn

I have been an ethnographer all my life. I also have been interested in peoples' emotions and intentions, how they create meaningful lives, and how they experience and cope with the problems of living.[10] During the 1970s, I had the good fortune of being at Stony Brook University, majoring in sociology. There I was able to pursue my interests and immerse myself in the ethnographic study of community. Positivism ruled in those days, particularly in sociology departments—it still does—and I was encouraged to emphasize systematic data collection and traditional analysis over imagination and storytelling. In 1982, while an assistant professor in sociology at University of South Florida (USF), my brother died in a plane crash. That event, and having a partner in the last stages of emphysema, led me to begin keeping notes on my relational and personal experiences of grief and loss, which eventually resulted in some of my first autoethnographic writing.[11] In 1996, I moved to the Communication Department at USF and there I was able to continue the work that connected my sociological eye with a communicative heart.[12] Autoethnography fulfilled me as it combined my interests in ethnography, social psychology of the self and role-taking, subjectivity and emotionality, face-to-face communication and interaction, writing as inquiry and evocation, storytelling, and my social work orientation toward social justice and giving back to the community.

Unlike the stories that Stacy Holman Jones and Tony Adams will tell below, I did not have "mentors" in autoethnography, and initially it was challenging to get this work accepted and published. What I did have, though, were like-minded colleagues and friends—Art Bochner, Norman Denzin, Laurel Richardson, Buddy Goodall, Mitch Allen, Ron Pelias, and many, many more—who encouraged and supported autoethnographic work within an intellectual environment where postmodern, poststructuralist, and feminist writers were contesting issues of authority, representation, voice, and method. Once Art and I joined our work and lives, the synergy propelled our autoethnographic and narrative projects forward.[13] We turned our energy to connecting social science and humanities; to making scholarship more human, useful, emotional, and evocative; to developing a research program in which we could mentor students in interpretive social science with a focus on narrative and autoethnography; and to contribute more meaningfully to the world in which we live.

Once immersed in Communication I was fortunate to have many supportive colleagues, especially Stacy, then a colleague in my department, who early on embraced autoethnography and continues now to carry the autoethnographic "torch" in so many wonderful ways. Together she and I were privileged to have many superb students, including Tony, who came to us already versed in autoethnography and eager to get on with telling their stories. I learn much from this younger generation of autoethnographers, and I am confident in their ability and desire to carry on the autoethnographic movement in academia.

I continue to write stories that start from and explore my relational and emotional life. In this book, I refer to my stories on minor bodily stigma, including tales of my own aging; emotional stories about loved ones in my life, such as caring for my mother and losing my brother; stories of relationships with neighbors, which bring up issues of social justice and extend my interest in ethics and method; and, most recently, stories about the lives of Holocaust survivors. In the latter, my focus has turned to "collaborative witnessing," a form of relational autoethnography that works to evocatively tell the experiences of others in shared storytelling and conversation.[14] I continue to do work that is a "calling" and the cornerstone of that work is autoethnography. In this book, I hope to further convey my passion for autoethnography, show how writing has positively affected my life, and open the possibility that it might affect yours in similarly constructive ways.

Stacy

I grew up in a research tradition that included personal experience, valued story, and sought the literary. In a collaborative graduate seminar on ethnographic methods, Nick Trujillo taught me to consider every moment of our work—conducting fieldwork (and hanging out), creating field notes, reading the literature, discussing our research in the classroom, all of it—as experiences worth writing about deeply, analytically, and creatively. He also insisted that what we were doing constituted a worthwhile turn in the larger conversation about ethnography and autoethnography happening in and around qualitative research.[15] Later, as I worked on my Master's thesis, Nick encouraged, cajoled, and demanded—again and again—that I write the story, that I keep writing the story, that I just write the story. And so I wrote stories, lots of them.

When I left California State University Sacramento in 1996 for the University of Texas (UT), I carried my love of story into the performance studies classrooms of Paul Gray, Lynn Miller, and Omi Ọsun Olomo. Omi taught me that working at the intersection of performance and ethnography meant understanding fieldwork as personal and knowledge as an embodied, critical, and ethical exploration of culture.[16] Performance was a stage and a means for writing, telling, and living the story of my research with others. While at UT, I met Carolyn Ellis and Art Bochner, who understood and encouraged my commitments to autoethnography and performance as complementary and of equal importance. And so, I wrote and performed and merged the two in/as performative personal writing—work that I have been doing ever since.

My work has focused on telling stories that clearly locate the personal in the field, the writing, and the political contexts of the research. In my essay on autoethnography for the *Handbook of Qualitative Research*, I told some of my story about coming to autoethnography as an effort to create research that changes the world.[17] Tony and I have continued to tell these stories, particularly in our efforts to write autoethnography as a queer method.[18]

Today my work focuses less on the story of *doing* research and more on storying lives *as* research. I consider the power of texts to call us into and out of being, as well as how identities and lives are performed in relation to others, particularly stories about the shifting and changing nature of queer identities and the relationships and families we create in and through adoption.[19] Throughout this book, I will share several stories about my research, along with excerpts of the texts I have published on these topics. It is my hope that as I share my stories you will observe ways of merging your personal experiences in and through your research.

What autoethnography is teaching me today is this: telling our stories is a way for us to be present to each other; the act provides a space for us to create a relationship embodied in the performance of writing and reading that is reflective, critical, loving, and chosen in solidarity.[20] I grew up and was nurtured in a research tradition that embraced autoethnography as a legitimate, important, and *telling* methodology. Although choosing autoethnography wasn't a professional risk during my graduate education or early in my publishing career, telling personal stories in/as research always carries personal, relational, and ethical risks. I view these risks as necessary not only for our research but also for living meaningful lives and changing the world in important and vital ways. I hope that this book will encourage you to embrace writing and telling stories as not only a way of life but also a way to make life better—for you and for others.

Tony

I first encountered autoethnography when I entered the Master of Arts program in Speech Communication at Southern Illinois University Carbondale (SIUC) in 2001. Lenore Langsdorf, my thesis advisor, advocated for the use of narrative and personal experience in research, and I took courses on performance theory and autoethnography with Ron Pelias. Elyse Pineau and Craig Gingrich-Philbrook were doing innovative work on auto-performance and embodiment, and I took classes alongside many contemporary autoethnographers, including Keith Berry, Jay Brower, Nicole Defenbaugh, Scott Gust, Ben Myers, Sandy Pensoneau-Conway, Satoshi Toyosaki, Adrienne Viramontes, and Amber Zimmerman.

I began my Ph. D. at the University of South Florida (USF) in 2004. In my first semester, I took a course on Narrative Inquiry with Art Bochner, and my final paper evolved into my first autoethnographic publication about the strained relationship I had with my father.[21] I took another course with Art on the Social Construction of Reality and completed an independent study with him the following semester on narrative ethics.[22] Art soon agreed to direct my dissertation on narratives of coming out and continued to work with me to publish my dissertation as a book.[23]

At USF I also took a course on autoethnography and another on qualitative research with Carolyn, and Stacy and I began to investigate the fertile relationship between autoethnography and queer theory.[24] Many of my peers were working in/with autoethnography, including Robin Boylorn, Andrew Herrmann, Chris McRae, Jeanine Mingé, Patrick Santoro, and Jillian Tullis, and I continued to find myself supported by the legacy of prior USF autoethnographers, including Christine Davis, Laura Ellingson, Elissa Foster, Christine Kiesinger, and Lisa Tillmann.

Although I attended graduate programs that cultivated and embraced the use of personal narrative and lived experience, I initially steered clear of autoethnography as the primary research method for my dissertation; stubbornly, and ignorantly, I thought that the method would thwart the possibility of having an academic career. I worried more about pleasing (imagined) traditional scholars at other schools than about pleasing the professors with whom I worked and doing the work I felt mattered. Thus, for the first two years of my doctoral program, I formulated a more traditional ethnographic study to investigate mediated representations of the environment found at The Florida Aquarium. Though this research was intriguing, it did not satisfy me in the way that autoethnographic research on relationships would do, once I allowed myself to embrace this approach.

On February 28, 2006, near the end of my second year in the doctoral program, my life changed abruptly: Brett Aldridge, an ex-boyfriend and close friend from my time at SIUC, passed away. His sister told me that he died of diabetes-related causes, but two of his friends told me that Brett might have committed suicide after telling his father he was gay.[25]

Although I recognized that I could not find out for certain how Brett died—his physical presence was gone regardless of how he passed—I did reflect on the onslaught of negative commentary I had been experiencing in regard to coming out and sexual orientation. I recalled various homophobic experiences in the classroom and with students who tried to save me from my homosexuality; discriminatory practices centering on sexual orientation that others relayed to me; and the criticism of family members in response to my coming out and their attempts to silence any discussion of same-sex attraction.

These reflections forced me to contend with some of the ways people were ostracized because of their sexuality and who, as could have been the case with Brett, might turn to suicide after experiencing such pain. I also realized that although my work on the environment and at the aquarium was important, the intimate, personal, and relational work of same-sex attraction mattered much more; lesbian, gay, bisexual, transgender, and queer (LGBTQ) persons were being harmed by the ignorance and hate of others, and I could not let these injustices proceed unchallenged. Thus, I turned to doing the kind of work that mattered most to me and to bringing my emotions and experiences into the research process. I turned to writing stories that others could use in times of relational distress, and I re-turned to the original principles of my graduate education, especially to doing and living autoethnography.

* * *

As our stories illustrate, autoethnography is a method that allows us to reconsider how we think, how we do research and maintain relationships, and how we live. Our stories of coming to the method tell of moments when excluding or obscuring personal experiences felt uncomfortable, even impossible. Our stories are not unique to us; they also illustrate a change in how researchers approach their work. As we show in the next section, autoethnography developed in response to a series of concerns and considerations about social scientific research and qualitative inquiry.

The Development of Autoethnography

Three interrelated concerns and considerations about social scientific and qualitative research contributed to the formation of autoethnography: (1) new and changing ideas about and ideals for research, a recognition of the limits of scientific knowledge, and an emerging appreciation for personal narrative, story, the literary and the aesthetic, emotions, and the body; (2) a heightened concern about the ethics and politics of research practices and representations; and (3) the increased importance of social identities and identity politics.

Changing Idea(l)s of Research

Throughout my (Carolyn's) education as a researcher, I questioned how *social science* could leave out the particular, nuanced, and complex elements of *social life*. Personal experience, storytelling, care and emotions, and bodies were considered "feminine" and unpredictable and, therefore, a barrier to producing objective and rational research, even though subjectivity, experience, emotions, and bodies are integral elements of research and rationality.[26] If our task as researchers, as *social* scientists, is to study the social lives of humans, then we cannot relegate elements of human lives or experiences to the periphery, nor can we bracket out the ways our lives and experiences are intertwined with our research projects and participants. I did not believe in the "self-regulation, guilt, pain, the denial of pleasure and the silencing of voice" that was required to produce so-called proper academic subjectivities.[27] Nor did I think that the worst sin I could commit as a researcher was to be "too personal."[28] I valued the personal, and I wanted to include—even to *feature* it—in my work.

Further, the idea(l)s of prediction and control in the hard sciences (e.g., chemistry, physics, and biology) do not translate to the movements and meanings of humans in social interaction or speak to the significance of human thought and action. Although we may be able to make educated guesses about cultural patterns and practices, we can never *predict* what other people might think, say, or do. Nor can we establish singular, stable, or certain "truth" claims about human relationships. *Social* life is messy, uncertain, and emotional. If our desire is to research *social* life, then we must embrace a research method that, to the best of its/our ability, acknowledges and accommodates mess and chaos, uncertainty and emotion.

Thankfully, I was not alone in questioning the assumptions and transferability of scientific methods to the social sciences and qualitative research, particularly in ethnography. In the 1970s and 1980s, the idea that researchers could separate (researcher) selves from the research experience created a *crisis of representation* in the human disciplines (e.g., anthropology, communication, gender and race studies, sociology, psychology)—an " 'identity crisis' "[29] that "prompted a rethinking of the form and purpose of sociocultural investigation and description."[30] As anthropologist Renato Rosaldo says of the crisis, "The once dominant ideal of a detached observer using neutral language to explain 'raw' data has been displaced by an alternative project that attempts to understand human conduct as it unfolds through time and in relation to its meaning for the actors."[31]

The crisis of representation called into question many objectives and practices of mainstream social research, including:

- The goal of seeking universal Truths, especially with regard to social relations.[32]
- The possibility of making certain and stable knowledge claims about humans, experiences, relationships, and cultures.[33]

- The prohibition against stories and storytelling as ways of knowing.[34]
- The bias against affect and emotion.[35]
- The refusal to acknowledge "local knowledge"[36] and how social identities (e.g., race, sex, age, sexuality, ability, class) influence how persons research, read and interpret, and write and perform.[37]
- The (standard) use of colonialist and invasive ethnographic practices—going into and studying a culture, leaving to write about (represent) this culture, and disregarding member concerns, relational ethics, and what the representation might do to the culture.[38]

Social researchers started to "radically rethink" how they conducted and represented their research;[39] they desired more realistic and responsible ways of researching the experiences of others, raised concerns about what any person could "know, verify, and responsibly present as cultural 'truth,'" and wanted "accounts that foregrounded dialogue, incompleteness, the impossibility of separating or collapsing life from/into texts."[40] As Laurel Richardson states, "Many of us no longer wish to become the kinds of ethnographers—distant, removed, neutral, disengaged, above-it—traditional ethnography would have us be."[41]

For ethnographers, it became "necessary and desirable to recognize that we are part of what we study," and, as researchers, to show how we are "shaped and affected by our fieldwork experiences. To deny the self an active and situated place in the field," as Paul Atkinson, Amanda Coffey, and Sara Delamont write, "is only fooling ourselves."[42] Ethnographic texts began to reflect how "the self and the field become one—ethnography and autobiography are symbiotic."[43] Although including the ethnographer's point of view within a text and telling personal and reflexive stories using the conventions of literature had been a common but discounted and ignored practice of women anthropologists,[44] ethnographers soon began to produce works that openly embraced storytelling, personal experience, aesthetics, and literary practices.[45]

Researchers also began to show why emotions are integral to doing and understanding social research.[46] As Tami Spry notes, emotions emerged in research "as a reaction to the dominant specter of objectivity and realist ethnographic methods."[47] Emotions are, of course, a part of social life and how we relate to/with others. "We are more honest as scholars," Kathryn Blee writes, "when we acknowledge the myriad ways in which our personal lives and emotions are intertwined with who, what, and how we study."[48]

Considering emotions in research also meant that researchers confronted the absence or erasure of bodies—the researcher's and the participant's—in ethnographic work.[49] For instance, ethnographers who focused on the experience of anxiety, disability, illness, death, and dying recognized that they could not ignore the ways emotions infuse and are intertwined with physical experience and embodiment.[50]

In addition to concerns and considerations surrounding the uncertainty and flux of knowledge, researcher positionality, the role of personal experience, storytelling, aesthetic and literary practices, emotions, and the body, the crisis of representation also prompted researchers to consider and develop ethical responsibilities toward their research "subjects."

Concerns about the Ethics and Politics of Research

Traditional ethnographers once worked as documentarians, entering a (foreign, "exotic") culture, observing and often participating in the lives and activities of the community, making recordings and writing field notes, and then leaving to "write up" and publish a representation of the group. Historically, this representation was not shared with members of the studied group. However, researchers eventually came to understand such practices as unethical and incomplete. The researchers took advantage of often-vulnerable others—and, as we note above, their representations of these others often were incomplete because they omitted the ethnographer's history of, presence among, and experience with others, as well as the ethnographer's decisions in recording and representing them.

The ethics of research and representation are not only the concerns of documentarians or ethnographers. My (Tony) undergraduate degree is in "Radio and Television." As part of the program, I worked as a news reporter, attending community meetings and interviewing people about preselected topics. After these encounters, I returned to the radio station and wrote news stories, framing interviewees' words as I saw fit. However, every time I interviewed someone, I felt invasive and self-serving. I was interviewing—and possibly exploiting—people for *my* benefit—that is, to complete my coursework and advance my reporting career. Then, in graduate school, I learned about interviewing as part of a field research methods course. Interviewing people for research projects felt similar to the work I did as a reporter: find others to speak with about my topic and use the information they provide for my benefit.

I still struggle with questions about if, and why, I have the right to interview and represent the words and perspectives of others in my work. I value others' privacy and dignity as much as I value my privacy and dignity. As a gay man, I do not want people regulating whom I love; as a feminist, I want others—my family, the government, the medical industry—to leave my body and others' bodies alone. I believe that we have a responsibility to intervene when others are inflicting or are living amidst harm, but I also recognize that what may be defined as harm for one person may not be harm for another.[51] As a researcher, I am confident about my right (and privilege!) to speak for myself, but I am less confident about my right to speak on behalf of others.

Concerns about the ethics and politics of researching and representing others have occupied researchers and institutional review boards for decades (see Chapter 3). And for good reason: Researchers have committed terrible acts against participants in the name of science and the progress of knowledge. For example, consider how Stanley Milgram's research on "destructive obedience" made people "sweat, tremble, stutter, bite their lips, groan, and dig their fingernails into their flesh."[52] Or consider the treatment of participants in the Tuskegee Syphilis experiment, a study that between 1932 and 1972 investigated the effectiveness of various treatments for syphilis. The researchers—all of whom were White—solicited only poor, African American men infected with syphilis to participate in the study; they treated these men as "subjects, not patients; clinical material, not sick people."[53] When an effective treatment for syphilis was discovered in the 1940s, the researchers did not offer the treatment to participants because they did not want to disrupt the research process. As a third example, consider Henrietta Lacks, an African American woman whose cancer cells were harvested without her permission and then preserved and reproduced for biomedical research.[54] Such harsh and life-threatening deception has made some cultural groups (e.g., African Americans) skeptical of research(ers). As Stephen Thomas and Sandra Quinn write, given that "strategies used to recruit and retain participants in the [Tuskegee] study were quite similar to those being advocated for HIV education and AIDS risk reduction programs today,"[55] some African American groups refuse to participate in such programs.

Dwight Conquergood characterizes "ethnographic research" as "absolutely embedded in issues of power and authority. The practice of fieldwork mediates a set of power relations that determines who is observing whom."[56] As Yvonne Jewkes writes, "It would be hard for me to deny that my attempts to build rapport and gain [a participant's] trust were underpinned by the instrumental purpose of persuading him to provide me with research data."[57] Sam Joshi characterizes ethnography as "a feather in the hat of Western epistemology—the fiction of an emotionally non-stick, tangle-free encounter between the observer and observed. To use this methodology," he says, "I have to go against my nature: It is only by behaving like a macho jerk that I can even accomplish my 'Ethnography' in the first place."[58]

In an attempt to respond to such concerns, Conquergood outlines four ethically questionable "stances towards the other" that often plague ethnographers. These include the

- "Custodian's Rip-Off," which happens when researchers appropriate cultural traditions and only search for materials to enhance their projects.
- "Enthusiast's Infatuation," which results in "naïve," "glib," and superficial research practices, including trivializing cultural differences among researcher and researched.
- "Curator's Exhibitionism," in which researchers focus on "the exotic, primitive, culturally remote," looking to sensationalize and "astonish rather than understand" others.
- "Skeptic's Cop-Out," a nihilist stance of detachment that suggests that we can neither learn about nor perform persons who are different from us.[59]

Instead of adopting or falling into one of these positions, Conquergood calls us to embrace a dialogic, conversation-driven approach to ethnographic fieldwork. Dialogism models the continuous, vulnerable, and overt play between research practice, identity, and difference. "The aim of dialogical performance," he says, "is to bring self and other together so that they can question, debate, and challenge one another."[60] Embracing and respecting cultural difference means researchers must be open to challenging and changing their experiences, identities, and cultures. As Deborah Reed-Danahay observes, no longer can researchers "assume a voice of objective authority, or a self-righteous certainty that his/her interpretation is 'true.' We know that the 'natives' have their own interpretations, and that our colleagues also may see things differently."[61] The practice of acknowledging individual ways of seeing, or standpoints, and valuing multiple perspectives lies at the heart of identity politics.

Considering Social Identities and Identity Politics

In the United States, the 1960s and 1970s are characterized as times of social unrest and counter-culture activities—the era of Black Power, disability rights, second-wave feminism, *Loving v. Virginia*, the Stonewall Riots, and Vietnam. One characteristic of this unrest was the battle to claim nonmainstream identities, thus contributing to the emergence of "identity politics." Identity politics focused on how identities *matter*—how identities influenced and governed whom you could love and marry; where and whether you could work, eat, or go to school; as well as what you could study. Identity politics led many of us to ask: How and why are some people treated "more humanely and considerately while others are met with silence, disregard, and abuse?"[62] Identity politics also turned these questions into a political mission, demonstrating how nonmainstream others can "use, deny, subvert, and refigure power relations" to create more just and equitable living conditions.[63]

Such unrest also called into question mainstream research practices and assumptions, creating a desire to understand "what aspects of the self are the most important filters through which one perceives the world and, more particularly, the topic being studied."[64] For instance, new concerns arose about accessibility and academic jargon.[65] Concerns were expressed about the privileging of prose and the bias against other kinds of aesthetic texts, including poetry, a privilege that, as Audre Lorde argues, has racist, classist, and sexist implications: Not everyone has the time or technique, the financial, physical, and social resources to write (White, male, upper-class) prose. Instead, poetry has functioned as the "major voice of poor, working class, and Colored women"; it is the most "economical" art form, a form that "requires the least physical labor, the least material," and a form that can be

> ... done between shifts, in the hospital pantry, on the subway, and on scraps of surplus paper.... A room of one's own may be a necessity for writing prose, but so are reams of paper, a typewriter, and plenty of time.[66]

Scholars also raised concerns about who gets a voice in and who is silenced by academic discourse[67]; they critiqued research that perpetuates heterosexual assumptions and other normative and alienating ideas about commitment, partnership, kinship, and family life.[68] They questioned how researchers accessed and represented particular groups, especially when the representations had the possibility of cultivating harmful stereotypes about and perpetuating ignorance toward these groups.[69]

Although there currently may be more structures to discourage prejudice and mistreatment and to engage difference in the United States, years, decades, and centuries of mistreatment and mistrust will take years, decades, and centuries to remedy. Questions continue about who can speak on behalf of others and whether groups can be excluded from particular communities or from activities such as schooling or the military. These continued inequities prevented many ethnographers from reverting to objectivist and/or colonialist research practices; as Robin Clair argues, the "days of naïve ethnography are over."[70]

The three interrelated concerns and considerations we have discussed—changing ideas about and ideals of research, increased concern about and care for the ethics and politics of research, and the rise of identity politics—contributed to the emergence of more flexible, open-ended, and ethical qualitative research methods, including autoethnography. Autoethnography offered researchers a method for articulating their personal connections to—and their investment in—identities, experiences, relationships, and/or cultures. Autoethnography also offered researchers a method for addressing the problematic application of scientific methods to social scientific research. This included the inability of these methods to create insight about the particularities, nuances, and complexities of identities, relationships, experiences, and cultures, as well as the methodological disregard of stories and storytelling and the bias against care, emotions, and the body. Autoethnography insisted on, and provided a forum for, addressing the ethics and responsibilities of research with human participants and for vigilantly trying to recognize the ways social positions and identities influence how we read, write, research, and evaluate experiences, cultures, and (research) texts.[71] In the next section, we present an account of the development and use of autoethnographic methods in response to these concerns and considerations.

A (Brief) History of Autoethnography

The first references to autoethnography correspond with the rise of identity politics. In 1975, Karl Heider used the term "auto-ethnography" to describe a study in which cultural members give accounts about their culture.[72] In 1977, Walter Goldschmidt noted that "all ethnography" is "self-ethnography" in that it reveals personal investments, interpretations, and analyses.[73] In 1979, David Hayano used "auto-ethnography" to describe anthropologists who "conduct and write ethnographies of their 'own people'" and who choose a "field location" tied to one of their identities or group memberships.[74] In these texts, Heider makes a case for the value of cultural members telling their stories, Goldschmidt argues that traces of the researcher are present in all ethnographic work, and Hayano describes the importance of a researcher's identities and the connection with similarly identified others. Although these views of autoethnography foreshadow insider-outsider distinctions in ethnography, the move to include personal experience is *implied* rather than explicitly embraced.

During the 1980s, researchers in sociology, anthropology, communication, performance, and women's and gender studies began writing and advocating for personal narrative, subjectivity, and reflexivity in research, though they did not often use the term "autoethnography."[75] Still, many scholars were interested in the importance of storytelling and enactments of culture, and they progressively became engaged by the personal traces in ethnographic practices. Rejecting the idea that ethnographers should—or could—hide behind or perpetuate an aura of objectivity, these researchers began to include themselves as part of their studies, often writing stories about the research process and sometimes about their personal experiences. At the end of the decade, scholars began to apply the term "autoethnography" to work that explored the interplay of introspective, personally engaged selves and cultural beliefs, practices, systems, and experiences.[76]

In the 1990s, researchers began to place more emphasis on personal narratives and the budding autoethnographic movement. I (Carolyn) published one book and more than two dozen essays about autoethnography, and I coedited two books about the use of personal experience in research—*Investigating Subjectivity* (with Michael Flaherty) and *Composing Ethnography* (with Art Bochner).[77] During this time, Bochner also published essays about the importance of personal stories and their relationship to theory.[78] Together, the two of us began editing the *Ethnographic Alternatives* book series, which published works that illustrated how and why personal experience should be used in research, including my (Stacy's) first book, *Kaleidoscope Notes: Writing Women's Music and Organizational Culture*.[79] Other key texts from this decade include numerous essays[80] and books,[81] as well as the first *Handbook of Qualitative Research*,[82] which included chapters on personal experience and research[83] and writing as a method of inquiry.[84] These texts (along with many others) better established a space for emotional and personal scholarship, and "autoethnography" soon became the descriptor of choice.

The first decade of the 2000s saw the publication of the second and third editions of the *Handbook of Qualitative Research*, both of which included essays on and references to personal ethnography, personal experience, personal narrative, personal writing, autobiography, and reflexivity, as well as chapters focusing specifically on autoethnography written by Carolyn and Art and by Stacy.[85] I (Carolyn) published two additional books employing autoethnographic methods and two more coedited collections about autoethnography.[86] Art and I also started *Writing Lives*, a second book series about autoethnography, published by Left Coast Press.

In addition to a second *Ethnographic Alternatives* series book, *Torch Singing: Writing Resistance and Desire from Billie Holiday to Edith Piaf,* I (Stacy) continued to publish essays and book chapters on or using autoethnography.[87] Further, *many* notable books employed autoethnographic methods in this decade as did essays and special issues of journals about autoethnography, reflexivity, and personal narrative.[88] In 2005 Norman Denzin started the International Congress of Qualitative Inquiry, an annual conference that recognizes the importance of reflexivity and personal experience in research.

In the past few years, autoethnography has become an important and legitimate method in many disciplines and research contexts. It flourishes in professional journals and at academic conferences. Numerous books and special journal issues are devoted to autoethnographic inquiry,[89] and researchers in disciplines such as anthropology, art and design, business, communication, criminology, education, geography, nursing, psychology, social work, and sociology have used autoethnography.[90] Courses devoted to autoethnography are taught at many colleges, and texts about research methods include chapters about the approach.[91] Further, since 2011, Derek Bolen has organized an annual "Doing Autoethnography" conference, and in 2013 Pat Sikes edited a four-volume collection of the foundational readings in autoethnography.[92] Our recently published *Handbook of Autoethnography,*[93] along with this book, will continue to legitimate the method by offering practical advice for using personal experience in research and by posing future possibilities for doing autoethnography.

Throughout nearly four decades of autoethnographic work, the method has offered qualitative researchers a forceful and compelling way to respond "to the various anxieties that arose from the politics of representation."[94] Qualitative research (or any research) can no longer maintain a distanced, so-called objective, self-serving stance, and no longer can researchers take advantage of vulnerable others without accounting for their own identities, experiences, social capital, intentions, and formative assumptions. As Richardson says, "speaking for 'others'" has become "wholly suspect."[95]

Further, the personal approach of autoethnography illustrates the investment researchers have in their research; by being personally, emotionally, aesthetically, and narratively connected to a cultural group or experience, autoethnographers may take more responsibility for and greater care in representing themselves and others. Of course, autoethnography does not provide an answer to all intellectual, aesthetic, emotional, or ethical concerns about research. However, as a method, mode of representation, *and* way of life, doing autoethnography and being an autoethnographer requires researchers to foreground research and representational concerns throughout every step of the research and representation process.

Further, autoethnography acknowledges how and why identities matter and includes and interrogates experiences tied to cultural differences. Autoethnographers often foreground the ways in which social identities influence the research process, particularly in terms of what, who, and how we study; what and how we interpret what we observe and experience; and how we represent our observations and experiences of cultural life.

It is our hope that our stories of coming to autoethnography, together with the considerations and concerns about social scientific research, as well as how autoethnographers have addressed these issues, have inspired you to do and write autoethnography. We hope this book will help you accomplish this work.

Using this Book

We have designed this text as both a guide to the practices of doing autoethnography and an exemplar of autoethnographic research processes and representations. We've done this by *telling about* key approaches, processes, ethical considerations and responsibilities, and representational issues in autoethnography and by *showing* how we have conducted our own research and handled these considerations. Thus, this book will help you learn about doing autoethnography, introduce you to us as researchers and authors, and describe how we learned the lessons we share in the text.

In Chapter 2, Autoethnographic Research Design and Philosophy, we outline the purposes and practices of autoethnography. Specifically, we discuss the core ideals of autoethnography and how autoethnographers go about accomplishing these ideals. We also discuss why researchers might choose autoethnography as their research approach.

In Chapter 3, Doing Autoethnography, we discuss the process of doing autoethnographic research. To begin, we focus on considering personal experiences that prompt us to begin our projects, and then move on to conducting fieldwork, doing initial research, addressing ethical considerations, and interpreting and analyzing our experiences and fieldwork.

In Chapter 4, Representing Autoethnography, we discuss modes of autoethnographic writing in all stages of a research project, from getting started to writing field notes and crafting autoethnographic stories. We also describe narrative and relational ethics involved in writing autoethnographic texts and offer suggestions about editing and sharing writing with others.

In Chapter 5, Evaluating Autoethnography, we offer our goals for creating and assessing autoethnographic texts. We use these goals to assess three of our autoethnographic projects. We conclude the chapter by reviewing the autoethnographic journey we have taken in this book and by describing how you might contribute to the future of autoethnographic inquiry.

In Chapter, 6, Resources for Doing and Writing Autoethnography, we provide a resource guide for autoethnographers, including a list of our favorite texts and journals, along with conferences and journals that welcome autoethnographic work.

Throughout this book, we make the case that doing autoethnography is more than a research method; it is a way of living. We write to show how telling autoethnographic stories is a way of making our research and our lives *better*. We believe that telling stories of selves and cultures is not a task to be taken up carelessly or without preparation and consideration of vulnerability, risks, and craft. We feel that autoethnography, as Audre Lorde writes about poetry, is not a *luxury*, but instead a method that "forms the quality of the light within which we predicate our hopes and dreams toward survival and change, first made into language, then into an idea, then into more tangible action."[96]

AUTOETHNOGRAPHIC RESEARCH DESIGN AND PHILOSOPHY

DESIGNING AN AUTOETHNOGRAPHIC project is intertwined with the purposes and practices of doing autoethnography. If we want to *do* autoethnographic research, we must know the core ideals of autoethnographic methods *and* how autoethnographers accomplish them. We also must know *why* researchers use autoethnographic methods. In this chapter, we describe the purposes and practices of the method and discuss why we choose to do and write autoethnography.

Core Ideals of Autoethnography

Autoethnography is a *qualitative* method—it offers nuanced, complex, and specific knowledge about *particular* lives, experiences, and relationships rather than *general* information about large groups of people. Qualitative research focuses on human intentions, motivations, emotions, and actions, rather than generating demographic information and general descriptions of interaction. As we discuss in Chapter 1, autoethnography emerged in response to concerns about colonialism, the need to recognize social difference and identity politics, an insistence on respecting research participants, and an acknowledgment of different ways of learning about culture. The *crisis of representation* motivated researchers to recognize the limits of the knowledge claims they make about the contexts, subjects, and findings of their research. The crisis considered the limits of *scientific* knowledge, particularly what can be discovered, understood, and explained about identities, lives, beliefs, feelings, relationships, and behaviors through the use of empirical or experimental methods; researchers recognized that social scientific research often failed to account for the "intuitive leaps, false starts, mistakes, loose ends, and happy accidents that comprise the investigative experience."[1]

The crisis of representation also motivated researchers to acknowledge how their own identities, lives, beliefs, feelings, and relationships influenced their approach to research and their reporting of "findings." This focus on representation encouraged qualitative researchers to search for more transparent, reflexive, and creative ways to do and share their research. Rather than deny or separate the researcher from the research and the personal from the relational, cultural, and political, qualitative researchers embraced methods that *recognized* and *used* personal-cultural entanglements. After all, as researchers we are interested in exploring and understanding the experiences that have salience in our lives, whether these experiences thrill, surprise, intrigue, sadden, or enrage us.

For example, when I (Stacy) began thinking about adopting a child, I wanted to learn all I could about the experience of birth mothers, adoptive mothers, and adopted children. I read memoirs and novels, nonfiction works that discussed how to adopt and provided advice about raising adopted children, and a variety of research reports (articles, book chapters, and edited collections) on transnational adoption. However, it was not until I became an adoptive mother and began to write about the "inside" experience *of* adoption that I could make sense of the knowledge "out there" *about* adoption.[2] Reflecting and writing allowed me to connect empirical knowledge generated through the observations and analyses of others—what Dwight Conquergood terms the distancing "view from above"—with personal knowledge "grounded in active, intimate, hands-on participation and personal connection," a "view from ground level, in the thick of things."[3] Autoethnography provided me—and can provide you—a method for exploring, understanding, and writing from, through, and with personal experiences in relation to and in the context of the experiences of others. In autoethnography, "proximity, not objectivity, becomes an epistemological point of departure and return."[4]

The impulse to create ground-level, intimate, and close-up perspectives on experience also led researchers away from using detached, generalized, and objective attitudes and languages. Many researchers searched for ways of doing and representing research that included questions, feelings, voices, and bodies. Autoethnographers, in particular, turned to narrative and storytelling to give meaning to identities, relationships, and experiences, and to create *relationships* between past and present, researchers and participants, writers and readers, tellers and audiences.[5]

Using narrative and storytelling to research and represent experience, autoethnographers also attend to *how* narratives and stories are constructed and told. As Craig Gingrich-Philbrook argues, autoethnographers must take seriously the *epistemic* (claims to knowledge) and the *aesthetic* (practices of imaginative, creative, and artistic craft) characteristics of autoethnographic texts.[6] For us, this means studying and practicing the methods and means for conducting *research,* as well as studying and practicing the mechanisms and means for making *art* (e.g., poetry, fiction, performance, music, dance, painting, photography, film).[7]

For instance, in addition to my (Stacy's) research on adoption narratives, I also studied the craft of writing *haibun*—a genre of writing that joins the poetic form of haiku with prose—by reading the work of poets and scholars who use the form in their writing, along with critical assessments of their work.[8] Here is an excerpt illustrating my interest in and work with haibun from my essay, "Lost and Found":

Measure

> You choose the stories again and again. You choose "Prose of Departure," a story within the stories within James Merrill's *The Inner Room.* The chosen stories unfold in a series of haibun which tell of lovers on a trip to Japan while a dear friend dies at home, trace interior sketches of pain and intimacy, and make love a dying art.[9] Haibun join the slow stretch of dialogue—the passage of time, the measure of sentences—with

the blinking, "ticking off syllables" of haiku, a form for "conscious evasion" of the world raging outside....[10]

You take the stories with you, stitching them into your own accounts and weaving them into the courses you teach, repeating their rhythms like a mantra, or a hymn.[11] When you ask the writing class what they think, they look back at you, blinking. They tick off their objections: the text is distant, obtuse, and vague.[12] The characters are at once tentative and righteous. There is nothing here they can *use*. Their criticism reminds you that writing and reading, identities and lives, are performed in relation with and to others. You search for another example, another story that embodies the tight, light knot that binds the space between two worlds, between love and loss.[13] You try the language of another haibun, connected in form, in subject, and in love with Merrill: Eve Kosofsky Sedgwick's *A Dialogue on Love*, a meditation on relationships, on queerness, on illness and beauty, on poetry and death. You ask,

"What's this piece doing?"
or even, "what does it know?"
leaving out, for now,

"What does my dream know?"[14] They look back at you, waiting, open, and expectant. You try to pare back, to simplify: "What is this book about?" They wait. You try,

It's writing loss in
and outside; it's making love.
It's about dying,

about AIDS, about being queer, about how love is bound up with loss.[15]

In this excerpt, the brevity of the poetry about the limits of knowledge and the depths of loss—the ticking off of syllables in the haiku—contrasts sharply with the more expansive sentences about the clarity and usefulness of prose.

* * *

Although this book will provide you with tools and resources regarding the craft of writing (Chapter 4), we encourage you to consult other resources on doing autoethnography, as well as to seek training in your preferred aesthetic medium.

Questions about research practice and craft require autoethnographers to be invested in—and accountable to—the creation of insight and knowledge and the engagement of compelling aesthetic practices. But these are not the only commitments autoethnographers must make when choosing to do autoethnography. They also must be equally committed to conducting their work responsibly and ethically; they must consider the personal, relational, and institutional risks and responsibilities of doing autoethnography. As Jillian Tullis notes, autoethnography "tethers" researchers to their experiences, participants, and texts, and requires "contextual, contingent and primarily relational" ethical engagement.[16] Such engagement requires us to work with participants in less researcher-centered and more participant-oriented ways—treating participants humanely and respectfully before, during, and after research projects.[17] We discuss the ethical considerations of doing and writing autoethnography in Chapters 3 and 4.

In summary, when designing autoethnographic projects, researchers focus on the following *core ideals*:

- Recognizing the limits of scientific knowledge (what can be known or explained), particularly regarding identities, lives, and relationships, and creating nuanced, complex, and specific accounts of personal/cultural experience
- Connecting personal (insider) experience, insights, and knowledge to larger (relational, cultural, political) conversations, contexts, and conventions
- Answering the call to narrative and storytelling and placing equal importance on intellect/knowledge and aesthetics/artistic craft
- Attending to the ethical implications of their work for themselves, their participants, and their readers/ audiences.

Designing Autoethnographic Projects

How do these core ideals relate to designing an autoethnographic project? Unlike scientific design, the nuance and complexity of identities, lives, relationships, and experiences do not easily or neatly translate to an experiment, survey, or list of interview questions. Autoethnographers, however, do have a common set of priorities, concerns, and ways of doing research. Typically, autoethnographers:

1. Foreground personal experience in research and writing
2. Illustrate sense-making processes
3. Use and show reflexivity
4. Illustrate insider knowledge of a cultural phenomenon/experience
5. Describe and critique cultural norms, experiences, and practices
6. Seek responses from audiences.

In the following sections, we describe and offer examples of each of these issues in doing autoethnography.

1. Autoethnographers Foreground Personal Experience in Research and Writing

As we noted above, our ideas for research projects are often—perhaps always—guided by the ideas, feelings, experiences, and questions we have in and about our lives. Rather than silence or disguise the personal reasons that lead us to choose our research projects, autoethnographers make use of personal experience and subjectivity in designing their research. As such, autoethnographers take up an array of topics.

Some autoethnographers share their experience about conducting their *fieldwork* alongside their insights about cultural phenomena.[18] Some write about the *feelings, attitudes,* and *beliefs* they have about/toward cultural phenomena, their experiences in a particular setting (e.g., a high school reunion), traumatic interactions such as abuse and neglect, or their experiences with health/medical conditions.[19] Some autoethnographers discuss their experiences with *identity,* such as what it means to be lesbian, gay, bisexual, or queer in the context of families, Black women in the academy, parents and children, lower social class, or as a person living with "minor bodily stigmas."[20]

Autoethnographers also write about *epiphanies*—those remarkable and out of the ordinary life-changing experiences that transform us or call us to question our lives.[21] In the process, epiphanies can motivate trauma, confusing us and moving us to sadness and discomfort, and sometimes resulting in a more satisfying life.[22]

2. Autoethnographers Illustrate Sense-Making Processes

Through the use of personal experience, autoethnography offers insight into how a person makes sense of cultural norms, experiences, and practices. Autoethnographers offer complex, insider accounts of *sense-making* and show how/why particular experiences are challenging, important, and/or transformative. In turn, autoethnographers provide a perspective that others can use to make sense of similar experiences.

For example, when I (Carolyn) confronted entrenched racism in the mountain community where Art and I built our summer home, I was moved to write about these experiences:

> "I'm not voting for no nigger," the 63-year-old White Man declares, as he pushes down on the footrest of his La-Z-Boy chair and comes to a sitting position. "A nigger will just take care of other niggers. You know that and I know that," he says, pointing first at Art, then at himself. "Anyway that nigger ain't gonna win. When White people are in the voting booth, they won't vote for a colored. Mark my words. Even if Obama would get elected—and he won't unless the Democrats pull something dirty—someone will kill him. There's going to be a civil war over this thing. Now tell me, when it comes, which side are you going to be on? Ours or theirs? Which one? Tell me. Ours or theirs?" He reclines back in his chair, seemingly satisfied.[23]

From interrogating my experiences with racism in this community, I wanted to show how/why particular experiences have been challenging, important, and transformative; figure out how to live among racist others; *and* respond in a way that honored my values by trying to remedy such racist wills. I wanted to turn my *insider* account toward larger, *outside* forces, considerations, and ways of living. I wrote:

> The rub for Art and me is how to respond to this racism in a way that is productive and transformational. I don't want to

have to avoid this man and his wife. Nor do I want to sit quietly without talking back. This community serves as a place where I live a portion of my life. I can no longer play the role of the newcomer, the ethnographer, who tries to understand a world from the eyes of the people who live there and who seeks to be accepted, often without fully voicing her concerns, values, and ideas. Where do we draw the line between living an ethnographic life—seeking to understand in a nonjudgmental way how people put their lives together— and our responsibility to speak out and reject beliefs that we feel are inherently wrong?

... How to be, and how to think and act, in order to escape the politics of difference is a very complex issue, its complexity revealed, I hope, in the lived experience of the stories I have told here.... [If] we fail to acknowledge, reveal, confront, and think hard about how to cope with our differences; if we give up on all those who are set and seemingly unyielding in how they think; if we ignore those who don't share our values, there will be no "reaching across the aisle," and we and others will just go our own ways with no interference.

Don't we all have a responsibility to reach out and try to fashion a way out of prejudices and values with which we disagree? Don't I, in particular, given my southern rural background and entrée into this mountain community, have a responsibility to keep coming back?[24]

Other autoethnographers also emphasize insider, sense-making processes. Elissa Foster attempts to make sense of her struggle between being a "good woman" and a "good feminist," highlighting how these identities can conflict when thinking about birth, mothering, and reproduction.[25] Boylorn tries to make sense of her connection to, and love for, her absent father and how his absence may have complicated her ability to date and trust men.[26]

In *The Daily Narrative*, Bud Goodall blogged about his day-to-day experiences of living in "Cancerland."[27] Goodall's writings offered insightful and moving descriptions of the cancer experience. He was able to speak for himself about coping with his diagnosis, enduring medical treatments, and living with the disease; he was not tied to what doctors said about him or what researchers reported about his experience. This is not to suggest that Goodall was more accurate in his representation of cancer, or that his experience was/will be everyone's experience. Rather, he offered readers unique, firsthand insight about living with and making sense of cancer in the midst of navigating his own uncertainty, pain, anger, and joy.

In many of the blog entries, Goodall reflects upon the limitations of his story. He speaks about the privileges of being able to work, of being "upper-middle class," of having good insurance. He describes being "surrounded by people I love" and notes that he has "a variety of entertainment options" to make it through each day. "When I think about people who have to go through Cancerland unescorted, or unloved, or without faith or insurance or a home or just plain alone," he says, "I say a quiet prayer for their deliverance. For some help to please come their way." Throughout his writing, Goodall shows how his perspective and experience of cancer are tied to his living conditions; he acknowledges how his social standpoint influences what he sees and how he lives. In these moments, Goodall highlights another priority and concern of autoethnography: he writes "reflexively."

3. Autoethnographers Use and Show Reflexivity

Autoethnographers use reflexivity to trouble the "relationship between researchers' 'selves' and 'others,'"; being reflexive means "taking seriously the self's location(s) in culture and scholarship."[28] Reflexivity consists of turning back on our experiences, identities, and relationships in order to consider how they influence our present work. Reflexivity also asks us to explicitly acknowledge our research in relation to power; as Bernadette Calafell explains, reflexivity means "skillfully and artfully recreating the details of lived experiences and one's space or implication" in control, contradiction, and privilege.[29]

For example, as a White, able-bodied gay man in his mid-thirties who has lived all of his life in the United States, I (Tony) am able to move through contexts in particular ways and with particular privileges. I do not often, if ever, worry about being followed in retail stores or being perceived as "trouble" when walking at night. I rarely, if ever, worry about others attacking me based on what I am (not) wearing. I do not worry about being perceived to have landed my job solely because of my race/affirmative action.[30] I do not worry about others questioning my citizenship or that my race will be held against me, should I ever be interrogated by the police. I can talk about race and racism and gender and sexism without thinking about others accusing me of playing the "race card" or of whining. Not having to think about race is a privilege that my Whiteness grants me;[31] not having to think about gender is a privilege of my maleness.

As an autoethnographer, I do my best to account for my identities, limitations, and perspectives and show readers that while I use my experiences to offer insight into cultural experiences, the way I make sense of these experiences is not the *only* way to make sense of them. In addition, I must acknowledge how and why my experiences identifying as a gay man guide my interest in and the decisions I make about research projects. For instance, I am keenly attuned to the heterosexual assumptions of everyday discourse. In classrooms and my office, in restaurants and bars, in online environments and at festivals and churches, I often hear statements such as "women love men who..." and "men love women who..."—and I cringe at such generalizations. I also cringe when I watch films that feature *only* heterosexual relationships and exclude stories and images of same-sex attraction. Strangers often ask whether I have a "girlfriend," and not whether I have a "girlfriend or a boyfriend." I dislike feeling as though my partner is disregarded in conversation, as though we are not a legitimate couple. I worry about one of us falling ill and having to go to a hospital, knowing that we must choose a hospital not based on the care it may provide, but on whether it has homophobic religious affiliations. I have made these assumptions, statements, absence of stories, questions, and worries the subjects of my research.[32] I do my best to reflexively engage questions such as "Why does everything have to be about sexuality?" and exhortations such as "It's only a movie," or "I only asked if you had a girlfriend, not a boyfriend," or "it's just a hospital, not a homophobic institution." I use reflexivity to scrutinize my experiences of self/culture, to illustrate how the autoethnographer is an "audience to her or his own experience" and can turn "back to signify this lived world" with and for readers.[33]

4. Autoethnographers Offer Insider Knowledge of a Cultural Phenomenon/Experience

As we note in the opening to this chapter, autoethnography is a method that affords an *insider's* perspective on the practices, meanings, and interpretations of cultural phenomenon/experiences.[34] Researching and writing from the lived, inside moments of experience allows autoethnographers to cultivate an "epistemology of insiderness," of being able to describe an experience in a way that "outside" researchers never could.[35] Further, insider knowledge can be used to call attention to the complexities of commonly held, taken-for-granted assumptions about these cultural phenomena.

For example, in 2005 and 2006 I (Tony) volunteered at The Florida Aquarium, a not-for-profit environmental education facility located in Tampa, Florida.[36] During this time, I cultivated relationships with a few of the paid workers at the facility, especially workers who had the same tasks as the volunteers. I also observed that many of these workers relied on their paychecks to survive. One day, I asked a worker if she had to work the next day. "It depends on whether or not you're coming into work," she replied.

I learned that the number of paid workers at the facility depended on the number of volunteers scheduled to work: If a volunteer was scheduled, a staff member would be asked to stay home or sent home without pay. The paid staff never could establish a set work schedule; their work was contingent upon volunteers. Further, staff members told me that pay raises were difficult to come by, especially because volunteers did the same work for free.

In my insider role as a volunteer, I learned that *my* volunteering directly influenced *others'* work schedules and pay. Although volunteering made me feel good, and the organization profited from my presence, my free help hurt others. I came to regard my volunteering as harmful and to resent the volunteer system the facility had established.

This example illustrates how insider experience helps generate insights that other methods might miss or actively discourage. If I, as an outsider (someone who did not have ties to the aquarium), asked to interview paid staff members about volunteers and volunteering, they might fear talking to me about the problems volunteers create for paid staff given that their critique of the volunteer program might further jeopardize their jobs. If I, as an outsider, interviewed aquarium volunteers, they might not identify any problems with the volunteer program unless they had learned how the program worked from paid workers. Further, given the culturally exalted status of "volunteering," many people—the volunteers *and* the workers—might find it difficult to speak against the practice.

Autoethnography also provides insight into social experiences that we *cannot* observe directly, because the experiences occur in their own time, uninterrupted by a researcher's presence. For instance, self-disclosure, as an event, is a difficult act to witness as it happens. It is difficult to observe coming out as lesbian, gay, transgender, bisexual, or queer to close friends and family members; everyday instances of discrimination; breaking up/dissolving a relationship with another person; informal and intimate patient-doctor interaction; or the last moments in a person's life. These experiences cannot be recreated in an experiment or laboratory and often are too sensitive to discuss in interviews or survey research. However, an insider can describe the nuance, complexity, emotion, and meaning of these experiences as s/he has lived them. For example, when my (Carolyn) partner Gene was critically ill and in the hospital, I recorded the private conversations that occurred between Gene, his doctor, and me. These conversations occurred in the hallway outside the hospital room, on the phone, and by the bedside in moments of crisis, and, in their immediacy and spontaneity, were hidden from researchers' eyes and ears.[37] As Lisa Tillmann writes about her experiences with bulimia: "I can show you a view no physician or therapist can, because, in the midst of an otherwise 'normal' life, I experience how a bulimic *lives* and *feels*."[38] Tillmann offers intimate and nuanced insights into her/the lived experience of an eating disorder, insights that other research methods could not easily, if ever, reveal.

5. Autoethnographers Describe and Critique Cultural Norms, Experiences, and Practices

Although most texts produce some kind of knowledge—every advertisement, movie, theatre production, or novel offers a window into and insight about society—autoethnographers *intentionally* use personal experience to create *nuanced, complex,* and *comprehensive* accounts of cultural norms, experiences, and practices. Autoethnographers offer these accounts—these "thick descriptions"[39]—in order to facilitate an *understanding,* and often a *critique,* of cultural life by encouraging readers to think about taken-for-granted norms, experiences, and practices in new, unique, complicated, and challenging ways.[40]

For example, as I (Stacy) continued my research and writing on adoption, I had to confront the ways adoption stories, adoptive relationships, and adoptions themselves left out, covered over, or otherwise silenced the injustices that occur in transnational adoption. Although there is much to celebrate in adoptive relationships, I felt responsible for writing about the practices, questions, nuances, complexities, and challenges of adoption and adoptive relationships. In my essay, "Lost and Found," I wrote:

You consider how you got here, how you arrived at the threshold of this request, this possibility, this gift. You pushed through the adoption paperwork, repeating the motions of a linguistic gestation: photographs, certified letters, figures, and fingerprints. You pushed against the ticking clock—not, as in recent years, the tick of aging out of adoption program regulations, but the clock of your heart, your hands, your mind. Preparing to meet—to love and parent—your son, you filled your days and thoughts with the words of expectant and adoptive mothers. Preparing to meet a daughter, you read books written by adult Korean adoptees.[41] And what you read makes you fall in on yourself, unable to stop looking, unable to sleep at night. You read how families and identities are lost and destroyed in the quest to manufacture a steady stream of available orphans through a "clean break" on the way to a "better life."[42] How married couples become single birth mothers, temporary choices become fabricated relinquishments, and given names become generic nomenclature meant to sterilize an exchange of human beings.[43] How being shipped a world away to be raised by people who do not look like you, or speak your mother tongue, or share your blood or your bonds *feels.* How returning to a birthplace where you look but do not look like you belong, speak but do not speak the language, and feel but do not feel one with your family creates a chasm of loneliness and longing so complete it can never be filled. How loneliness and longing become the human currency exchanged for international aid, military support, and economic development. How barren white women and sterile white men eager to meet the demands of compulsory parenthood pay the wages of this exchange. You read yourself. You read him. You read her.

And you write. You write so that someday he might read your words and understand—what? That you didn't *know*? That you thought that love might make loss bearable?[44] That you love him not because you couldn't have children of your *own*, but because he is not yours, because children are never someone's to own. That you do not believe your own joy somehow becomes his mother's joy or that loss is his property or responsibility, alone. That had you understood all of these things—the pain, the injustice, the suffering, the grief of transnational adoption—you would've reconsidered that privileged, violent choice. That even though you believe one person's unwillingness to contribute to an unjust system makes a difference, you wonder how your refusal might change her life. Will she be relinquished? Adopted? If you weren't his mother, who would you be? If you aren't her mother, who or what will occupy the cavern filled by your love?[45]

Similar to critical ethnographers, autoethnographers use their research to facilitate "social consciousness and societal change," aid "emancipatory goals," and negate "repressive" cultural influences; to, as Bernadette Calafell says, "create spaces of resonance, possibility and activation for the reader"; and to write to acknowledge their own "privilege, disempowerment, and accountability" in cultural life.[46]

6. Autoethnographers Seek Reciprocal Responses from Audiences

Autoethnographers invite participants and readers/audiences to engage in the unfolding story of identities, experiences, and worlds, to creatively work through—together—what these experiences show, tell, and can mean; they treat research as a socially—and relationally—*conscious* act, and attempt to cultivate reciprocal relationships with their participants, readers, and audiences.[47] By reciprocity, we do not mean the *exchange* of stories, experiences, or resources—a "giving back for something received" that is commonly criticized in fieldwork relationships.[48] Instead, autoethnography seeks reciprocal *responses* from multiple audiences through *relationships* and *participation*. Like the positive and productive relationships in our lives, reciprocal relationships are marked by a sense of mutual responsibility and care.[49]

I (Carolyn) have been engaged in a relational autoethnography project with Jerry Rawicki, a Holocaust survivor, about his experiences during and after the Holocaust.[50] We call this project and our approach "collaborative witnessing," a process in which both the story-teller and story-listener share, as fully as possible, in the construction of experience and meaning. As the autoethnographer, the collaborative witness, I write for and with Jerry, listening and working with him in care and compassion. In the essay, "More than Mazel? Luck and Agency in Surviving the Holocaust," I demonstrate this relational process as I reflect on Jerry's sense of meaning and his reluctance to claim agency in his survival:

I ask Jerry, "Did you have a sense that your life was meaningful?"

"I didn't think much, if anything, about meaning then," Jerry replies. "I'm not sure we, in our broken bodies, were capable of that kind of thinking. Really any thoughts I had were mired in that primal will to survive, to just live another day."

"Did you think about death a lot?"

"No, I didn't, at least not in the traditional 'going to see my Maker' sense. Death was not the problem, survival was. Nobody talked about death, which was so omnipresent that it lost its 'allure.' Looking at the dead, or worse yet, at those starving and near the end of their lives, I thought about the extent of human suffering rather than the 'ever after.'"

...Stunned by the depth of what Jerry says, suddenly I experience a new level of understanding. I imagine Jerry as a fourteen-year-old boy trying to stay alive amidst other broken, crying, and dying bodies. Of course, I did not know that boy, but I hear the stories he tells now as an older man and I feel the emotion with which he tells them. From viewing Holocaust movies, documentaries, and photos, I also have an image of how he might have appeared and acted back then. Still I have to wonder if I have fully considered what it meant to have these experiences at such a young age. I realize how difficult my questions are as I ask Jerry to recall being that boy who was obsessed with living another day, remember what was going through his head or heart, and explain his behavior.

....I recognize that Jerry does not want to be seen as a hero. He thinks of himself as an ordinary man doing the best he could given the circumstances....And that is a portrait I must honor as well, though he has become so much more to me.[51]

Why Do Autoethnography?

In addition to understanding and embracing the core ideals of autoethnography and engaging the aforementioned approaches for doing autoethnography, researchers must also consider *why* they want to do autoethnography. Although the reasons for coming to and engaging in autoethnography are as diverse as the researchers who hold them, we believe several fundamental reasons exist for doing autoethnography:

1. To critique, make contributions to, and/or extend existing research and theory
2. To embrace vulnerability as a way to understand emotions and improve social life
3. To disrupt taboos, break silences, and reclaim lost and disregarded voices
4. To make research accessible to multiple audiences.

In the following pages, we elaborate on each of these reasons.

1. Autoethnographers Want to Contribute to, Extend, and/or Critique Existing Research and Theory

In contrast to memoirs, autobiographies, personal diaries, and blogs, autoethnographic projects seek to contribute to a *scholarly* _conversation_. Although other forms of personal writing may offer scholarly insight, autoethnographers often engage extant research and theory in explicit ways; they intentionally try to contribute to, extend, and/or critique existing research and theoretical conversations. Some autoethnographers accomplish this by using the language and formatting conventions of traditional social-scientific forms of writing—that is, structuring a work using a literature review, research questions, methods, data, and findings format.[52] They adopt this language and format because it is recognizable to scholars across many disciplines.

Other autoethnographers use recognized scholarly writing conventions, such as in-text and endnote citations, in conjunction with stories, poetry, photos, and other nontraditional or experimental scholarly forms.[53] My (Stacy's) work often makes use of endnotes as a way of engaging existing research and theory in relation to the stories and experiences that I tell. Consider, for example, an essay about how my relationship with my father has changed following his stroke and my coming out to him as queer.[54] Using endnotes (presented in the notes for Chapter 2 at the end of this book), I make sense of my experience with my father in conversation with Judith Butler's writing about the relationality of identity and the risk and possibility of asking for (and giving) recognition:

> During [a] phone conversation, my father asks how my daughter and I like living in the renovated house. I tell him "We're getting used to it," and my father says, "Does the baby know you're a queer?" using a word his grandmother— my great grandmother—and not he, at least not before the stroke—would have used.
>
> "Yes, Dad. The _baby_ is seven and she knows I'm gay."
> "You can't be a _gay_. You were married for 15 years for Christ sakes."
> "Twelve."
> "Twelve what?"
> "I was married for twelve... never mind. Yes, the baby knows I'm gay," I say, then revise. "Knows I'm queer."
> "Gay. Queer. Whatever you call yourselves these days. Your mother and I should have known."
> "Should have known what?"
> "Should have known about you."

> "How could you have known? I didn't know—who or what I am, who or what I love. I still don't."
>
> "Well, we knew one thing."
>
> "What's that?"
>
> "We knew you were strange. *You* were always strange."
>
> "And what would *you* know about being strange?"
>
> My father laughs. "A helluva lot. All these braces and bags and metal? You should see me. I look like a monster."
>
> "Thank goodness you are a lovable monster."

> My father does not say anything. And I do not say what I am thinking: that since the change, since the shifts in our identities and our relationship, we have been asking each other to see us for who and what we are, as we always have been, as we were, *before*.[55] Though I am trying to know that when we ask for this kind of recognition, we petition the future *in relation* to each other.... In the asking, we become something new.[56]

* * *

Still other autoethnographers contribute to and extend existing research and theory entirely through story or other aesthetic means.[57] I (Carolyn) have written several short stories that introduce theoretical questions and offer analysis without referring to other academic work. For example, "Maternal Connections," an essay about caregiving for my ill mother, critiques research that describes caregiving as a sterile act or as a burden by showing caregiving as a process that awakens the love people can have for each other.[58] Likewise, the story, "Lechem Hara (Bad Bread), Lechem Tov (Good Bread)," extends existing conversations about the Holocaust and defining evil by describing a person's conflict between generous self-sacrifice and the instinctive drive for survival.[59]

2. Autoethnographers Embrace Vulnerability as a Way to Understand Emotions and Improve Social Life

As autoethnographers, we try to contribute to existing research and theory by using personal experience to describe, understand, and challenge cultural practices and beliefs. We also conduct research in order to better understand social phenomena or to explore the questions we have about our experiences; similar to many qualitative researchers, autoethnographers address "research questions." Sometimes these questions are explicit, such as when we ask: "What does it mean to come out of—and, consequently, stay in—the closet?"[60] or "How does a gay person experience contradiction [paradox] in interaction?"[61] Sometimes, though, these questions are less formal or explicit, such as when we ask: "How have I experienced trauma and/or the loss of a relationship?" or "How can I invite readers and audiences to use my stories and experiences for their own sense making?"[62]

The goal of autoethnographic projects is to embrace the *vulnerability* of asking and answering questions about experience so that we as researchers, as well as our participants and readers, might understand these experiences and the emotions they generate.[63] "I tend to write about experiences that knock me for a loop and challenge the construction of meaning I have put together for myself," I (Carolyn) write in *The Ethnographic I*. "I write when my world falls apart or the meaning I have constructed for myself is in danger of doing so."[64] When we embrace this kind of vulnerability in our research and representations, we commit ourselves to improving the lives of others as well as our own.

For example, I (Tony) published two autoethnographic essays about the troubled relationship I have with my father.[65] In both essays, I use a relational perspective—a perspective that assumes that *all* people involved in a relationship perpetually and mutually influence each other in innumerable and uncertain ways—to describe the ways my father and I hurt each other with our words and actions. Prior to writing these essays, I blamed my father for our problems. However, doing autoethnography—reflecting on my experiences and using them to discern some of the cultural expectations for being "fathers" and "sons"—I began to understand how I, too, was responsible for my/his/our problems. I used autoethnography not only to learn about myself but also to figure out how we, *together*, made our problems, *together*.

I did not want to write my story only to work through my own anger, pain, and/or confusion about our relationship; I also wanted to offer *others* ways of working through their feelings about *their* relationships. If I had not had this goal, I would have no need to publish the essays—I could have written through my emotions on a blog or in a personal diary. I published my stories so that others might use them as "equipment for living"[66]; as stories to "live with" during times of relational distress.[67]

By telling stories—often vulnerable stories—about aspects of our identities and experiences, autoethnographers purposefully open themselves up to "criticism about how [we've] lived" and, as a result, to being "wounded or attacked."[68] Autoethnographers make these choices in order to call attention to the vulnerabilities, questions, injustices, silencing, and shame that others might endure. Autoethnographers embrace vulnerability with a *purpose*.[69] "Vulnerability doesn't mean that anything personal goes," as Ruth Behar writes. "The exposure of the self who is also a spectator has to take us somewhere we couldn't otherwise get to. It has to be essential to the argument, not a decorative flourish, not exposure for its own sake."[70]

For instance, in the second and third chapters of my (Tony's) book,[71] I describe my past sexual practices with men and women in detail, noting how I deceived and manipulated some of these partners. I tell stories about hiding, lying, and engaging in reckless behaviors (e.g., driving drunk and having unprotected sex). I make some unfortunate and upsetting parts of my life known— parts that others hold me accountable for—because I want to describe the painful and turbulent experiences that might happen to a person with same-sex attraction. I reveal my experiences—as unflattering as they may be—so that others might learn from my mistakes and avoid such behaviors.

As we will describe in Chapter 3, autoethnographers must consider not only what is important, fair, and just to say, but also what risks to our relationships, reputations, positions, and personal safety we are able and willing to endure.[72] As Tami Spry notes, the space of personal writing is one "of intense personal and cultural risk" and, simultaneously, one of "profound comfort." For Spry, this personal space has enabled her to "speak about the personally political in public, which has been liberatory and excruciating, but always in some way, enabling."[73]

3. Autoethnographers Disrupt Taboos, Break Silences, and Reclaim Lost and Disregarded Voices

In addition to promoting and extending personal/particular understandings of cultural identities, relationships, and experiences, autoethnography also allows researchers to reclaim voice by adding nuanced personal perspectives to and filling experiential "gaps" in existing research.[74] Unlike more traditional research, autoethnography refuses and disrupts canonical narratives, writes against hegemonic beliefs and practices,[75] and describes cultural experience as it is *particularly*—rather than *generally*—lived. Further, in breaking the silence around understudied, hidden, and sensitive topics, autoethnographers create a textual space for talking back to neglected cultural experiences and, simultaneously, offer accounts that allow others to "bear witness" to these experiences.[76]

For example, in my (Tony) recent autoethnographic work, I write against the assumption that coming out is a discrete and linear process.[77] Contrary to much existing research, I show how coming out can be a never-ending process, contingent upon each new audience, and not something that can be accomplished with one sweeping disclosure. I also write against the idea that a person's struggles with same-sex attraction will end with coming out.

In the last few years, the three of us have written against the assumption that the grief and loss a person may experience upon another's death does and should end.[78] We write to disrupt the silence around expectations of grief and loss and illustrate how these emotions can still constitute many of our mundane experiences years and even decades after losing people we love. We refuse to rationalize our grief or to believe in singular and stable stories of life and death. Instead, we write about being undone by death, make a case for unrecognized and unspeakable grief, and show why others should not/can never define for a person when and how the experience of grief happens.

4. Autoethnographers Make Research Accessible to Multiple Audiences

Art Bochner, my (Tony's) dissertation advisor, once asked: "Do you want 5 or 5,000 people to read your work?" Art's question is a direct critique of traditional, esoteric academic articles from journals that often sit on people's shelves or are skimmed quickly online, their impact and potential to create change in people's lives lost because of their lack of availability and accessibility. Art's question made me understand that I did not want to write in ways that kept others out of or away from my work. Although

Western text-centrism rarely takes into account other forms of understanding and knowing,[79] my duty as a scholar and as a member of society is to do my best to create and share accessible, written work with as many others as I can.

Goodall says that becoming writers means "cultivating readers, and cultivating readers means communicating with them and for them, not above them or beyond them. For this reason, we need to train our next generation of scholars to become better storytellers."[80] Access and availability can happen through the use of engaging writing, as well as an autoethnographer's ability to bridge the academic and the affective by addressing the *heart* (emotions, the sensory and physical aspects of experience, intuition, and values) and the *head* (the intellect, knowledge, the analytical).[81] "Making our stories public outside of academe expands our reach, our influence, our capacity, and our audience," Robin Boylorn writes. "I have learned that closeted auto/ethnography, the kind that is hidden behind academic doors (and locked access journals), limits the potential of the work."[82]

Rather than producing esoteric, jargon-laden texts, many autoethnographers recognize a need to speak also to *non*-academic audiences. They satisfy this need by writing and performing in engaging, creative ways. Such techniques make research more *valuable* because more than a select and trained few will read the work.

Another aspect of accessibility centers on *which* selves, identities, experiences, and cultures we write about. Members of under-represented identity categories (including, but not limited to, gender, race, ethnicity, religion, class, sexuality, age, and ability) have long lamented the lack of representative stories about their lives. Writer Chimamanda Adichie describes the dangers of having, or believing in, a single story about any experience, or any group of individuals or cultures. Upon encountering a roommate when she left Nigeria to study in the United States, Adichie says,

> What struck me was this: She had felt sorry for me even before she saw me. Her default position toward me, as an African, was a kind of patronizing, well-meaning pity. My roommate had a single story of Africa: a single story of catastrophe. In this single story there was no possibility of Africans being similar to her in any way, no possibility of feelings more complex than pity, no possibility of a connection as human equals.[83]

From this and other experiences with *single stories*, Adichie counsels, "Many stories matter. Stories have been used to dispossess and to malign, but stories can also be used to empower and to humanize. Stories can break the dignity of a people, but stories can also repair that broken dignity."[84]

A third aspect of accessibility means taking into account the storytelling traditions and ways of using language and ways of knowing our audiences might engage. Although narrative rationality (see Chapter 4) gets at the idea that storytelling is a way of being that rivals rational and social-scientific thought,[85] we recognize that there are many ways to tell a story: Some stories are *linear*, following a five-part Western dramatic structure (including an exposition, rising action, climax, falling action, and denouement) while other stories are *circular* or even "*chaotic*."[86] These stories use nonlinear, nonchronological, and anti-conflict resolution sequences. As writers, we must consider what storytelling *forms* are most familiar and accessible to our intended audience(s).[87]

A fourth aspect of accessibility has to do with the text-centrism of autoethnography, which not only diminishes the in-the-moment, embodied, and fleeting textures of experience and fieldwork, but also ignores the ways texts have been used to diminish, silence, and control marginalized others. "The dependency of indigenous peoples on other people's records which hold their cultural history breeds hostility," Keyan Tomaselli writes. There are "suspicions about textual (cultural, linguistic, spiritual) theft," and "texts come to be seen as both means to liberation *and* subjugation."[88] In response, some autoethnographers create work that does not rely solely on text, but instead uses other forms of representation and research output, including performance, music, dance, video and film, and photography.[89]

For example, Rebecca Long, a black, Sudanese refugee living and working in Australia and Anne Harris, a white, US American-Australian, adopted, and queer scholar in education create autoethnographic films that explore their experiences and relationships. They note: "Videos, disseminated through the Internet, on YouTube, and on social networking sites, are perhaps the most egalitarian public pedagogical tool available today. They can reach millions. They are relatively uncensored. They do not require funding or peer-review... They do not require high levels of literacy, or what we educators call competencies, before they can be watched, made or distributed."[90]

We are not suggesting that we abandon the practice of creating autoethnographic texts, but instead encouraging autoethnographers to consider the accessibility of their texts, and asking what value or benefit our work might have for our participants and readers, as well as ourselves. As Tomaselli writes about the value his research had for its indigenous participants: "We pointed out that we could not help them materially, but that we do and will continue to write in styles that they can understand, that we would return copies of the pictures taken, and that we would ensure that their voices are heard in the corridors of power: provincial, national, in academia and development NGOs."[91]

* * *

Although we have discussed separately the ideals of, approaches to, and reasons for doing autoethnography, all are interrelated. For instance, an autoethnography that reclaims a silent or lost voice often does so in the context of scholarly conversations that silence or leave out these voices.[92] Most autoethnographers write to help others and to make life better, and, given the use of personal experience, explicitly seek to reach audiences both inside and outside the academy.[93] Further, many autoethnographies, in allowing the author to maneuver through painful, confusing, and uncertain experiences, often are written with the intent to critique and change these experiences not only for the author but also others.

In addition, autoethnography is appealing for reasons other than those we outline above. For instance, Andreas Philaretou and Katherine Allen, echoing Audre Lorde's observations about poetry (see Chapter 1), argue that autoethnography is attractive because of its "relatively low cost compared to other more mainstream quantitative and qualitative methods. For this reason," they write, the method "may be particularly appealing to researchers in resource-poor institutions," thus creating a space for marginalized groups to speak.[94] After all, not everyone has a room of her own in which to write.[95]

Taken together, the core ideals of, ways of designing, and reasons for engaging autoethnography illuminate the challenges and possibilities of the method. In the next chapter, we describe the process of doing autoethnography, beginning with experience and then moving into and through research, fieldwork, and the responsibilities and ethics of the autoethnographer.

3

DOING AUTOETHNOGRAPHY

THE TERM AUTOETHNOGRAPHY invokes the *self* (auto), *culture* (ethno), and *writing* (graphy). When we do autoethnography, we study and write culture from the perspective of the self. When we do autoethnography, we look *inward*—into our identities, thoughts, feelings and experiences—and *outward*—into our relationships, communities, and cultures.[1] As researchers, we try to take readers/audiences through the same process, back and forth, inside and out.[2]

For example, when I (Stacy) was about to become an adoptive mother, I wanted to understand my experience in relation to the experience of others I encountered in my research and met along the way: social workers, doctors and government officials, adoptive parents and children, and prospective parents experiencing the adoption process. Closer to home, I wanted to connect with my grandmother who, until the time I told my family about my plans to adopt, I had not known was an adopted child herself. My research interests and writing created an opening, a chance to talk with my grandmother about an experience that had a profound effect on her life, but one that she had not discussed in detail with anyone in our family.[3] This inside-out journey then extended to the people who have read my and my grandmother's adoption stories and who have since offered stories of their own.[4]

The inside-out trajectory of autoethnography also describes how we begin a research project. Often, research projects begin with events that turn *us*—our thinking, feelings, sense of self and the world—and *others*—our friends and families, members of our social, political, and cultural communities, and others who are different from us—*inside-out*. Autoethnographies begin with the thoughts, feelings, identities, and experiences that make us uncertain—knocking us for sense-making loops—and that make us question, reconsider, and reorder our understandings of ourselves, others, and our worlds.[5]

In this chapter, we describe the process of doing autoethnography, starting from experiences that turn us inside-out. We then describe autoethnographic fieldwork and consider the ethics of autoethnographic projects. We conclude by discussing how we interpret meanings and analyze what happens in our fieldwork. Although we recognize that *doing* autoethnography is inseparable from *writing* autoethnography, in this chapter we focus on the field-based, methodological considerations of autoethnography. In Chapter 4, we will consider autoethnographic writing and representational practices.

Starting Where You Are and Finding Yourself in Story

Autoethnographers sometimes begin projects with personal experiences that we want to understand more fully, deeply, and meaningfully. As noted in Chapter 2, sometimes these experiences are *epiphanies*—transformative moments and realizations that significantly shape or alter the (perceived) course of our lives.[6] Epiphanies create impressions that stay with us, "recollections, memories, images, feelings" that persist "long after a crucial incident is supposedly finished."[7] These epiphanies prompt us to pause and reflect; they encourage us to explore aspects of ourselves and others that, before the incident, we might not have had the occasion or courage to explore. For example, the death of my (Stacy's) grandmother was a crucial incident in my life; writing to remember and memorialize our relationship prompted me to consider other losses that I was not ready or able to consider until, or because of, her passing, namely the decision to not adopt a second child and the sense of loss that I felt about this decision. As I note in my writing about these losses, "If we are, indeed, at least 'one loss behind' in our grieving, becoming aware of our ongoing (and perhaps unfinished) grief can help us revisit losses as they exist in relationship."[8]

Or consider how the death, possibly by suicide, of my (Tony's) former boyfriend Brett prompted me to write about the consequences of entering, staying in, and coming out of the closet.[9] After Brett died, I embarked on an investigation of how I came into the closet, considering my early experiences of same-sex attraction and learning that I better not speak about my attraction, or else I would face ridicule from and possible abandonment by friends and family. As a teenager, I made many efforts to date women and to try to find the perfect "wife." But when I recognized that I would harm not only myself but also the woman I might marry because of my same-sex attraction, when I finally allowed myself to think of myself as gay, I experienced an epiphany: my recognition of and personal embrace of same-sex attraction significantly altered how I thought I would live my life.

Even if we do not have an epiphany that sparks an autoethnographic research project, we can still use autoethnographic methods. For example, Derek Bolen organizes his autoethnography around mundane "aesthetic moments" that constitute his relationship with his father—everyday experiences that may not be epiphanical and, as such, may be "overlooked because they lack transformative power."[10]

At the very least, beginning any project requires us to do the simple, yet deeply reflective work of starting where we are. As Soyini Madison notes,

> The experiences in your life, both past and present, and who you are as a unique individual will lead you to certain questions about the world and certain problems related to why things are the way they are. It is important to honor your own personal history and the knowledge you have accumulated up to this point, as well as the intuition or instincts that draw you toward a particular direction, question, problem, or topic—understanding that you may not always know exactly why or how you are being drawn in that direction. Ask yourself questions that only you can answer: "What

truly interests me? What do I really want to know more about?" "What is most disturbing to me about society?"[11]

Whether by epiphany, aesthetic moment, or intuition, we begin autoethnographic projects by starting where we are. From there, we begin to situate ourselves in *story*—our own story, the story told in existing writing and research on our topic or experience, and the stories told by others. Many, perhaps most, researchers do this work simultaneously, moving inward and outward and inward again, from epiphany, aesthetic moment, or intuition into an "interpretive community," the group of researchers who also write about our topics and whose conversations we want to join.[12] Bud Goodall describes the process of searching for an interpretive community, reading the work others have published about a topic, and looking for a way to enter the conversation as a *search for clues* in the "research literature story."[13] This process involves searching for a *storyline*—a plot, recurring theme(s), interdisciplinary spinoff(s)—and looking for an opening or a "gap" in the story where you can address a topic or experience that is missing, not well understood, or not told thoroughly or correctly.[14]

In addition to looking for the clues and gaps in existing research stories, autoethnographers also examine other relevant personal and cultural texts, including photographs, personal diaries, popular press books, blogs, films, and podcasts. Autoethnographers use these texts to determine how their experiences and stories contribute to, complement, and contrast with others' experiences and stories. For instance, Ragan Fox consults various "institutional artifacts" from his high school experience—a map of the school's architecture, a guidance counselor's account, report cards, yearbook photographs—to illustrate how homophobic educational systems can influence the creation, persistence, and transformation of gay identities. Fox describes this work as "auto-archaeology," and he likens the use of these artifacts, combined with the use of his personal experience, as an "archaeological dig" that shows "how one gay identity was performatively rendered in high school."[15]

It is here, in the spaces in existing stories—as told in research, artifacts and texts, films, books, and blogs—where autoethnographers add their voices to ongoing conversations. It is here where autoethnographers begin their fieldwork in an attempt to follow these clues, bridge these gaps, and/or remedy uncertain and unsatisfying cultural accounts.

Doing Autoethnographic Fieldwork

Like ethnographers, autoethnographers study culture; they often focus on the collective relational practices, common values and beliefs, and shared experiences of a group of people with the purpose of better understanding the group and themselves.[16] Like ethnographers, autoethnographers study culture at "ground level, in the thick of things" through the empirical (observation- and experience-based) method of *fieldwork*.[17] Like ethnographers, autoethnographers cannot begin fieldwork until they locate and gain access to a "field." Sometimes the field might be discursive and relational, constituted or dominated by language and interaction rather than physical space.[18] At other times, the field may be a location, site, or occasion for encountering cultural others.[19]

Making Contact

Accessing the field may require making contact with others, acquiring their permission to talk with and accompany them in their everyday lives,[20] and creating representations of their experiences alongside and in contrast to your own. Accessing the field means making your orientation to research and your goals for a project known to yourself and to others. "Being a fieldworker in my everyday life means that I attend to the social patterns around me, analyze my own actions, and piece together the observations I make and the words I hear," Sheryl Kleinman writes. "Being a *feminist* fieldworker means that I attend to the subtleties of inequalities (in race, class, gender, sexual orientation, ability, age, etc.), including the ways in which I live out sexist programming."[21]

Madison recommends beginning your efforts to make contact with others by creating a *lay summary*, which details "who you are, what you will be doing, and what [the participant's] role will be in the process."[22] The summary—designed for the "people who are central" to your project—serves as a guide to your project and should, to the best of your ability, address the following questions:

- *Who are you?* Answering this question involves sharing details about your personal background, institutional affiliation/sponsorship, and any other information regarding your cultural, ethnic, or personal identity that participants might find relevant to working with you.
- *What are you doing and why?* Answering this question includes telling your personal story of what brought you to the field (i.e., the topic, site, and/or occasion), the methods that you will use in exploring this field, and what you hope to accomplish with the project.
- *How did you choose your site/occasion/participants?* Answering this question includes disclosing how you came to this topic, site, occasion, and group of participants (e.g., by way of personal recommendation, advertised event, or causal encounter).
- *How often and how long will you be/stay in the "field?"* Answering this question includes detailing how much and how often you would like to participate in events, observe others, and conduct interviews.
- *What will you do with the "results" of your project?* Answering this question includes describing the form the stories, information, and experiences you gather will take, how this information will be shared, and the anticipated audience(s) for this information.
- *How will your work benefit or put your participants at risk?* Answering this question includes describing how you believe your presence will influence participants' experiences, how your project might enrich or contribute to their lives, how interacting with and disclosing to you might negatively affect participants, as well as what you plan to do to mitigate such risks and negative effects.
- *What efforts will you take to protect the confidentiality and, if necessary, the anonymity of the site, occasion, and participants and how will you seek permission for participation in your project?* Answering these questions includes detailing how you will remove, alter, or safeguard identities, details, and happenings in public (re)presentations of your work, along with your methods and mechanisms for seeking participants' permission to write, record, and represent their words, actions, and experiences.[23]

A lay summary is helpful if we become *participant-observers* in a culture that is new or not entirely familiar to us. However, issues of access and responsibility are important even when we are members—insiders—of a culture. For example, my (Tony's) experiences identifying as a gay man grant me access to numerous informal and impromptu interactions in which people who identify as lesbian, gay, bisexual, and queer (LGBQ) have asked me about my experiences with and advice about disclosing their sexuality. I never know when someone will want to talk about personal struggles with the closet, coming out, and same-sex attraction. Because I am "one of them"—that is, a gay man, a perceived "insider"—I presume that these others feel safe in sharing their coming out dilemmas and secrets with me, trusting that I will not ridicule or out them to others. Still, thinking through the questions included in the lay summary has allowed me to foreground issues of privacy and confidentiality during and after these impromptu disclosures.

Some communities, field sites, and occasions are closed off to researchers who are not perceived as insiders and/or as trustworthy or safe. These sites could include private therapy sessions, confidential support groups such as Alcoholics Anonymous, hate groups such as the Ku Klux Klan, doctor-patient interactions, undocumented citizens, and groups bound by marginal and possibly deviant desires.[24] If an autoethnographer wanted to study these groups, having a guide for accessing these private and sometimes vulnerable populations is both necessary and important. Later in this chapter, we will return to the ethics of fieldwork.

Talking With Others

Goodall writes that fieldwork is "about adapting yourself to the swirl and mix of a social world."[25] Entering a site and "hanging out with others," talking with them and "sharing and learning about their everyday practices" are some of the first and richest moments of autoethnographic fieldwork.[26] Further, informal conversations can offer researchers unique insights into identities, experiences, and cultures. For example, the informal, unsolicited conversations I (Tony) have with LGBQ persons provide "unplanned" and "surprising"[27] glimpses into the coming out experience, glimpses that allow me to attend to "life itself"—that is, to the world of "everyday encounters."[28] By treating these conversations as meaningful, I move beyond the "rarefied atmosphere of the interview" and explore "people's lives *outside* the research context."[29]

When you have such conversations, take notice of them—either in the moment by recording key details, or later, by detailing these exchanges in field notes (which we discuss in Chapter 4). Make sure to note not only the words that are spoken, but also the hesitations and moments of silence, tones and fluctuations of voice, patterns of emphasis, facial expressions and gestures, resounding images, movements, and bodily stances of the speakers.[30] Also make yourself available to the speaker, setting aside your own preoccupations, experiences, and research agenda so that you may *listen* mindfully to what the speaker says and to the story or experience being told.

Listening Out Loud

Della Pollock, a performance and cultural studies scholar who works extensively with oral histories and the intermingling of memory and remembering, describes a story-sharing process called "listening out loud" that she uses with project participants.[31] This approach, which focuses on listening, telling, and retelling, is also helpful to autoethnographers. The approach begins with a conversation in which participants learn about each other—their identities, lives, and experiences—by conversing without the aid of pen, paper, or other recording devices. Instead, participants use "only the technology of the ear" and "listen body to body, heart to heart"; they work to "absorb" the "other person's story" in order to learn something about each other. The process then asks participants to re-tell each other's stories using first-person voice ("I") and beginning with the statement, "This is what I heard."[32] The goal of the re-tellings is not to get the story "right" or to imitate what the teller said, but instead to incorporate "others' memories into the body of our own and then again into others' through ... reperformance," to embrace how persons and stories are connected and differentiated, familiar and misrecognized. In other words, the retellings embody the inside-out movement of stories and storytelling. Pollock says the process often yields a "hard lesson:"

> ...a story is not a story until it is told; it is not told until
> it is heard; once it is heard, it changes.... The "I" I become
> in telling your story is one *who doesn't and can't possibly—
> in any kind of full or total sense—know you,* who learns the
> limits of representation—and begins to enjoy and to remem-
> ber the selves that emerge within those limits...[33]

Talking with others in conversation and listening out loud are
processes that can lead to and into longer and more developed
exchanges, including interviews.

Interviewing Others

Autoethnographers might use a variety of interview types ranging
from *oral histories* in which individuals recount social, historical,
and political experiences and events from their own perspectives;
to *personal narratives* in which participants offer personal reflections on an identity, event, or experience; to *topical interviews* in
which participants comment on specific subjects, issues, or processes.[34] These interview types can and do overlap.

Before and during such interviews, autoethnographers also
can employ a range of techniques, including researcher-centered
formats that employ systematic and sequential processes for
selecting interview participants and asking predetermined questions, such as Spradley's "Developmental Research Sequence."[35]
Some autoethnographers choose to be more collaborative,
involving participants in a range of interactions including, but
not limited to:

- *Emergent interviewing*, in which informal interactions
  lead into more structured question-and-answer sessions
  or in which interviewers visit with participants in their
  everyday environments and contexts, conversing and
  asking about experiences, practices, and perceptions as
  they happen[36]
- *Sensory-based interviewing*, in which researchers and
  participants focus on sensory experiences, surroundings,
  metaphors, or memories[37]
- *Participatory photo (or photo-voice) interviewing*, in
  which participants are asked to provide or take photos

of their identities, experiences, cultures, and other aspects in their lives; the meanings and significance of these photos are then discussed collaboratively with researchers[38]

- *Interactive interviewing*, in which researchers and participants share personal/cultural experiences and tell (and perhaps write) their stories in the context of their relationship.[39]

Interviews are a way to connect our personal experiences, epiphanies, and intuitions to those of others. Sometimes these connections confirm our experiences; other times, interview conversations contradict or conflict with our experiences. In both instances, the insights we acquire from talking with and listening to others can deepen and complicate our own stories. For example, Amir Marvasti interviewed people about what it means to be and live as a person of Middle Eastern descent in the United States. He complements his interviews with his experiences, showing how they align with and rub against what some of the interviewees said. "My original intention was to use interview data as well as my personal experiences to show how Middle-Eastern Americans manage [stigma] in the aftermath of September 11th." Marvasti writes,

> While working on the first draft, I told my Iranian friend Ahmad, with whom I was having lunch, that I was working on a paper titled "Stigma Management Strategies of Middle Eastern Americans." He nodded... After a short pause, he asked: "Why 'stigma'? What is the stigma?"
>
> I was a little surprised that he failed to see the obvious. I explained, "After September 11th, people from the Middle East, especially Muslims, are treated with suspicion and subjected to ethnic profiling. That's why we are stigmatized."
>
> He replied in a matter-of-fact tone. "Not always. Sitting here with you, talking in this school cafeteria, I don't feel stigmatized."[40]

In interviews that complicate and extend our stories, talking with and sharing experiences can lead some autoethnographers to collaborate with participants in fieldwork and in writing. One type of collaboration autoethnographers can use is "collaborative witnessing."

Collaborative Witnessing

I (Carolyn) have worked with Holocaust survivor Jerry Rawicki for five years. We call our process "collaborative witnessing," a type of research relationship in which a survivor and researcher become "co-storytellers" who collaboratively discuss and write their stories in order to understand meaning, challenge and create knowledge, and engage in a compassionate and caring relationship.[41] Collaborative witnessing, especially of traumatic experiences, requires "being with" the teller;[42] it requires us not only to live *with* but also *in* the stories we tell and hear from others.[43] With Jerry, I committed not only to being a listener but to being a co-storyteller, which means that I had to do everything I could to empathize and put myself in his perspective,[44] to feel resonance with his story and feel the story's emotions and nuances,[45] and to learn why and how his stories matter to him and to us. I committed to doing and writing autoethnography with Jerry as if I were a person in his story.[46] Such work—as with each of the fieldwork processes and techniques we describe above—requires a careful consideration of the ethics of doing autoethnographic research with others.

Doing Autoethnography Ethically

As I (Tony) have written before, "writing about the self always involves writing about others."[47] Autoethnographers—researchers who write about the self/personal experience—must, therefore, make ethical considerations central to their work.[48] Although autoethnographies may not always fall under the purview of institutional review board (IRB) and approval processes,[49] researchers must adhere to the basic ethical principles and guidelines for conducting research as outlined by the National Commission for the Protection of Human Subject's Belmont Report.[50] These guidelines include:

- *Respect for persons*, which means we must treat research participants as autonomous persons and acquire their consent to participate in our research projects or provide protections for persons who have diminished autonomy, including seeking consent from their guardians to participate in research

- *Beneficence*, which means we must work to ensure participants' well-being by doing no harm and maximizing possible benefits of the research for participants, including protecting their identities
- *Justice*, which means we must work to ensure a fair distribution of research benefits and burdens.

However, acknowledging and meeting the ethical standards of respect for persons, beneficence, and justice when we use and write about personal experiences—experiences that inevitably implicate our family members, friends, partners, co-workers, neighbors, and other intimates—is not always easy. As such, in addition to these basic ethical principles and guidelines, autoethnographers have developed considerations for seeking consent, limiting risks and maximizing benefits, and protecting participants. Some of these considerations include process consent, an ethics of consequences, and protecting the privacy and identities of participants.

Process Consent

"Process consent" happens when researchers check in with participants during *each* stage of a project, from design to fieldwork to drafting and sharing of an autoethnographic text, to ensure participants' *continued* willingness to take part in a project. Process consent views consent as dynamic and ongoing, one that persists for the life of a project and that happens in a form and context that is accessible to and comfortable for participants. In other words, autoethnographers must never assume that written consent forms are the most appropriate or only way to discuss and obtain consent.[51]

For example, in my (Carolyn's) work with Jerry, I routinely consult with him to ensure that he is willing and able to talk with me about his experiences of the Holocaust and as a survivor. I am also keenly aware of how discussing these experiences may affect him. Not wanting to incite further trauma, I monitor our conversations carefully, trying to be sensitive about when it is okay to ask a question, when it is important to remain silent and wait for a response, and when it is best to change topics. I monitor his life situation as well, because what is okay to talk about at one time might not be okay to talk about at another time. For example, when Jerry's wife was dying, I did not want to ask him about the death of his mother and sister at Treblinka. Further, I consider how our work might be read by his family members and how our work might affect, or be perceived by, other survivors. In this research, my guiding principle is to do no harm and to add positively to Jerry's and other survivors' lives.[52]

Ethics of Consequences

Autoethnographers must also consider what Kim Etherington terms the "ethics of consequences"—that is, accounting for the positive and negative reasons for participating in a study and acknowledging and working to minimize the power differentials and varying goals that inevitably exist between researchers and participants.[53] For instance, in my (Carolyn's) work with Jerry, we had to address our different audiences and goals:

> ... the audience I [Carolyn] wrote for initially was composed of Holocaust scholars. I sought to deconstruct "luck" [as a narrative explanation of why Jerry survived the Holocaust while others perished] and show the agency that underpinned the explanation of luck... I thought that relying on luck as the sole explanation, as Jerry had done, resulted in buttressing the unfounded stereotype of Jews as passively failing to resist during the Holocaust. Thus I found myself trying to persuade Jerry to modify his strong conviction that his survival was simply a matter of luck.
>
> While Jerry valued the research aspects of this project, his audience consisted of family members who had encouraged him to publish his stories, general readers who might pass on his stories to the younger generation, and other survivors who might react personally to his experiences. Most likely this audience had less interest in debates about luck and agency... than they had in stories of Jerry's experiences. As well, Jerry was attuned to the voices of his relatives who had been killed in the Holocaust... he was intent on presenting himself without pretensions and making sure he took no credit for his survival. He was cautious not to imply that he might have had special skills or powers that those who died lacked. "That would be wrong," he said, "just wrong."[54]

Protecting the Privacy and Identities of Participants

In addition to seeking the consent of participants throughout the process of doing autoethnography and working to minimize the risks and maximize the benefits of research for others, autoethnographers must develop strategies for protecting the privacy and identity of their participants. Although our insights may be grounded in our experiences, our recollections, accounts, and interpretations might embarrass, harm, or expose others.[55]

For example, I (Carolyn) have written about the discomfort I felt about not sharing my writing about taking care of my elderly mother with her before it was published.[56] When students asked about my mother's reactions, I also felt uncomfortable telling them I had not shown her the essay. Though I had my reasons—wanting to protect our relationship and not wanting to upset her with some of my descriptions of her deteriorating condition—my reasons felt ethically suspicious. Eventually, I did read the essay to my mother, along with a second story I wrote about taking care of her.[57] Although my approach was not without contradiction—I skipped some things as I read, and then left the printed essay for her to read on her own—she seemed happy with what I had written and wanted to show it to other family members. I think my focus on her life and our relationship; my desire to understand myself, her, and us; and the attention I lavished on her in the process contributed to the strong love that continued to develop between us before she died.[58]

Although Carolyn was eventually able to read her work to and talk with her mother about her autoethnographic representations, I (Stacy) was not able to share my work on adoption with my grandmother before she died. Further, I am only now able to share and talk about this work with my twelve-year-old child, who was a baby when I began writing about adoption. Even though the perspectives on adoption are my own, my inability to share my work with my grandmother is especially painful because she, more than anyone else in my family, was a supportive, careful, and critical reader of my writing; I know that her comments would have improved my work. Although I was, and am, thoughtful about what I reveal about my child, we have recently had difficult conversations about the availability of my work online,[59] its potential accessibility to school friends, and its potential as a source of embarrassment.

Including details such as a name, gender, race and/or ethnicity, age, role or title, or other identifying features of participants in project summaries, presentations, performances, and written representations may mean that others will be able to identify your participants.[60] Revealing such information about persons, events, and/or sites might thus inflict harm on others. For example, in some contexts, coming out as lesbian, gay, bisexual, transgender, or queer (LGBTQ) can still be a contentious act: a person could be fired from a job, ostracized from family, verbally abused and/or physically harmed.[61] As such, when I (Tony) include others' experiences with coming out, I often heavily mask their identities. In addition to participants' names, I might change how and where a conversation happened, the age of a participant, and other identifying characteristics.

Further, I (Tony) once advised a student doing autoethnographic research with international students about their experiences in the United States. During her project, this student was exposed to her participants' recreational and illegal drug use.[62] As a result, these participants—students on our campus—could have faced punishments, by the school or by law enforcement, if they could be identified in the research. In her thesis, my student took great care in masking her participants' identities through composite characters[63] and by creating a single and general story about international student experience; she made it difficult, if not impossible, for any reader to identify an individual student.

In addition to addressing both the *procedural* ethics (IRB review; other processes for ensuring respect, beneficence, and justice for research participants) and *situational* ethics (processes for engaging with others ethically as projects unfold), autoethnographers must also attend to *relational* ethics in their research projects.[64]

Relational Ethics

As I (Carolyn) have written elsewhere, a relational ethic "recognizes and values mutual respect, dignity, and connectedness between researcher and researched, and between researchers and the communities in which they live and work." Acknowledging relational ethics means acting, as researchers, from "our hearts and minds, to acknowledge our interpersonal bonds to others."[65]

One approach researchers use to enact relational ethics is "friendship as method."[66] Friendship as method asks researchers to approach their relationships with participants as they would a friendship, including:

- Prioritizing the relationship, including being there for participants and not making inappropriate demands on their time, resources, or emotions
- Nurturing the relationship by whatever means appropriate and being willing to change patterns of interaction to accommodate the relationship
- Addressing possible conflicts in the relationship and the research process/project explicitly
- Acknowledging issues of confidentiality, loyalty, and critique in ways that meet both the demands of the friendship *and* the demands of research
- Maintaining the relationship after the research is complete or no longer possible.[67]

In friendship-as-method, there is "no leaving the field."[68] As with any research orientation, friendship-as-method has limitations and risks, including being scrutinized as friends as well as researchers and the difficulty of negotiating the multiple demands of research and friendship. Researchers also might encounter difficulty in acquiring IRB approval for a friendship-as-method study and in determining which times, contexts, and topics are appropriate to research. Although friendship as method does not satisfy *all* of the ethical dilemmas that can arise in autoethnographic projects, it *is* a relationally ethical approach designed to care for, respect, and do justice to/for our participants. Other relationally ethical approaches to doing autoethnography include:

- Sharing recollections, field notes, presentation and performance texts, and written representations with participants so that they may read and comment on them[69]
- Creating representations that use composite characters, fictionalized narratives, and/or third-person and other distancing or abstracting writing techniques to obscure the identities and respect the privacy of participants[70]

- Conducting research and writing representations collaboratively with other researchers and/or participants.[71]

Thus far, our discussion of ethics in autoethnography has centered on our relationships as researchers to intimates, participants, collaborators, and communities. As we treat those we encounter in our research in ethical ways, we must also consider how to care for, respect, and do justice to and for ourselves.

Caring for the Self

Autoethnography is a way of caring for the self. We often write to work something out for ourselves, and when we do, we must take into account how we care for ourselves, as well as how we experience tension and conflict with others. At times, such as in Stacy's previous example about her grandmother, we may not have the opportunity to obtain another person's consent to share our stories involving them. At other times, we may believe that it is not feasible or safe to share stories about our personal experiences with others. For example, consider Shelly Carter, who feared for her safety and wanted to protect her own privacy and identity and, as a result, wrote an article about her abuse using a pseudonym.[72] Or consider Carolyn's example of sharing only parts of "Maternal Connections" with her mother.[73] Or consider instances when we decide that the need to share our stories does *not* outweigh our responsibilities to care for ourselves and others, as was the case of a student in my (Carolyn's) class who wrote a story about being abused by a sibling and ultimately chose not to publish her work because of the harm it might do to their relationship and to her sibling. In these instances, autoethnographers must balance their need to heal and to get on with life with considerations about protecting themselves, their relationships, and others' privacy.

How do we make the decision that writing and publishing our work is an appropriate way to proceed? There is no singular or prescriptive set of rules for determining when and how we share our work. Each case should be considered on its own—and researchers must account for both the goals and potential consequences of a project. Further, we should discuss these issues with other researchers and consult accounts of ethical considerations written by others.[74] A helpful approach to this process is to work from "specific cases to guiding principles and back again, over and over."[75] This inside-out process helped me (Carolyn) decide what to tell and what to leave out of *Final Negotiations*, a book about my relationship with my partner Gene, who struggled with emphysema and eventually died. I "moved back and forth between considering the constraints of telling and the possibility of healing, between loyalty to Gene and creating the best self I could become after his death," and I "considered what I needed to tell for myself, while honoring my implicit personal trust with Gene the best I could."[76]

As these examples illustrate, doing autoethnography can create personal and professional risks and vulnerabilities. These risks and vulnerabilities also are felt in the way participants and readers/audiences *respond* to an autoethnographer's representations of personal/cultural experiences.[77] Because autoethnography requires us to examine our identities, experiences, relationships and communities, the *personal* risks of doing autoethnography can be significant.

Some autoethnographic projects might prompt us to revisit traumatic events or experiences and we might find ourselves unsettled again, unable to cope or adequately manage our thoughts, feelings, and behaviors when we are revisiting these experiences. For example, April Chatham-Carpenter writes candidly about being pulled back into anorexia as she wrote about her (past) experiences with the disease. She notes,

And, just like that, seemingly all of a sudden, I would start cycling downwards into wanting, really wanting, to be thin again, and to do whatever it took to get there. I realized what I was doing, but liked thinking about the temptation. "It's okay, as long as I don't act on it," I would tell myself. How was I going to do this research without being harmed by it? How was I going to keep myself from going down that road again if I continued to focus on anorexia so intently for my research?[78]

Chatham-Carpenter stayed with her project because of the potential benefits that such an open and honest account of an insider's experience with an eating disorder offers to others struggling with eating disorders; she completed her autoethnography through disciplined efforts to keep herself safe and by focusing on the belief that others would benefit from her account.[79]

Sophie Tamas is more ambivalent about the possibility and benefit of writing through pain and loss. She worries that writers who present the messy, unfinished business of trauma as a "clean," "reasonable," and "readable account of loss" might "reinforce the expectation that our trauma ought to make sense, and if it doesn't we must be somehow inadequate or failing."[80] Still, Tamas persists in such writing, noting that as an autoethnographer she often writes "in the voice I warned me about."[81]

The personal vulnerabilities and risks of doing autoethnography also extend into our intimate and professional relationships. Consider, for example, Barbara Jago's chronicling of her personal and professional struggles with depression. She wonders how readers will receive her stories and, in particular, whether she is undermining her credibility as an author, teacher, scholar, and human being.[82] Ayanna Brown and Lisa William-White write about power differentials and institutional racism in academic institutions through an examination of their own experiences with power and racism.[83] In a later essay, William-White describes the critical, recriminating, and subtly aggressive reactions colleagues and administrators had to the first article.[84] These autoethnographers enumerate the costs of trauma and the weight of oppression for themselves and for their readers.[85] Still, others may wonder: Is putting oneself at personal, relational, and professional risk "worth it?"[86] An autoethnographer can only answer such a question for her/himself.

A final consideration about self-care in autoethnography centers on our inability to leave the field once we begin working with a particular topic, context, or community. As we have described, we do autoethnography in the context of research *and* the context of relationships; ethically, it may be difficult or impossible to leave the relationships we have established in the field once we have finished a project or received the information—the "data"—we need.[87] Further, autoethnographers may become so identified with a field topic or site that they find it difficult to escape reader/audience responses.

For example, more than two decades ago, my partner, Art Bochner, and I (Carolyn) published an essay on the constraints of choice in abortion.[88] Writing through the experience together helped us heal and strengthen the bond of our relationship. However, following the publication of the essay, we found ourselves not only open to the critique and disapproval of others, but also stuck by/bound to the published text, unable to account for the ways we have since changed. "You become the stories you write," I said in a later essay. "Art and I became the couple who had an abortion and wrote about it. No matter that we might feel differently now than then and see ourselves as changed from the characters presented in the story, this portrayal of ourselves is edified in print."[89]

Other autoethnographers become so identified with a topic or site that they find it difficult, if not impossible, to ever leave the field. As Patricia Leavy writes,

> ...given the nature of the courses I teach which, at times, can be quite personal for students, I have sat in my office countless times as female students have poured out their experiences to me, often in tears—experiences including but not limited to devastating breakups, infidelity, body image struggles, depression, domestic violence and sexual assault.[90]

Similarly, given that I (Tony) use autoethnography to write about my experiences with same-sex attraction and coming out, and given that I self-identify as gay in many contexts, I can never leave the field of same-sex attraction and coming out.[91] Coming out is a never-ending process, one that changes with each context and every new audience, and an act of disclosure that requires me to repeat the same kind of disclosure again and again. Although I can stop using autoethnography to write about my experiences with same-sex attraction and coming out, as long as sexuality remains a meaningful social identity and as long as assumptions of heterosexuality and heteronormativity infuse many contexts, I will still be held accountable, by myself and others, for (not) disclosing my same-sex attraction in particular ways, at particular times, and in particular places. Further, as a self-identified gay man, I will continue to hear others' coming out stories, especially if these others know about my research interests and the autoethnographic work that I have done and still do.

* * *

In this chapter, we have discussed doing autoethnography, starting from the initial moments of gaining access to and entering the "field," interacting with others, and ethical ways of doing our work while cultivating care for participants and ourselves. What we have not yet examined are the meaning-making processes we engage in while doing autoethnography. In the final section of this chapter, we describe autoethnographic interpretation and analysis.

Interpreting Meaning and Analyzing Fieldwork

Your conversations, interviews, and fieldwork will generate a wealth of information. But how do you organize, use, and make sense of such an unwieldy and perhaps overwhelming "mass of information?"[92] How do you tell the story of yourself within/alongside a story of culture?[93] It may be helpful to begin the work of interpretation and analysis by creating themes for the ideas, interactions, and insights that you have generated in the field.

Several helpful guides exist for thematizing autoethnographic fieldwork.[94] Here, we focus on making sense of fieldwork through *story*. As Goodall says, a story-approach to thematizing fieldwork asks you to tell the story of culture in relation to "the story of *you*, as a *researcher*, as a *person*."[95]

When I (Carolyn) begin to write a story, I ask myself, "What is going on here?" Then I write to describe an identity, relationship, occasion or event, location or context in detail. My writing is usually prompted by a topic or experience that has grabbed hold of me and will not let go, or a topic/experience I think has the possibility of teaching me something, or one that will allow me to connect with the experiences of others. As I write, I work to hold myself and my imagined reader *in* the experience—not letting myself or my readers exit the movement or emotions of the story—until we have had a sufficient opportunity to be engaged in and by it.

Once I have introspected as deeply as I can to create a sense of an event—both as it happened then and as I re-experience it now, after time and reflection—I begin another level of the editing process. Here, I attempt to create the best *story* of the experience I can, turning "this happened" and then "this happened" into a meaningful and coherent narrative. The editing and rewriting

I do at this stage is an important part of understanding "what's going on" (in the field, in my recollection, in the story as I am telling it), as well as what the experience might mean. During this stage I also become deeply engaged in the wider processes, themes, and perspectives that might illuminate aspects of my experience. I then think carefully about how my experience might question, add to, or illuminate aspects of these processes, themes, and perspectives.

For example, in my autoethnographic work on minor bodily stigma, in which I wrote about hating my voice, I explained

> I doubt that I would have been able to move outside the category of minor bodily stigmas without first immersing myself in it. Categories too often limit us without our being aware of their influence; once we are aware, too often we assume there is no use in trying to break through them. Telling and analyzing my personal story not only helped generate and make visible the category of minor bodily stigma, it also provided a way through. The categorical story offered a name to my experiences where before there was only dread; the personal story connected real people with feelings to the labels, where before there were only tactics of concealment and denial. This research helped me understand the inextricable connections between categorical and personal knowledge.[96]

* * *

As we mention in the opening of this chapter and throughout this book, it is difficult, if not impossible to separate *doing* autoethnography from *writing* autoethnography. In this chapter, we emphasize the importance of grounding ourselves in the *now*, concentrating our attention on doing autoethnography openly, actively, and ethically by focusing on *being* with ourselves and others in the field rather than *reflecting* on our field experiences in our writing. To borrow a phrase from writer and performance scholar Lynn Miller, doing autoethnography asks us to "focus less on where we're going and more on where we are."[97] In the next chapter, we describe autoethnographic writing and representational practices—additional and alternative processes for telling stories of self in culture.

4

REPRESENTING
AUTOETHNOGRAPHY

WRITING IS A part of the autoethnographic process from the beginning of a project through its completion. Viewed as a mode of inquiry, writing is a way of coming to know an experience better or differently.[1] Autoethnographies often begin as journal entries, narratives, poetry, blogs, or other forms of personal writing in which authors explore their experiences with the goal of understanding those experiences. Sometimes the occurrences that prompt us to write are profound—times when we lose a loved one, face an illness, welcome the birth of a child, move to a new city or enter a new relationship, change careers, and/or experience a host of other epiphanic moments.[2] As Spry notes, writing provides a means for processing, creating meaning around, and enduring profound experiences: "After years of moving through pain with pen and paper, asking the nurse for these tools the morning after losing our son in childbirth was the only thing I could make my body do."[3] At other times, the experiences that call us to write are more mundane "aesthetic moments,"[4] such as the rhythms of long-standing friendships, the habits of work or exercise, the memories and feelings prompted by reunions, or the everydayness of cooking and being with family.[5]

In this chapter, we discuss modes of writing in all stages of the autoethnographic process—from getting started, into editing, all the way to "finishing" an autoethnographic text. We also explore various forms of autoethnographic representation, including decisions about voice, writing with and through theory, and issues of narrative fidelity and relational ethics.

Writing Processes

Getting Started

I (Stacy) once asked Carolyn for writing advice. She said, "Keep butt on chair." She has told this story before, in *The Ethnographic I*:

> I open a new document and label it "Writing a Methodological Novel." I stare at the blank screen, pondering how to make my writing practices visible. I open a manila folder containing field notes on writing I have kept since the beginning of this project. After reading through them, I stare again at the blank screen. I want to put off this chapter; then again, I want to finish the book.... A deep breath, then a sigh, reflects how daunted I feel by the task. Where do I start?....
>
> I look at my watch. It is after ten. Maybe one more cup of coffee. Empty cup in hand, I rise, then resist, and sit back down. "Keep butt on chair," I say, reciting my writing mantra.[6]

In addition to keeping their butts on chairs, many writers recommend a daily writing practice. Stephen King suggests that new writers create a daily goal. "I suggest a thousand words a day," he says.

> I'll also suggest that you can take one day a week off, at least to begin with. No more; you'll lose the urgency and immediacy of your story if you do. With that goal set, resolve to yourself that the door stays closed until that goal is met.[7]

Making time to write—just as you make time to exercise and prepare meals and study—is an act of prioritization. Making time indicates that what you are doing is important—so important that it warrants a permanent place in your routine. A writing routine gives your work a reassuring structure. Novelist Aimee Bender observes that

> ...writing can be a frightening, distressing business, and whatever kind of structure or buffer is available can help a lot. For almost 17 years now, I've been faithful to a two-hours-a-day routine, every morning, five or six days a week. I get up, sit down, check e-mail briefly, turn off my email and Internet, look at the time on the computer, write the two-hour marker on a little pad of paper on my desk, and begin.... Writing every day can be a powerful action, a gesture of belief in one's own imagination.[8]

Bud Goodall recommends a similar routine for ethnographers, noting, "You have to practice your art, as does any other artist, which in my view means you dedicate at least part of each day of your entire life to nothing else."[9]

As we mentioned in the introduction to this chapter, getting started on an autoethnography often begins with personal writing around an epiphany, mundane aesthetic moment, or intuition that you find interesting or about which you have questions. Getting started can be as simple as *paying attention to what holds our attention*—in writing, in thinking and feeling, in our bodies. Experiences often hold our attention because we have trouble understanding or explaining them; we want to better, or differently, know what some thing, event, or person means to us, and we can generate this understanding by writing.

When we find ourselves asking about an intriguing experience, we also try to connect with others who have had, and have written about, similar experiences. In connecting with others, we move from what is happening *inside* our bodies, hearts, minds, and lives and *out* into what is happening in culture. Indeed, we are always in culture and culture is always in us, but a new awareness around an experience encourages us to connect our selves and others' selves in tangible and meaningful ways. As we noted in Chapter 3, this need and desire for connection illustrates the relationship between the situated self (auto), culture (ethno), and writing about selves and cultures (graphy).

As I (Carolyn) explained in Chapter 3, I often begin with an experience that "knock[s] me for a loop," an experience that has me asking, "What's going on here?" I write to describe the experience in great detail. I write to hold myself and my imagined reader in the experience, then write to get a more general view of what is happening within and alongside my deep, processual reflections, turning a sequence of happenings into a more coherent and engaging story.

However, your writing may not begin with self and expand to culture, or expand from fieldwork and field notes and interviews to analyses and conclusions, all presented in a seamless story. My (Stacy's) autoethnographic writing does not often unfold in this way. Instead, I begin with fragments of stories, clips of conversations that replay in my thoughts, feelings or embodied memories that resurface with time, lines of texts, and stories that I return to again and again.

In my writing sessions, I often create textual structures that *purposefully* delay the possibility of creating a storyline or a clear conclusion.[10] Instead, once I have an experience that calls me to write, I focus my "getting started" writing sessions on generating the beginnings of multiple stories and storylines, avoiding attachment to any one idea or character or scene so that I can let the story that wants to be told unfold throughout the writing process.

My (Tony's) writing technique often combines these two approaches. Like Carolyn, sometimes I start with an experience that "knock[s] me for a loop" and I ask myself, "What's going on here?" This is how I approached my writing about the sudden death of an ex-partner, troubling coming-out interactions with friends and family members, and difficult or counterintuitive fieldwork observations. But like Stacy, I am sometimes called to write about debilitating experiences, feelings, or memories from my past that come to haunt me unexpectedly. In these moments, I try to write without any end goal, and I do so by writing about and around these experiences, feelings, and haunting memories, focusing on clips of conversations, and taking notes on the texts that I read alongside my questioning, uncertainty, and discomfort. Sometimes with a project, I do not know where I am going, and that's okay; I trust and immerse myself within the writing *process*.

* * *

In the next sections, we describe some of our favorite writing techniques; these approaches can be used to start a writing project, as well as throughout the writing process.

Text Spinning and Collaging

Begin by gathering a few (3–5) books and/or essays that you have read recently or find yourself revisiting. These materials could be philosophic or theoretical texts, short stories, poetry, scholarly articles or book chapters, fiction or nonfiction—any kind of writing. Select texts that *call* to you because the ideas, claims, and conclusions are exciting, complex, or frustrating; the writing is compelling; the work speaks to you emotionally, intellectually, or politically; and/or the texts seem to have some connection to the experiences you are writing about. Then:

1. Read through these works, writing or typing passages that you have underlined or noted.
2. Work through each source, or work with multiple sources at one time, building and spinning out a collection of notable passages until you have several entries.
3. Look over this list of entries, connecting and grouping—collaging—the disparate material in ways that make sense to/interest you.
4. Do this collaging until you feel inspired to begin writing a story, taking the collaged idea(s) as a starting point for your account. Alternatively, if you are already writing stories, look for moments to connect the citations to the stories you have crafted, incorporating the citations into, alongside, before, or after your stories.
5. Do not worry if you do not use all of the material you have cited or all of the stories you have written. You can continue spinning and collaging in multiple writing sessions, beginning by reading over what you have done in a previous draft and then adding to the document you are creating.[11]
6. Stay open and pay attention to the emerging logic of your choices, thinking about what connects the work and words you are writing.

Over time, your collaging will develop into an internal through-line or logic. This through-line/logic could be anything—a theoretical idea; a repeated experience or way of describing an experience; a recurring character, object, feeling, space, or place. Use this through-line/logic as you continue to develop your writing project.

For example, in my (Stacy's) essay, "Lost and Found,"[12] the recurring appearance of suitcases, phone calls, and letters connect seemingly disparate narratives about Walter Benjamin's disappearance and death and the lost possibility of adopting a child:

Cartera Grande

> ...Upon learning that the woman who crossed the French and Spanish border with Benjamin was living in Chicago, [anthropologist Michael] Taussig called her from a pay phone. She knew—or thought she knew—the reason for Taussig's call. He was after Benjamin's case—a large handbag, a *cartera grande*—his only baggage. Benjamin lugged this heavy black case over the Pyrenees, chanting, "I cannot risk losing it...it is the manuscript that *must* be saved. It is more important than I am."[13] After Benjamin's death, the authorities found and cataloged the *cartera grande* and its contents—a pocket watch, a pipe, a pair of glasses in nickel frames, several photographs, an x-ray, some papers and money—but no manuscript. And, as Taussig reminds, "no body either."[14]

> No body, no great
> work, no words. Just a suitcase
> full of emptiness,
> full of the collected pain of the past. Full of fragments of
>   stories....

Hold

> He insists: *you* call
> the social worker and say,
> "the adoption's off."

You agree, trying to diffuse [your husband's] anger and sadness and ignore your own. But each time you pick up the phone to call, the recriminating sound of the dial tone taunts you. You push the receiver back into its cradle.... You settle on a letter. In it, you say without explanation that you have some things to work out before moving forward. Unable to let go of wanting this relationship...in spite of knowing the irreconcilable losses she will suffer as your daughter...you ask to place the adoption on hold.

Call Waiting. Before his death, before the discovery of his missing name, missing body, missing grave, missing briefcase, missing manuscript, and missing *life,* Benjamin made four phone calls and wrote one letter.[15] No one knows whom he was calling or whether he got any answers; no one received his parting text, except by delayed delivery.[16] No one, that is, but Benjamin and even this knowledge has vanished, disappeared. Still, not knowing does not stop you from looking for who and what is gone, for writing in and over lost texts, trying to understand. Not knowing keeps you waiting for the phone to ring, waiting for the call—of adoption, of death, of story, of what is possible.[17]

* * *

When I started writing stories about the decision to not adopt a second child, I was reading Walter Benjamin's ideas about the storyteller and accounts of his exile, mysterious death, and missing manuscript and briefcase. I did not know whether or how these stories were related, but I did not press myself to figure out *why* I was writing what I was writing. I simply continued to write until one day, reading through the story fragments and excerpted texts, I noticed that suitcases, phone calls, and letters appeared in both stories. I began to think about what these cases and calls might mean and soon recognized a way to thread together the fragments of text/experience.

Found and Parallel Poetry and Stories

A variation of the text spinning and collaging technique described above is to create found and parallel poetry and/or stories from your source text(s). A found poem or story is composed of *words and phrases* found in another text(s); a parallel poem or story is composed using the *structure* of another text(s) while focusing on a distinctly different topic.[18] Transforming a text into another form—for example, from prose to a poetic form that requires line breaks and stanzas—invites writers to pay attention to language, rhythm, beat, and breath, as well as to how the text is both a physical and visual representation that mirrors our experiences, images, and bodies.[19]

When I (Stacy) began to assemble fragments of the "Lost and Found" essay, I experimented with the "haibun" form, showcased in Eve Sedgwick's *A Dialogue on Love* and James Merrill's "The Inner Room"—two texts that I had been using in my spinning and collaging exercises. As I note in Chapter 2, haibun joins the expansiveness of a paragraph to the economy of haiku[20] poetry; the prose allows for a wide vision while the haiku asks for a more limited scope. Sedgwick describes Merrill's use of this form as "prose spangled with haiku...his very sentences fraying

into implosions
of starlike density or
radiance, then out

into a prose that's never quite not the poetry."[21] For my essay, haibun were a fitting form for exploring—both up close and expansively—the themes of losing and finding. Haibun also mirrored—or performed—the ways stories create and deliver a relation with the people, identities, and loves we have lost, as well as with those relations that might still, or yet, be.

Consider the relationship of form and content as you arrange your text(s) in poetic form or parallel structure. Read through the text(s) side-by-side and aloud. Pay attention to what form highlights and obscures, what feelings and ideas it inspires, and how writing structure connects with the experience you want to relay. Experimenting with form can help you find a story form that most readily captures the feeling, movement, and potential meaning of an experience.

Images and Imaging

Writing activities that allow us to move *outside* of our immediate thought processes (including the impulse to critique what we have already written) are also helpful for beginning and sustaining writing projects. Any stream-of-consciousness, free-writing exercise can help us move *inside-out* and back again; autoethnographers might find the image-based work of Lynda Barry's *What It Is* and Michael Taussig's *I Swear I Saw This* particularly helpful because of how these works direct our attention to context and surroundings—that is, to the ethnographic world around and beyond our immediate experience.[22]

Barry's writing session helps writers focus on images in context. She recommends:

1. Beginning with a prompt (a noun—such as "dogs I have known" or "phone numbers" or "cars"—or a verb— "telling," "missing," or "finding out"). Use this prompt to make a list of the first 10 images you think of/about. Review this list and pick one of these images.

2. Picture your image by answering who, what, when, why, where, and how questions: Who is in the image with you? What time of day is it? What time of year? When did you arrive in the image? When did others arrive? Why are you in the image? Why are others there? How are you positioned, speaking, and/or moving in the image? How are you and/or others relating in the image?

3. Get inside your image by writing about the scene: What is in front of you? To your left? To your right? Behind you? Above you? Below you?

4. Set a timer and write uninterrupted for 10 minutes about, in, and through your image, beginning with the words "I am...."[23]

Barry advises against reviewing these writings for a few days or weeks (in order to prevent the critic's voice from creeping into the texts), though this delay is something only you can decide. These image-writings can also be the "seeds" of larger projects, a starting point for writing more consciously and completely about the images, ideas, and themes that resonate with you.

These techniques (text spinning and collaging, found and parallel poetry and stories, and images and imaging) are just a few tools for joining self and culture in your writing. In the next section, we focus on writing about experiences in the field.

Merging Self and Culture, Personal Experience and Fieldwork

As we mentioned in Chapter 3, when we enter the "field," we often begin our work by talking with others, sharing and learning about the experiences that capture our attention, and exploring our own and others' memories of these experiences.[24] Writing accompanies these interactions, as we record our conversations with others and take notes on or work to remember them with the purpose of then writing about these conversations, interactions, and experiences at a later time. We liken this process of writing to the work of the documentarian, in which recording the *details of an experience* dominates the project.

We also write to *reflect and analyze* our experiences and conversations, shaping field notes and other recordings into stories about/around a theme (or themes), characters, voice, dialogue, and plot. In the following sections, we explore strategies for writing to know and to show what happens to our selves and participants in conversation, interaction, context, and culture.

Looking for Themes

Field notes and transcripts of interviews may be so voluminous that it may be difficult to decide how to use these materials in, or which materials to leave out of, your writing. Begin by reading through your field notes looking for *clues*: repeated images, phrases, and/or experiences. Assemble these clues into a handful of groups or categories. As we discuss in Chapter 3, this grouping/categorizing work is known as *thematizing*. Thematizing helps us imagine a logic or pattern to our narrative and to explicitly connect personal experience with culture.[25] Thematizing also helps us to identify and create characters and to write these characters into dialogue and interaction.

Creating Characters

In addition to looking for and following themes, notice the "characters" that appear and reappear in your stories. These can be literal characters, including yourself (the researcher) and your participants. Characters also might be found in identities and subject positions. For example, Sophie Tamas describes her search for characters when writing a script for a group of women working against gendered violence:

> I went home and tried to write a play, in which they could all shine...I couldn't do it. I couldn't figure out how to

make it work, how to tell a story that let you hear all their voices.... When I explained where I was stuck in writing this play, [my clever brother] said, why don't you think of them as subjectivities rather than subjects?

So I did. I went home and wrote a play about a typical small-town Canadian married couple.... But I had three actors play each partner.... Each one played a subjectivity— a voice or persona. Sometimes they comforted or bickered with each other. Often they interrupted one another, competing for what I'd now call the dominant narrative. Each had their own characteristics and priorities, and as the plot moved along—as we followed them through their lives— each partner worked toward greater internal unity. It was a simple device but it worked.[26]

Goodall writes that the characters we create are "rhetorical" figures "'responsible' for the narrative and 'accountable' to readers for what the narrative says and does to them."[27] In short, characters and the relationships and meanings they create constitute the soul of good autoethnographic writing.[28] The character of your *narrator* is a mechanism for connecting yourself and your experience to others—other characters in the story, as well as readers—and a medium for creating knowledge, understanding, and meaning around what happens in our lives/cultures.

Choosing Narrative Voice

Autoethnographers often write using *first-person* voice or point of view, positioning the *researcher* as the narrator of the story.[29] First-person point of view is decidedly subjective because the narrator reports what she or he sees, experiences, knows, and feels, providing readers with I/eye-witness accounts.[30] First-person narrators invite readers to put themselves inside the action and in the minds, hearts, and bodies of the narrators.[31]

Autoethnographers also use *second-person* voice or point of view; here the *reader* is addressed directly as "you." Second-person narrators ask readers to imagine that they, themselves, are living through a scene, event, or experience.[32] The use of second-person voice creates a space of ambiguity around the presumed narrator, inviting readers to see themselves as people capable of thinking, feeling, acting, and saying the things the narrator says while distancing themselves from controversial, painful, and shameful personal experiences that may be difficult for authors and readers to claim as their own.[33]

Autoethnographers often use *third-person* voice or point of view to describe the experiences, thoughts, feelings, and actions of *characters*.[34] Third-person narrators lend an air of objectivity, even anonymity, to an account. The story seems to come from someone outside, looking in on and analyzing the action, providing an "outsider's insider" perspective.[35] Third-person narration can help distance readers from the story and encourage them to accept the narrator's personal/cultural analysis as accurate, complete, and true.

Some autoethnographies combine first-, second-, and third-person voice in order to capitalize on the multiple characters, points of view, and positionings in the account.[36] Each kind of narration is a "personal rhetorical imprint of who we are in and on what we write"[37] that motivates readers to feel that they are being addressed, understood, and considered in a unique and moving way.

Writing Dialogue

In addition to narrative voice, autoethnographers should consider how and why to include dialogue in their stories. When, how, and why characters speak, as well as what they say, are all questions to consider. As Anne Lamott observes, "One line of dialogue that rings true reveals character in a way that pages of description can't."[38] Stephen King says that dialogue is key to defining characters and has the advantage of *showing* your characters in action and interaction, rather than only *telling* us about them.[39] King also advises writers to listen to the talk of others, focusing on accents, rhythms, dialect, and slang, and to cultivate an "ear" for hearing and writing talk.[40] Further, dialogue must be *honest*— it must represent the speech of your characters, even when crass, biased, or harmful: "Talk, whether ugly or beautiful, is an index of character; it can also be a breath of cool, refreshing air in a room some people would prefer to keep shut up."[41]

King also advises that the adverb, a word that modifies a verb, adjective, or other adverb, is not a writer's "friend."[42] Writers often include adverbs in their stories—for example, "she closed the door *firmly*"—when they are uncertain about how clearly they have described a scene or an action. The mood, emotion, and context of the scene should be communicated in the *story*, rather than in clarifying adverbs. Adverbs, especially when used in dialogue—for example, "she said angrily" or "he said pitifully"—make stories feel stilted and clunky.

Consider how I (Tony) mix description and dialogue in a scene in which I recount asking Brett, my first long-term boyfriend, if he told his family that he identified as gay. As I noted earlier, when Brett died in March 2006, his family said that he died of juvenile diabetes. However, two of Brett's friends told me that just before his death, Brett informed his dad that he was gay. These friends believed that Brett might have committed suicide because of his father's hostile reaction:

> Before our relationship, Brett lived with a man for four years. Because of this, I *assumed* he had come out to his family, *assumed* he told them he was gay. After his death, I replay previous conversations with Brett in my head:
>
> "Are you 'out' to your family?" I ask.
> "They know," he responds.
>
> *and*
>
> "How do your parents feel about your sexuality?" I ask.
> "We don't talk about it," he responds.
>
> *and*
>
> "I'd like to meet your family," I say.
> "Maybe one day," he suggests.
>
> Brett never told me he had *said* anything to his family about his sexuality. He only said "they know," nothing more. What did "they know" mean?[43]

Here I use parallel, short, simple, and adverb-free dialogue to break from *telling* about my knowledge of Brett's death to *showing* the tension and uncertainty I felt (and still feel) about Brett's untimely death. I want readers to sense how trapped I feel about knowledge that I do not have, and now, after Brett's death, may never have; I want to show *all* of the times that I asked Brett about his family's knowledge of his sexuality; I want readers to see how

I relied on a possibly faulty assumption, namely, that Brett's family did indeed know about his same-sex attraction; and I want to show some of my regret about never asking: "Brett, have you ever told your parents that you identify as gay?"

King recommends simplifying dialogue attributions to the "he said" and "she said" variety, working to tell the *story* so that readers know how characters would say their words, "fast or slowly, happily or sadly."[44] Further, if the turns in a conversation are brief, you can often dispense with the "he saids" and "she saids" to allow the rhythm of the dialogue to shine, as in this example from my (Stacy's) essay, "Always Strange":

> My daughter reads the first few chapters of *A Wrinkle in Time*, a story about a brilliant scientist father who goes missing and the strange and stubborn daughter who sets out to find him. She calls my father [to talk about the book]. She listens while he talks... [then she] holds the phone out to me. "Grandpa wants to talk to you."
>
> "Hi Dad, how are you?"
> "Not too good."
> "No? What's not too good?"
> "I can't help with this book, honey."
> "You can't?"
> "No. I've read the first chapter several times, but I can't remember what happens."
> "Oh, Dad, that's okay."
> "My brain just doesn't work as well as it used to."
> "I've read that first chapter and it's confusing."
> "It's not confusing for you, but it is for me. I used to be able to read anything, but now [after the stroke] I can't. Tell her I won't be able to help with her homework."
> "Don't worry, Dad. I can help her. I've never read *A Wrinkle in Time*, and I should."
> "I'm sorry."
> "No, *I'm sorry*. I didn't mean for this to be a frustrating experience for you."
> "I just don't read much any more. But honey?"
> "Yes?"
> "Make sure she finishes that book."
> "I'll make sure she finishes it. We both will."

Shaping the Plot and Story

As you thematize, create characters, make choices about narrative point of view, and write dialogue, make sure to ask: "What story are you telling about yourself and your fieldwork?" "What does your experience suggest about culture?" "What does the culture/context teach you about your experience?" and "What is your role in shaping the possible meanings of your story?"

Any story we construct is partial, privileged, and rhetorically crafted for an audience. As we mentioned in Chapter 3, Goodall believes that ethnographic writing is composed of two stories: one story about culture and one story about you, the researcher within culture.[45] As writers, we must try to balance these stories or decide whether one of the stories will take precedence over the other. The unfolding of these stories in scene, sequence, and context constitutes the plot of the narrative. Rather than impose a (pre-determined) plot on your stories, writer Anne Lamott advises us to let plot grow out of the writing process and through character development—in other words, to allow writing to be a process of inquiry:

> I say don't worry about plot. Worry about the characters. Let what they say or do reveal who they are, and be involved in their lives, and keep asking yourself, Now what happens? The development of relationship creates plot.... Find out what each character cares about...because then you will have discovered what's at stake. Find a way to express this discovery in action....[46]

As we note above, Goodall likens the search for a plot—through characters in relation and in action—to searching for clues in a larger *mystery*: as writers, in writing, we do not necessarily know how our stories will turn out.[47] The task of creating plot and story—replete with narrators, characters, and dialogue—is the search for the *how, what,* and *why* of our selves, experiences, and cultures.

For example, in *The Ethnographic I*, an ethnographic novel, my (Carolyn's) main storyline followed a fabricated class I was teaching on autoethnography. In the story, I tried to show the experience I had with the class and the students. The plot had to fit what plausibly might happen in a classroom while conveying academic and practical information about doing autoethnography. At the same time, the "novel" part of the book had to offer readers an engaging and evocative story, one that would carry readers along and motivate them to care about what happened. As I wrote, I gave myself freedom to let the plot unfold without advance outlines, and I resisted previewing or telling too much too quickly in order to heighten the dramatic arc of the story. Then, seeking coherence and continuity, I outlined and reorganized each chapter around a theme, describing methodological issues of autoethnography and covering no more material than I might in one class session. I wrote to create a sense of ongoing development and continuity rather than resolution. To increase coherence, I also concentrated on the development of each character. Before publication, I printed out all that I had written about individual characters across chapters and read about each character in total to make sure the character's story made sense in its entirety. Then I compared the characters' stories to see if they worked together. Thus, the *narrative* plot was primarily character-driven while the *academic* plot was guided by methodological themes and a discussion of the projects each character conducted.[48]

Forms of Autoethnographic Representation

Once your writing begins to take shape and after some initial thematizing—that is, once you have found a logic or storyline that connects the characters, experiences, fieldwork, interviews, and ideas you are writing about—you might begin thinking about forms of autoethnographic representation (if you have not already). The forms an autoethnography might take are as diverse as the kinds of texts you read and enjoy, whether you want to create a more traditional research report or monograph or want to use creative forms such as narrative, poetry, performance, spoken word, song, film, photography, or dance.[49]

Because autoethnography is the study of culture through the lens of the self, separating the *content* of the text from the *form* of its representation is not desirable or possible.[50] As we mentioned in Chapter 1, the idea that researchers could separate selves and cultures motivated a *crisis of representation* in the social scientific and humanistic disciplines. John Van Maanen's

Tales of the Field was an early text that addressed this crisis by offering researchers a typology of ethnographic representational forms that, to varying degrees, *merge* the mode of representation with the researcher's voice and focus. Van Maanen offers three forms—or "tales"—researchers use to represent themselves, others, cultures, and fieldwork experiences: realist tales, impressionist tales, and confessional tales. *Realist tales* focus on the culture being studied (and less, if at all, on the researcher), use third-person narration, and document fieldwork experiences from an omniscient, objective, and authoritative perspective. *Confessional tales* focus on the researcher (and less on the culture), use first-person narration, and demonstrate the ways researchers are limited and vulnerable. *Impressionist tales* focus equally on the researcher and the culture, merging the features of realist and confessional tales to create a focused and imaginative rendering of fieldwork and personal/cultural experience.[51] Although these forms can and do overlap, each type of tale foregrounds particular relationships among selves, others, cultures, experiences, and fieldwork.

You may have noticed that Van Maanen borrows the terms "realist" and "impressionist" from the visual arts. These terms chart the movement away from *realist* painting, which uses formal and highly staged or stylized scenes in order to create a *comprehensive or complete* version of reality, toward *impressionism*, which focuses on the details of everyday subjects and field happenings to create a general picture of cultural experience; the goal is to create an impression, rather than a true and certain reproduction, of an experience. Although Van Maanen did not employ visual art terms exclusively in his typology— choosing the term *confessional* tales for researcher-focused representations—here, we embrace movements within visual arts as a scheme for describing and understanding the diversity in autoethnographic representational forms. As we note above, representational forms can and do overlap; rather than reading these forms as discrete and exclusive, we encourage you to consider how each form allows you to focus your writing processes, as well as how combining multiple forms/types of representation might help you accomplish your writing goals.[52]

Realism

Realist autoethnographies use perspective—primarily the researcher's perspective, but also the perspective of participants—to create a sense of *verisimilitude*, the feeling or illusion of reality. Realist autoethnographers use personal experience as a way into, and/or a means for, describing and understanding cultural experience as *fully, complexly,* and *evocatively* as possible, creating what Clifford Geertz termed "thick descriptions" of cultural life.[53] In realist autoethnographies, authors most often use third-person voice, though they may also include first-person narration. Realist autoethnographies move from story to interpretation, often (though not always) creating texts that separate experience and analysis. Although realism encourages writers to create a vivid and comprehensive portrait of experience, the mode does not often embrace storytelling as the *only* form of representation. Instead, realist texts include story *and* analysis, showing *and* interpretation. Realist texts take many forms, including:

- *Research reports* and *reflexive interviews*, in which the researcher's experiences are used to complement, extend, and/or contextualize fieldwork, interviews, and analysis[54]
- *Analytic autoethnography,* in which a researcher acknowledges membership in a research community, reflects on research experience in the context of fieldwork, and describes the theoretical contributions of research in distinct and separate moments of the narrative[55]
- *Ethnodramas,* which use the techniques and craft of scriptwriting and staging to create a live performance of participants' experiences in conversation with the researcher's interpretations of those experiences[56]
- *Layered accounts,* which juxtapose fragments of experience, memories, introspection, research, theory, and other texts.[57] Layered accounts reflect and refract the relationship between personal/cultural experience and interpretation/analysis.

Impressionism

Autoethnographers writing in the mode of impressionism are interested in creating an *overall experience* for readers, focusing as often on everyday subjects as on the epiphanies that shake, test, and change us. Impressionist painters use brushstrokes and depth of color to create a sense of light and movement—rendering an *impression* of a scene and the passage of time (rather than the particulars of a subject or site). Impressionist writers use language, rhythm, and silence to create the sense of research/field experiences. Impressionist texts often rely on first- or second-person narration to evoke unique ways of seeing, knowing, and experiencing self and culture. Impressionist texts take readers into the sights, smells, tastes, and movements of a place, space, or context, and they foreground the fragmented, uncertain, mundane, and mosaic qualities of cultural experiences. Whereas realist texts often separate story and analysis, showing and interpretation, impressionist texts immerse readers in an experience as a means of understanding it; they rely on the impressions they mark/make *as* their mode of interpretation and analysis. Impressionist autoethnographies can take many forms, including:

- *Temporal, sensory,* and *physical accounts*, which explore personal/cultural experiences through the lenses of time, the senses, and the physical body.[58] These texts seek to immerse readers in the sights, sounds, smells, and textures of the experience related in the account.
- *Narratives of space and place,* which show how spaces and places infuse, inform, and shape our identities and experiences.[59] These narratives focus on the impressions that these spaces and places make on the autoethnographer and on the reader.
- *Interactive interviews*, in which two or more people come together to share stories about experiences, cultures, and epiphanies with the goal of providing a nuanced and impressionistic view of these experiences, cultures, and epiphanies.[60] Interactive interviews allow all participants in the interview process to participate meaningfully in the interview, with little, if any, distinction between interviewer and interviewee.

- *Co-constructed narratives* and *collaborative autoethnographies*, which are stories told by multiple narrators that pivot around a common experience, social issue, or epiphany; these stories present multiple perspectives on the experience, issue, or epiphany, as well as offer impressions of the responses to the stories being told without separating story and analysis.[61]

Expressionism

In the visual arts, both realist and impressionist works might be seen as moving from an *outside*—a scene, an external physical world—to an *inside*—a sense of "reality" or an overall impression of an experience or context. By contrast, expressionist works move from the *inside-out* and focus on evoking moods and expressing emotions. Expressionist paintings often feature vivid colors and unexpected, even jarring juxtapositions to highlight the interior and particular experience of the artist (as opposed to a realistic or "natural" external reality).

Expressionist autoethnographies focus on expressing a researcher's internal *feelings* and *emotions*, presenting personal/cultural experience from a thoroughly subjective perspective. Rather than document a physical or empirical reality, expressionist autoethnographies seek to engage readers emotionally and explore the meanings of a storyteller's identities, challenges, joys, and epiphanies. Written primarily in first- and second-person narration, expressionist texts resemble what Van Maanen calls *confessional* texts—texts that take us into a narrator's perspectives on the research process, the storied experience, and the researcher's interactions and relationships with others, as well as how the story and the storyteller are situated in, produced, and changed by cultural beliefs and practices. Expressionist autoethnographers use writing to examine and move through pain, confusion, anger, and uncertainty with the goal of making life better. These texts rely on evocation and feeling, and they use story as the mechanism for interpretation and analysis. Expressionist autoethnographies take many forms, including:

- *Confessional research accounts,* which focus on the researcher's particular experiences of fieldwork and how he or she changes as a result of doing fieldwork[62]
- *Collaborative witnessing,* which involves focusing compassionately on participants' experiences with the goal of developing and sustaining deep and committed relationships with research partners[63]
- *Emotional renderings,* in which the emotional lives and journeys of the researcher and participants form the crux and mood of the narrative[64]
- *Devotional texts* that pay tribute to others, identities, caregiving and/or the creation and sustenance of spiritual communities.[65] Devotional texts chart the subjective, loving, and charged relationships among selves and others.

Conceptualism

In conceptualist art, ideas dominate; they become the "machine that makes the art."[66] Conceptualism returns us to the "outside" world, questioning taken-for-granted assumptions about what art is, how it is created and valued, and what it might mean and for whom. Conceptualism also reimagines the role of the artist in culture. Rather than viewing artists as craftspersons who create material objects (e.g., paintings and sculptures) within a system of tangible and reliable value (as defined by critics, museums, and buyers), conceptualist artists are innovators who create new and often unexpected ideas, perspectives, and experiences.

In conceptualist autoethnographies, personal stories become the mechanism for conveying and critiquing cultural experiences, breaking silences, and reclaiming voices. Conceptualist autoethnographies use first-, second-, and third-person narration and are highly reflexive. Conceptualist texts question the role and purpose of research and writing, the formality of research texts, the role of the author as artist, and the lessons that autoethnographies can offer writers and readers. In conceptualist texts, interpretation and analysis are the inspiration for story; showing and interpreting are tightly coupled. Conceptualism also emphasizes the importance of audiences in creating and completing texts, thus making a variety of collaborative readings possible. Conceptualist autoethnographies may take several forms, including:

- *Performative writing,* in which the writing itself approximates—performs—the experience(s) and culture(s) being discussed. Performative writing is "writing as doing," rather than "writing as meaning."[67] In performative autoethnographies, the idea, concept, experience and/or culture under consideration guides the form and structure of the work.
- *Insider texts,* in which members of marginalized and subordinated groups create representations that illuminate the workings and abuses of power in culture, research, and representation, and that work to correct the inaccuracies and harms of previous research.[68]
- *Critical autoethnographies,* which foreground overt critiques of cultural identities, experiences, practices, and cultural systems, as well as address instances of unfairness or injustice.[69] Critical autoethnographies foreground a writer's standpoint and make this standpoint accessible, transparent, and vulnerable to judgment and evaluation.[70]
- *Community autoethnographies,* in which researchers collaborate with community members to investigate and respond to a particular, often oppressive, issue.[71]

As we note above, our discussion of the forms of autoethnographic representation is not exhaustive, nor are the categories we offer fixed or certain. As you create your own autoethnographic representations, we encourage you to reimagine and extend these categories and forms.

Story as Theory and Theorizing Stories

As your autoethnography takes shape, consider as well how you will articulate the relationship between theory and story. For autoethnographers, theory and story share a reciprocal, symbiotic relationship. Theory asks about and explains the nuances of an experience and the happenings of a culture; story is the mechanism that illustrates and embodies these nuances and happenings. Conceived in this way, theory is *not* an add-on to story. Instead, theory is a way to understand—think with and through, ask questions about, and act on—the experiences and happenings in our stories.[72]

Autoethnography is a method for putting theory into action; autoethnographic texts can thus pose a challenge to entrenched beliefs, practices, and ways of understanding experience. In some autoethnographies, story and theory are told *together*; here, story *is* theory and theory *is* story.[73] In other autoethnographies, story and theory are put into direct conversation, with authors using the vocabulary of theory and the mode of story to create nuanced and compelling accounts of personal/cultural experience.[74]

In this section, we discuss techniques for linking story, self, theory, and culture. The techniques that make the most sense for your writing will depend on the cultures you write about, your fieldwork experiences, and the forms of representation that connect most meaningfully with the stories you want to tell. Further, this is not an exhaustive list of how to work with theory; make sure also to examine autoethnographies and texts in which you believe the theory-story relationship is successful and compelling.

Living with Story: Story *as* Theory

In Chapter 2, I (Tony) mentioned that I published autoethnographies in order to offer others stories to use as "equipment for living,"[75] as stories to "live with" during times of relational distress.[76] This assumption—that we can live *with* story—is one way to understand the connection between story and theory: stories *are* theories that we use to understand experience.

We can each attest to the ways our lives have changed because of living with others' stories; the stories have become our theories, frameworks for understanding, interpreting, and analyzing personal/cultural experiences. For instance, after reading Boylorn's autoethnography on race and reflexivity, I (Tony) am reminded of the need to recognize the ways race infuses and alters everyday interactions.[77] Bochner's autoethnographic work about his relationship with his father also served as an impetus and guide for my writing about my own father; in sharing stories about *his* father, Art taught me how to understand and love *my* father.[78]

For me (Stacy), reading Ronai's[79] and Ellis's[80] work as a graduate student and young scholar encouraged me to write with honesty, vulnerability, and integrity; however, it was not until many years later that I understood how these works about parent-child relationships and complicated love and loss would become core themes and commitments in my life and research. I (Carolyn) am constantly inspired by the stories students' write about their lives. Their stories have taught me about experiences I have not had, such as losing a father at an early age, coping with eating disorders, coming out as gay, and losing a home to foreclosure.[81] Their stories have made me a better teacher, mentor, and person.

These examples show how autoethnographic stories have changed what we think and how we live; they have become the theories we use to understand experience, working on and with us and encouraging us to be more just and humane. In these autoethnographies, the stories are the theories; the authors did not feel a need to explicitly include the language and arguments of a particular theoretical framework. Nonetheless, other autoethnographies do use the language of theory and the conventions of storytelling to create a conversation that shows the links among self, story, theory, and culture. In the following sections, we outline a few techniques for combining theory and story.

Citationality: Writing in the Poetics of Theory

Citationality focuses on the poetics of theory by treating theory as a *language available to you* as you write your stories. This approach uses *citation* (the quoting of texts) as a means for articulating ideas, feelings, and conclusions. This approach does not work with all theoretical writing; however, it often works well with the writing of critical theorists whose projects aim to *enact* the intervention of theory *in the writing* itself.[82]

For example, in my (Stacy's) work, critical scholars, including Roland Barthes, Walter Benjamin, Jacques Derrida, Julia Kristeva, Judith Butler, Michael Taussig, and Kathleen Stewart, provide particularly *poetic* theory.[83] For me, the language, the rhythms of the sentences, and the movement of the ideas in these author's works are beautiful and compelling. I use these theorists' words in and as my/our work, combining my language with theirs and citing their work either in the main text or in endnotes. Consider, for example, this passage from "Lost and Found,"[84] which features the words of Taussig and Stewart (shown here in italics—refer to the notes for Chapter 4 at the end of this book for a discussion of these ideas and citations):

> These stories tell a journey into a possible future. They make pilgrimages into what happens on the way, assembling temporary *monuments* to risk, to loss and longing.... You tell these stories as *a memorial, as a way to slow down*[85] and to resist the impulse to represent and evaluate long enough to perform what takes
> *hold in and of us*
> *in a world that's always now,*
> *always being made*
> *and suffered,*[86] composed and inhabited. What this work knows, if it knows anything, is change, is letting go, is telling stories [about]... *"something not quite already given and yet somehow happening."*[87]

Many autoethnographers, including Craig Gingrich-Philbrook, Tami Spry, Sophie Tamas, Stacy Wolf, and Jonathan Wyatt and Ken Gale, focus on the poetics of citation, moving seamlessly between their voices and the language of theory, poetically merging story and theory so that story becomes theory in action.[88]

Writing in/as Reverie and Mining Connections

Another approach to merging theory and story is to use a theoretical idea/image as a starting point for mapping the movement of an idea or a series of observations. Such writing presents a meditation—or, *reverie*—prompted by a single idea/image that charts and follows a line of thought. An alternative metaphor for this approach is *mining* a single idea for the connections that it incites in thinking and for understanding experience. To use this approach, begin with a single (and often simple) phrase, idea, or image, and follow where it leads in your writing.

I (Tony) use this technique in the essay, "Mothers, Faggots, and Witnessing (Un)Contestable Experience." I mined the experience of being called "faggot" in four ways to illustrate the possible relationships between intention, context, and meaning. I began each iteration with the same series of sentences:

"I fucked your mom, faggot!" someone screams at me from a passing car. It's 10 p.m., and I'm walking on a residential street in Tampa, Florida.
I check my location: Morrison Avenue. I take note of my surroundings: Any place to run? I grab my cell phone to call the cops...[89]

In the first iteration of the experience, I describe my self-identification as a faggot who was indeed walking to a gay bar. I also describe wondering/worrying if I had time to call the cops and if I could hide or lie about my sexuality in order to stay safe.

In the second iteration, I consider the cultural conditions that may have contributed to my concerns about safety—my ability to recognize "fucking" and "faggot" as derogatory terms—to understand the degraded and turbulent social status of women and faggots, and to know whom I should call for help (e.g., the cops rather than a hair stylist or a taxi driver).

In the third iteration, I write about how I would describe the person who screamed at me—a teenager, I think. I discuss the misogynistic and homophobic practices that I used to engage in when *I* was a teenager, particularly how calling others faggots and making fun of other boys' mothers was a way for me to simultaneously show power over others (the faggots, boys, and mothers) and to garner respect from my peers.

In the fourth iteration, I consider the ways that I could use the experience to my advantage by having the teenager arrested and me being the witness to his crime. Trying to have the screamer arrested could give me a more complex and evocative story to tell, though I felt guilty for wanting to get even with and exploit the teen and guilty for wanting to exercise power over him.

In each iteration of the story, I connected my words, ideas, and feelings with existing research and theoretical ideas, letting my insights around one brief experience create ever-expanding possibilities, relationships, and contexts.[90]

Writing as Foundation/Elaboration/Juxtaposition

A third approach to merging story and theory is to consider the ways theory supports, elaborates, and/or contradicts personal experience. In this approach, theory provides a *foundation* on which to elaborate or provide a counter narrative to the meanings and implications of your stories. This approach to using theory is often found in autoethnographies that use footnotes or endnotes, glossaries, appendices, and/or split or collage texts—all of which provide explanations, make connections, and provide supplemental or counter narratives—in addition or juxtaposition to a primary personal narrative.[91]

The use of footnotes as foundation can be seen in my (Stacy's) previous example from the essay, "Lost and Found," or in another excerpt from this essay in which I use R. D. Laing's theory-poem "Knots" as inspiration for a poem on adoption. In a series of footnotes I write:

[1]The title of this section comes from the portion of R.D. Laing's poem "Knots" which reads, "The patterns delineated here.... /are all, perhaps, strangely, familiar.... Words that/ come to mind to name them are: knots, tangles, /fankles, *impasses*, disjunctions, whirligogs, binds."[92]

[2]Laing writes into the knot of mine-not-mine, me-not-me that I imagine as a conversation on gratitude and entitlement in adoption. He offers: "All I have has been given me and is mine.../It is not mine/but it has been given me and I have it/therefore I am grateful for what I have, or/have been given./But I resent being grateful/because if I have been given it, it has not always been mine.[93]

These footnotes are connected to a poem about adoption I share in the main text of the essay:

Lost: to adoption,
to each other, mine not mine
not given, grateful.
Found: in searching, in
letting go, opening to
what's not already gone.
Knotted: in word, in
sacrificial strands of silk
carefully bound, stitched....

Consider also Eve Tuck's and C. Ree's use of both a glossary and an appendix,[94] Jeanine Mingé and Amber Zimmerman's layering and "revisiting" of narratives of/in the spaces of Los Angeles,[95] and Amy Kilgard's use of collage as a kind of/means for creating performance.[96]

Considering Story, Participants, Readers, and Yourself in Writing

When we write autoethnography, we must consider not only our commitment to providing readers with texts that link story and theory, but also our responsibility as authors for telling stories that exhibit narrative rationality and espouse relational ethics. As we note throughout this text, our identities, experiences, and stories are intertwined with the identities, experiences, and stories of others; our writing must be both faithful to experience and respectful of relationships.

Narrative Rationality

According to Walter Fisher, humans are storytellers in search of narrative rationality—stories that are plausible, trustworthy, reliable, and "true" to experience. Narrative rationality consists of two elements—narrative *probability* and narrative *fidelity*. Narrative *probability* exists when a story is coherent, "hangs" together, and is free of contradiction; of the story, readers ask: "Could the story have happened in the way the narrator and characters describe?"[97] Narrative *fidelity* considers the "truth qualities" of a story—"the soundness of its reasoning and the value of its values"; of the story, readers ask: "Do the actions and interactions in the story happen for 'good reasons'?" and "Are the lessons of the story relevant to and valuable for my life?"[98] According to Fisher, if a story meets the "tests" of narrative probability and narrative fidelity, readers will more likely "accept" the story and incorporate it into their lives.[99]

As autoethnographers interested in the symbiotic dance of self and culture, we must be mindful of the ways in which our stories—especially our characters, descriptions, dialogue, interpretations, and conclusions—illustrate narrative rationality. Even though our stories can and do change with time, space, and context; even though memory is fluid and fallible and revision is always possible,[100] we must, to the best of our ability, create probable, trustworthy, and resonant autoethnographic tales.

Relational Ethics in Writing

In addition to *narrative* rationality, we must consider the *relational ethics* involved in writing autoethnography.[101] When writing autoethnography, Tami Spry encourages autoethnographers to:

- Avoid *self-indulgence* by critically reflecting on our motives for and methods of writing; disclosing information about selves, others, and contexts; and, to the best of our ability, connect our motives, methods, and disclosures to larger cultural issues.
- Avoid *blaming* and *shaming* when representing experience by learning about our selves, interrogating our connections to others and to larger cultural systems, and examining "our involvement in perpetuating or being subject to oppressive systems."
- Avoid *heroics* by humbly and critically reflecting on fieldwork experiences.
- Avoid framing self/others as victims without offering a critical analysis of injustice and oppression.
- Avoid *self-righteousness* by acknowledging our identities and privileges as researchers.
- Avoid *disengagement* with self/others by learning about the histories, cultures, and politics of the experiences and cultures you represent.[102]

I (Carolyn) confront several of these concerns in an essay about my neighbors in a mountain community, where I encounter differences in attitudes about religion, gender, ethnicity, and race. I question the ethics of showing racist and sexist attitudes in the stories I present about the mountain people; still, I make the case that presenting their views is an important part of understanding, and possibly changing, racist and sexist attitudes. I attempt to understand their values from their perspectives, calling on what I know about my own rural family and upbringing. I take seriously my responsibility as a rural, southern-raised woman to explain my position and affect their attitudes without alienating them. I question my motives for including information about the mountain community that might be perceived as negative and I focus on the positive values of being a good community member and helping neighbors, vital aspects of this culture. I ask questions about why I feel more protective of my family than I do of these neighbors. Finally, I seek to understand how I am similar to, as well as different from, them and speculate how I might have been more like them had I continued my life in a rural southern culture. I ask how the mountain folks see me, as well as how I see them, and how they might condemn some of my behaviors. The final portrayal is a messy representation filled with ethical dilemmas and questions that—I hope—helps readers think more complexly about their values and experiences, how they story and re-story themselves and others, and ways to respect and accommodate vast differences in our research.[103]

As we note above, your writing must be faithful to your experience and respectful of and responsible to your participants and readers. Once you have written an autoethnographic story (or stories) that you believe meets these guidelines, it is time to edit and share your work.

Editing and Sharing Your Work

Stephen King distinguishes between two types of writing: writing with the door shut and writing with the door open. When writing in door-shut mode, your goal is to write as much as possible without any interference. This mode of writing should result in what King terms an "all-story" draft.[104] King recommends, if possible, that you take a day, week, or month-long vacation from the all-story draft. Following this vacation, you can return to edit the draft, looking for ways to simplify, clarify, and sharpen the writing.

Once you edit the "all-story" draft, working to carefully, ethically, thoughtfully, and aesthetically craft the story so that its themes, characters, voice, dialogue, plot, and theoretical insights tell an evocative and meaningful tale of self/culture, you are ready to share your work with others. Share your all-story draft with your "first readers"—people who will be supportive as well as lovingly critical and exacting with the work—along with key participants or characters represented in the story. King refers to this sharing process as door-open mode. He also suggests asking your *ideal reader*—the reader you may have thought of and wrote to in this draft—to read the work. "You can't let the whole world into your story," King says, "but you can let in the ones [who] matter the most."[105]

Ask your first readers for feedback on how the story is crafted; what thoughts and feelings the story generates; what insights the text offers about the relationships among self, culture, and context; and how well and responsibly the account represents the lives and identities of others. As you engage this process, embrace King's door-open metaphor: stay *open* to the reactions and suggestions you receive from readers, understanding that this is the first step in an ongoing feedback process—one that also includes feedback from participants, mentors, reviewers, editors, and critics.

Think carefully about how to address the feedback you receive, staying mindful of the goals of your work and open to how the process of revision can move the work closer to what it should become. When I (Stacy) am in the midst of revising and addressing feedback from my first readers—among whom I count Tony and Carolyn—I often return to writer Raymond Carver's thoughts about revision and craft:

> Evan Connell said once that he knew he was finished with a short story when he found himself going through it and taking out commas and then going through the story again and putting commas back in the same places. I like that way of working on something. I respect that kind of care for what is being done. That's all we have, finally, the words, and they had better be the right ones, with the punctuation in the right places so that they can best say what they are meant to say. If the words are heavy with the writer's own unbridled emotions, or if they are imprecise and inaccurate for some other reason—if the words are in any way blurred—the reader's eyes will slide right over them and nothing will be achieved.[106]

Carver's argument about the precision and accuracy of writing, along with a commitment to making our stories as good as we can, turns our attention to questions about the quality and effectiveness of autoethnographic research and representation. In the next chapter, we consider how to assess the engagement, effectiveness, and insight offered in/by autoethnography.

5

EVALUATING
AUTOETHNOGRAPHY

EVALUATING RESEARCH IS a necessary yet contested terrain.[1] The difficulty of evaluating autoethnography, which includes the experience of the researcher, is perhaps more difficult than evaluating traditional research projects. Critics of the method routinely have refused to evaluate autoethnography as *scholarship*. These critics base their refusal on the narrow view that personal, autobiographic, and aesthetic work cannot be assessed for its explanatory power, scholarly insight, or ability to cultivate social change. Indeed, some critics have worried that including storytelling and first-person narration in research sacrifices the analytic purpose of scholarship. For those opposed to the method, featuring—even *celebrating* narratives—invites scholarship in which stories are

...stripped of social context and social consequences. [Narratives] are understood in terms of an individualized view of the self. Narratives are the means by which a narrating subject, autonomous and independent.... can achieve authenticity.... This represents an almost total failure to use narrative to achieve serious social analysis.[2]

Though those writing narratives rarely presume a context-free, autonomous, and independent subject or author, some people still question the relationship between storytelling and scholarship. Consider, for example, an ongoing debate I (Tony) have with a colleague. It began when my colleague, who was not aware of my autoethnographic research, informed me that any research using first-person narration was inadequate, solely because of its inclusion of first-person voice.

"But what if the research is comprehensive, well-argued, and full of passion and conviction?" I asked.

"Then it shouldn't use first-person narration," she replied. "First-person narration introduces partiality and bias."

I informed my colleague that I use "I" in my work. "I do not want to hide myself behind the text or claim that my work is objective or value-free," I told her. "Dismissing an entire project solely for the use of 'I' is unfortunate and naïve."

She disagreed; we continue to disagree. Students tell me that this colleague does not allow them to use "I" in their writing. I tell these students that although I believe such I-restriction is uncalled for, the restriction is her perspective and a writing requirement for her courses.

Others have found themselves defending the use of first-person voice. Aslihan Agaogl describes how his dissertation supervisor told him the use of "I" in a dissertation was inappropriate and wrong; there are no "'I's in academic writing." Agaogl then notes that his training in creative writing taught him that third-person (distanced, passive) narration is "not acceptable." "Good writers" do not use passive voice; "good writing" uses active, first-person narration. "When you alienate the 'I' from your dissertation," he continues, "you are taking a big risk: turning your writing into a mere juxtaposition of facts and figures."[3] As David Shields observes, "We commonly do not remember that it is, after all, always the first person that is speaking" in our research.[4]

The use of first-person voice and the practice of sharing personal narratives also is criticized outside of academia. Consider the debate generated around dance critic Arlene Croce's criticism of the dance piece *Still/Here* created by Bill T. Jones. Croce opens her *New Yorker* essay by writing, "I have not seen Bill T. Jones's *Still/Here* and I have no intention to review it."[5] Jones's use of video footage featuring the personal narratives of people living with terminal illnesses in relation to the dancer's movements on stage rendered the work, for Croce, "beyond the reach of criticism."[6] Croce refuses to view and review so-called victim art:

> I can't review someone I feel sorry for or hopeless about... [people] I'm *forced* to feel sorry for because of the way they present themselves: as dissed blacks, abused women, or disenfranchised homosexuals—as performers, in short, who make out of victimhood victim art.[7]

Responses to this diatribe reminded Croce that "art comes bundled with autobiography, fiction, morality, [and] politics."[8] Scholarship—especially and particularly autoethnographic scholarship—comes bundled with these gifts *and* burdens. In addition to dismissing the personal, Croce positions herself as above (as more informed and better educated) than both the artist who created the work and the audiences who saw *Still/Here*. Such attempts to position critics and other evaluators as separate from or above authors create illusory boundaries and "borders" between scholarship and criticism.[9] As Craig Gingrich Philbrook notes,

> What we think of as evaluation... never stands above autoethnography. Instead, it always occurs alongside, on the same plane and in the same world as the autoethnographic work under consideration, whether it contests or reaches out to that work in coalition.[10]

In this view, autoethnographic evaluation and criticism present "another personal story" about the experience of an experience.[11]

Rather than think of evaluation as a power play or a pronouncement from/by an all-knowing entity—despite the power we sometimes bestow on those "delegated/assigned a judgmental authority" in the academy—we would be better served to believe, as Gingrich-Philbrook writes, that

> Any evaluation of autoethnography... is simply another story from a highly situated, privileged, empowered subject about something he or she experienced. To evaluate autoethnography in a genuinely useful way, you have to open yourself up to being changed by it, to heeding its call to surrender your entitlement.[12]

Further, although Michael Patton notes, "Judging quality requires criteria,"[13] we recognize that evaluation criteria are political: they privilege some voices and research projects while discouraging and silencing other voices and projects.[14]

In the spirit of demonstrating openness to being changed by the work we create and evaluate, in this chapter we present our goals for autoethnographic texts. We then assess three of our autoethnographies in terms of these aims as a way of showing how we, as autoethnographers, were successful *and* unsuccessful in creating effective and compelling autoethnographies. In these evaluations, we accentuate how the practices, considerations, and responsibilities of doing and writing autoethnography are, like all skill-based endeavors, *crafts* that we continue to improve. We conclude this chapter by briefly reviewing our journey in this book, pausing to consider where autoethnography might take you—and us—in the future.

Goals for Assessing Autoethnography

Based on the core ideals, research design considerations, and reasons for doing autoethnography we outline in Chapter 2, we have created four categories of goals that we use to assess the value and success of an autoethnography. Rather than creating a closed set of "criteria" against which we might measure autoethnographic texts, we offer these goals as both "descriptive/prescriptive" and "practical/theoretical" objectives—descriptive/prescriptive in terms of evaluating what an autoethnography might and should aspire to be, and practical/theoretical in terms of evaluating if/ how an autoethnography has achieved its purpose(s).[15] Our goals for evaluating autoethnographies include:

- Making contributions to knowledge
- Valuing the personal and experiential
- Demonstrating the power, craft, and responsibilities of stories and storytelling
- Taking a relationally responsible approach to research practice and representation.

We discuss each of these goals in the following sections.

Making Contributions to Knowledge

As we note throughout this book, we do autoethnography to reflect on and create understanding about identities, relationships, and/or experiences. We also do autoethnography to share our reflections and understandings with others. As such, contributing to knowledge means extending *existing* knowledge and research while recognizing that knowledge is both *situated* and *contested*. Contributing to knowledge also means valuing the *particular, nuanced, complex,* and *insider* insights that autoethnography offers researchers, participants, and readers/audiences.

Valuing the Personal and Experiential

Autoethnographers value the personal and experiential in their research. This includes featuring the *perspective of the self* in context and culture, exploring *experience* as a means of insight about social life, and recognizing and embracing the risks of presenting *vulnerable selves* in research. Using—and even foregrounding—*emotions* and *bodily experience* as means and modes of understanding is also an important way to accomplish this goal.

Demonstrating the Power, Craft, and Responsibilities of Stories and Storytelling

Autoethnographers foreground the *power of stories* to describe and critique culture. We look to stories to show *sense-making,* the processes we use to create *understanding,* and the *reflexivity* in considering a researcher's location in research and representation. Here, reflexivity includes both acknowledging and critiquing our place and privilege in society and using the stories we tell to *break long-held silences* on power, relationships, cultural taboos, and forgotten and/or suppressed experiences. Accomplishing these goals requires autoethnographers to place as much importance on developing the *craft* of writing and representation as they do on developing and honing their analytic abilities.

Taking a Relationally Responsible Approach to Research Practice and Representation

Autoethnographers take a *relationally responsible* approach to our engagements and representations of self, participants, and readers/audiences. This means working to make our research relationships as *collaborative, committed,* and *reciprocal* as possible and *safeguarding the identities* and *ensuring the privacy* of our participants. A relationally responsible approach also means making our research *accessible* to a variety of readers and viewing our work as an *opportunity to engage and improve* the lives of our selves, participants, and readers/audiences.

Assessing the Goals in Practice

Many authors discuss the criteria we should use to evaluate autoethnographic texts.[16] However, with the exception of the occasional review of an autoethnographic book or performance, we do not see many autoethnographers explicitly assessing autoethnographies based on how completely or how well they achieve the goals of autoethnography.

In this section, we evaluate three autoethnographies we have published, noting where our work met and where it failed to meet the goals we hold for autoethnography. We do this to illustrate that although we are committed to the value and practices of autoethnography, we also recognize that our understandings of the method and of our research have changed with time. We want to show how our work has shifted as we have honed our abilities as researchers and writers and as we have changed as people. By attending to the craft and possible meanings of each text, we offer constructive evaluations with the hope of enhancing, refining, and reconsidering the practices of autoethnographic research and representation.

Tony: *Narrating the Closet*

When I started writing about coming out of the closet, I knew from reading numerous memoirs about and research on coming out that I could not write just another "coming out" story. I knew that I had to *contribute to knowledge* about coming out by saying something new about the experience or writing against these memoirs/this research. I also needed a "new angle" toward coming out; my experience, alone, of coming out was not "sufficient to justify a narrative."[17]

In my book, I work backward from coming out and against the metaphorical construct of "the closet" in order to investigate experiences of coming out that were not often, or explicitly, discussed in existing texts. I begin by observing, wondering:

> ...if a person is said to have come out of the closet, then it must be assumed that the person earlier went into the closet—one must go in before coming out. But how does a person enter the metaphorical space? Is a person birthed into the room? If a person has no idea of what same-sex attraction is or means, or has no familiarity with such terms as "lesbian," "gay," "bisexual," and/or "queer," would the person be able to describe her or his experience as precloseted? Does a closet form only via hindsight, a reconstructed looking-back? What conditions must be met before a closet can exist, before a person could ever fathom coming out? When the closet is framed as the *origin* of same-sex attraction—a framing best noted by Sedgwick's title *Epistemology of the Closet*—precloseted experiences and epistemologies are often disregarded.[18]

Experiences of entering or going into the closet were rarely discussed, at least explicitly, in the research I encountered. As such, I use my *personal experiences* to represent *particular, nuanced, complex* and *insider* insights about precloseted experiences in an attempt to *contribute to the knowledge* about the experience of the closet.

Throughout the text, I try to attend to the *power, craft* and *responsibilities* of storytelling. My training in journalism helped me improve the clarity and structure of my writing, and as I completed my graduate degrees I worked to hone my narrative writing skills. As an autoethnographer, I want to tell a compelling and evocative story of coming out by attending to the *craft* of writing.

For example, in the third chapter "Living (In) the Closet: The Time of Being Closeted," I switch from using first-person narration to second-person narration. I make this switch for two reasons. First, I want to bring readers into my story, inviting them to live my experiences alongside me, feeling how I felt and suggesting how they might, under similar circumstances, act as I did. Second, I want to create some distance from sad, shameful, and even unethical experiences (e.g., lying to others, driving while intoxicated, having numerous reckless sexual encounters). Although these experiences are bound up with, and constitutive of, my coming out experiences, they also make me feel *vulnerable*. Writing using first-person narration made me feel *too* vulnerable about my shameful actions; using second-person narration allows me to tell my stories fully and openly while providing me with a feeling of safety.

I think that moving from first-person to second-person voice also works for readers. A student told me that, after reading this chapter, she "would never want to have dinner with me"; to her, I was manipulative and unethical. She also shared that later chapters softened her opinion of me, something that, *personally*, I was glad to hear. As a *storyteller*, though, I expect and desire her harsh response: I want to convey a *vulnerable*, miserable self, and hearing this reader's reaction makes me I feel I succeeded in my writing.

Although these are ways in which my text fared well in terms of our evaluative goals for autoethnography, I would also like to acknowledge three possible limitations—even failures—of the text. First, I wrote the book from the perspective of a White, gay, 30-year-old, able-bodied man, and I tried to show moments when my race and age and sex and ability influenced what I said and how I interpreted the actions and identities of others. However, some people tell me that women's experiences are not well represented in the book. Others say I do not sufficiently address race and racial influences on coming out. Still others believe I present a generational (age-based) perspective on coming out—a perspective not necessarily shared by or applicable to gay men in their eighties or their twenties. Even though I tried to write *reflexively*, I now believe that I was not *reflexive* enough; I should have interrogated my race, age, sex, and ability more than I did, and, at the very least, used a more complicated, intersectional approach to understand my experiences.

Second, my book is not as critical of homophobia or others' decisions to not come out as some may want it to be. I did not want to dismiss or eliminate contact with family members for homophobic remarks. Counter to some calls for people to come out and make their lesbian, gay, bisexual, and/or queer identities visible, I did not want people to feel pressure to come out to particular others. Although I feel my ideas and arguments are relationally responsible, I recognized how others can perceive my ideas as *relationally irresponsible* concessions to homophobic others and to insidious heteronormative cultural structures; by *not* being aggressively critical, my work does not do enough to *engage* and *improve* the lives of others.

Third, although I received "informed consent" for my formal interviews, I included, without consent, several of the brief conversations about coming out that happened in my office, at restaurants, and via e-mail or Facebook. I struggled with whether it was *relationally responsible* to include these conversations without asking for permission. For example, a student—Maria—came to my office to seek coming out advice: She was not out to her parents and she had a girlfriend/partner of more than five years. Maria then disclosed that two years prior she was diagnosed with cancer and was only expected to live a few months; she struggled with knowing that even as she faced/prepared for death, she could not disclose her same-sex attraction to her parents or tell them about her partner.

I thought Maria's story captured the essence—the narrative truth—of coming out situations in which a person might be more comfortable with disclosing a life-threatening illness than their same-sex attraction. And so I used a variation of Maria's experience when writing my book, though I changed any details that might identify her, including her illness, age, and location.[19] I felt confident that my account effectively masked her identity. However, I did not ask Maria for permission to write about her experience. Years later, I still wonder if I exploited Maria's experience for my benefit (that is, as "data" for my arguments about coming out). Yet I still believe that sharing her experience might help others who struggle with similar coming-out circumstances.

As I continue to do and write autoethnographies about sexuality and same-sex attraction, I will take these limitations into account. I have since forced myself to be as reflexive as possible with all of my writing, to frame and understand my experiences from multiple perspectives, and to observe even better the possible ways in which my social privileges influence my experiences and the stories I tell. I will continue to be more mindful of the differing criticisms that I might receive about my autoethnographic work, especially criticisms that could suggest that my arguments are not radical enough. And I will be vigilantly observant about whether and how I represent others, as well as the choices I make to mask these others in my text.

Stacy: "Lost and Found"

In my essay "Lost and Found," I write about how relationships are created, questioned, and transformed in the telling and performance of stories. I write specifically about how a series of changes, losses, and discoveries, including the decision not to adopt another child and the loss of my grandmother (who was herself adopted), illustrate how identities and lives are performed *in relation* to others.

In terms of the first goal, which focuses on making contributions to *knowledge*, I work from the idea that knowledge is not only situated and contested, but also relationally created. The writing works to tell the story of theory—for example, Walter Benjamin's ideas about the storyteller and Judith Butler's ideas about giving accounts of ourselves for and to others—in relation to my stories about the experience of adoption, my decision not to adopt a second child, and the lessons my grandmother taught me about adoption. Using my *particular, nuanced, complex,* and *insider* knowledge of adoption, my essay extends existing research and *contributes to knowledge* about identities and relationships in the context of adoption.

My essay also foregrounds both the *personal* and *experiential* and embraces *vulnerability* in the representation. In the text, I convey the sadness and the joy I feel about my relationships with my adopted child, the child I chose not to adopt, and my grandmother. I focus on the *emotions* and *bodily* experiences of both losing and memorializing my grandmother. However, although I believe the risks involved in making myself and my loved ones *vulnerable* in the text are worthwhile, given the insights they offer about the experience of adoption and loss, I have had moments of regret about just how much I chose to reveal. For example, when the essay was reviewed on *The Critical Lede*, I found myself cringing as the reviewers discussed my work. Although their comments were supportive and useful to me as an author, hearing the complicated story of my identity and experience chronicled in a laundry list of transgressions and losses left me feeling exposed. Still, I believe that the essay meets the goal of valuing the personal and experiential, and, for the most part, I find the risks of vulnerability acceptable.

Believing in the power of *storytelling* as a way to describe and critique culture is a central part of the argument and logic of "Lost and Found." I write to make sense of the changes in my relationships, the loss of my grandmother and the possibility of adopting another child, and my discovery of a new queer identity. I write *reflexively* about taboo topics (leaving my marriage to pursue a queer), about the *silences* around the experience of and losses of adopted children, and about the hidden power structures and exploitations of racial and economic privilege in transnational adoption. However, I wonder whether I go far enough in meeting the challenge and commitment of reflexivity, particularly when writing about transnational adoption. Although I ask whether the "world needs one more page filled with the worry and guilt of one more adoptive parent," I read my writing as just that—pages given over to worry and guilt—and question how my writing might contribute more meaningfully work against creating such systems of loss and injustice.[20] Finally, as I note in Chapter 4, I chose to use the poetic form of *haibun* to write about the immediate and expansive ways in which stories create relationships. Once I made this choice, I read widely about the use and aesthetics of *haibun* and worked to develop skill in writing this form, responding to the call for autoethnographers to attend to the craft of their writing. Thus, while my essay does a good job of demonstrating the power and craft of storytelling, it does not sufficiently address the responsibilities of reflexivity in representation.

In terms of the final goal, which focuses on the *relational responsibilities* of autoethnographic research, "Lost and Found" is perhaps the least successful. I believe the essay argues that *all* relationships can and should be collaborative, committed, and reciprocal. As I previously note, I wrote the essay with the explicit purpose of understanding and connecting my experience to the experiences of other adoptive parents, adopted children, and queer people. The touching and inspiring responses I have received about this work in classrooms, via e-mail, and at conferences suggest that I achieved this goal.

I could not share this work with or get consent from my grandmother before she died, though I feel confident that she would have approved of how I represented our conversations and the lessons she taught me about writing and living. I feel less sure about what she would say about my descriptions of her physical appearance during her stay in the hospital or about my decision to write about the last moments of her life. In addition, I worry about how my child (whom I avoid identifying by name in the work, as well as here in this text) will feel about being included and portrayed in this essay. I also am concerned about my work being a source of embarrassment if it is ever accessed by school friends, a perhaps remote but nevertheless petrifying possibility for a pre-teen. Thus, I am not sure that I did all I could have to write and act in *relationally responsible* ways and to *safeguard the privacy* of my loved ones.

Finally, while the essay underscores the importance of creating stories readers can *use* in their own lives, I have received feedback that this essay is not accessible given its use and love of theoretical language. Although I am committed to the goal of showing critical theory in action and choose, as I note in Chapter 4, to use theory as a foundation for the work, the theory in this essay might alienate some readers. Further, the use of poetry—a form I love and consider to be as essential as laughter or good wine or breathing—might also turn some readers away.

In sum, although "Lost and Found" is successful in meeting many—if not most—of the goals of autoethnography, it falls short in several important ways. I am taking the lessons of writing this assessment forward with me as I write new autoethnographies. Also, I am choosing to view "Lost and Found" as an important moment in my development as a scholar, teacher, mother, and partner, and as a loving and meaningful tribute to my grandmother.

Carolyn: Collaborative Witnessing and Ethical Research

In the preceding sections, Tony evaluates his book and Stacy evaluates one of her essays. Given how long I have been doing autoethnography, I would like to speak to a few essays I detail throughout this book, and then discuss how my recent work responds to some of the limitations in my earlier studies. When I wrote "Maternal Connections," the first essay about my mother, I used a short story to *contribute to knowledge* about caring for a parent. My story questions the idea of caregiving as a burden, instead portraying caregiving as a loving and meaning-making relationship. In portraying a maternal connection, my story introduces concerns and offers an analysis of caregiving across generations. The story also became an historical essay in that it describes a generation of women who chose careers over having children and offers a discussion about career and motherhood at a particular point in our culture. Given the responses and tales this story engenders from many, I believe this work contributes to knowledge and offers readers an example of story *as* theory.

"Maternal Connections" also emphasizes the *personal and experiential* in describing my relationship with my mother. The story foregrounds our emotional relationship, showing how we "fall in love" with each other. The story *embodies* illness in its descriptions of my mother's ailing body and physical functions alongside my introspection about my body and comparison to my mother's body. My mother is *vulnerable* in my descriptions and revelations about her and her illness. As a loving daughter trying to take care of my mother, I am vulnerable as well in that I risk harming our relationship and how others will view me: Will my mother be embarrassed by my descriptions? Will readers wonder whether I have exploited my relationship with my mother?

In this story, I call on literary writing techniques to show the *power, craft, and responsibilities* of stories to describe and critique culture. I do not include theory or reference the research literature, but instead call on sensory details, movement, emotions, dialogue, and scene setting to convey an experience of taking care of a parent—one that many of us will have at some point—and the contradictions for baby-boomer women, many of whom chose a career over having a family. Writing in this way led me to reflect on the choices I made as a career woman and on my relationship with my mother, even improving our relationship in the process. The short story form makes the story accessible to a large audience and hopefully provides a benchmark for others thinking about relationships with and responsibilities toward parents.

That I did not show the story to my mother before publishing it also introduced concerns about representing others in *relationally responsible* ways, especially those who can be recognized in our stories. I addressed these concerns in a second story about my mother, which I later shared with her along with "Maternal Connections."[21] In the second story, I speak about what it means to share our stories with our loved ones, as well as our *responsibilities* to them and to readers. I also raised the issue of valuing our *relationships* over our research projects, and what such valuing might entail. I portray how difficult it is to read her the entire printed text, especially the parts that might hurt her. Though not fully resolved, I end the second essay by introducing the idea that we must look at each particular text and relationship, always thinking and trying to rethink what we say and do. I conclude the essay by expressing my belief that my relationship with my mother was more important than telling readers everything about her/our relationship.

These two essays made me think deeply about how I want to relate to those who participate in my studies and my responsibilities to them. My current research with Holocaust survivors takes into account what I learned in writing about my mother. My work with and about survivor Jerry Rawicki is now either constructed *with* Jerry or shared with him many times throughout the writing process.[22] I want to *contribute to knowledge* about trauma, in particular the Holocaust, examine survivor testimonies, and explore, with Jerry, the role of the *personal* and *emotional* in his experience of this horrific event. When he and I write together, we focus on writing and rewriting, turning his testimonial anecdotes into literary tales that will *engage* the reader, evoke *response*, and be remembered by others. Because my primary goal now is to use collaborative witnessing to *make people's lives better*—especially the lives of our participants—I have not faced the same contradictions as I had in former work between what to tell and what to keep quiet. My decisions are made *with* Jerry. Nevertheless, situations still arise where I must make ethical decisions about the best way to present information, be aware of when Jerry needs me as a friend rather than a research partner, know when to turn off the tape and leave the video recorder at home, be in tune with *relational ethics* and consider who must give consent and how, and try to ensure that I do no harm in asking Jerry to retell his traumatic experiences. I also am committed to staying open to the different meanings, experiences, interpretations, audiences, and goals that Jerry and I have. Though I do not always succeed, I try to treat our relationship with deep ethics at all times, and I try to remember to call on our differences as a way to write richer and more complex stories rather than viewing them as a threat or something to be resolved.

* * *

As the evaluation of our work shows, it is perhaps unrealistic to believe that a single autoethnography can meet all of the goals we have outlined for the method. However, as our insights about autoethnography develop, the number of skilled autoethnographers grows, and the availability of exemplary autoethnographic texts increases, we believe that we will encounter autoethnographies that meet many, if not most, of these goals. These works, in turn, will become stories we aspire to emulate and to re-tell using our own voices, experiences, and insights.

Autoethnographic Futures

Throughout this book, we explore the core ideals and best practices of autoethnography. We describe key autoethnographic approaches, processes, ethical considerations, and representational responsibilities. We *show* how we use or address these issues in our work. We share our stories of coming to autoethnography, concerns and considerations that led to the development of the method, and a brief history of autoethnography (Chapter 1). We outline the purposes and practices—the core ideals—of autoethnography, how autoethnographers can accomplish these ideals, and why researchers might choose to do autoethnography (Chapter 2). We describe the processes of doing autoethnography, conducting fieldwork, researching ethically, and interpreting and analyzing our experiences (Chapter 3). We explore the various modes, techniques, and ethical issues used and involved in writing autoethnography (Chapter 4). We detail our goals for creating autoethnography and assess our work using these goals (Chapter 5). In this last section, we describe the future of autoethnographic inquiry and offer some concluding reflections on doing autoethnography.

First, we hope you will join us in further establishing auto-ethnography as a rich and viable method for social research by teaching, talking about, using, and showing the power of autoethnography. Review and cite others' autoethnographic work, showcase your own, and insist (gently) that others take this approach seriously as a method for research and writing projects. Although you might encounter people (e.g., colleagues, professors, editors, reviewers) who try to discourage you from using the method, recognize that there are just as many people who appreciate and support autoethnographic work. If the responses the three of us receive to our work, and the increasing numbers of articles, books, and citations are any indication, the number of people who support autoethnography is growing daily. At the same time, carefully consider critiques of the method and find ways to address these criticisms in your work.[23]

Second, do not focus on or worry about publication. Anne Lamott laments that writers often only want to be published, and she notes that life will not change much—if at all—after publication.[24] Instead, concentrate on doing the best autoethnographic work you can do. Doing good work includes reading others' autoethnographies and examining how they use and represent personal experience; developing your writing skills and analytic talents; making time for writing every day; carefully editing your work, making sure that every word counts; and soliciting and addressing feedback from others.

Third, turn your attention toward the injustice being done to us and to others and use autoethnographic research to describe experiences of exclusion, disconfirmation, and degradation. Create work that not only makes the case for cultural change but also embodies the change it calls into being. Tell stories of compassion and hope, vulnerability, solidarity, and communion; stories that "write to right" injustices.[25]

The three of us live, and love, autoethnographically. We value stories, personal experience, and critical research. We work to make our writing and research accessible so that it might improve others' lives. We value our relationships with and respect the privacy of our participants, our friends and families, and others who populate our stories. We write to interrogate and end harmful cultural beliefs, practices, and experiences. For us, this is what research is and what research should do.

We hope that this book inspires you do autoethnographic research and to live the autoethnographic life. We look forward to reading your autoethnographies and hearing your responses to this text. Until then, read, write, research, do fieldwork, seek consent, be vulnerable and reflexive, and dedicate yourselves to telling and listening to stories.

6

RESOURCES FOR DOING AND WRITING AUTOETHNOGRAPHY

THROUGHOUT THIS BOOK we have worked to provide a comprehensive account of sources that detail what autoethnography is and does, alongside examples of compelling autoethnographic stories. We also have discussed works that serve as guides for conducting autoethnographic research and writing. In this final chapter, we list some of our favorite resources related to autoethnography. We include our favorite monographs, articles, chapters, and special issues of journals, along with conferences and journals that welcome autoethnographic work. These lists are not exhaustive; they offer resources that influence how we do our research and exemplars that engage us and evoke our emotions. As your autoethnographic research and writing unfolds, add your own favorites to these lists.

Resources for Doing Autoethnography

Adams, Tony E. "The Joys of Autoethnography: Possibilities for Communication Research." *Qualitative Communication Research* 1, no. 2 (2012): 181–94.

Allen-Collinson, Jacquelyn. "Autoethnography as the Engagement of Self/Other, Self/Culture, Self/Politics, and Selves/Futures." In *Handbook of Autoethnography*, edited by Stacy Holman Jones, Tony E. Adams and Carolyn Ellis, 281–99. Walnut Creek, CA: Left Coast Press, 2013.

Anderson, Leon. "Analytic Autoethnography." *Journal of Contemporary Ethnography* 35, no. 4 (2006): 373–95.

Anderson, Leon, and Bonnie Glass-Coffin. "I Learn by Going: Autoethnographic Modes of Inquiry." In *Handbook of Autoethnography*, edited by Stacy Holman Jones, Tony E. Adams and Carolyn Ellis, 57–83. Walnut Creek, CA: Left Coast Press, 2013.

Bartleet, Brydie-Leigh. "Artful and Embodied Methods, Modes of Inquiry, and Forms of Representation." In *Handbook of Autoethnography*, edited by Stacy Holman Jones, Tony E. Adams and Carolyn Ellis, 443–64. Walnut Creek, CA: Left Coast Press, 2013.

Behar, Ruth. *The Vulnerable Observer*. Boston, MA: Beacon Press, 1996.

Berry, Keith. "Spinning Autoethnographic Reflexivity, Cultural Critique, and Negotiating Selves." In *Handbook of Autoethnography*, edited by Stacy Holman Jones, Tony E. Adams and Carolyn Ellis, 209–27. Walnut Creek, CA: Left Coast Press, 2013.

Bochner, Arthur P. "Criteria Against Ourselves." *Qualitative Inquiry* 6, no. 2 (2000): 266–72.

———. "Narrative's Virtues." *Qualitative Inquiry* 7, no. 2 (2001): 131–57.

———. "Perspectives on Inquiry III: The Moral of Stories." In *Handbook of Interpersonal Communication*, edited by Mark L. Knapp and John A. Daly, 73–101. Thousand Oaks, CA: Sage, 2002.

Bochner, Arthur P., and Carolyn Ellis. "Personal Narrative as a Social Approach to Interpersonal Communication." *Communication Theory* 2, no. 2 (1992): 165–72.

Butz, David. "Autoethnography as Sensibility." In *The SAGE Handbook of Qualitative Geography*, edited by Dydia Delyser, Steve Herbert, Stuart Aitken, Mike Crang and Linda McDowell, 138–55. Thousand Oaks, CA: Sage, 2010.

Carless, David, and Kitrina Douglas. "A History of Autoethnographic Inquiry." In *Handbook of Autoethnography*, edited by Stacy Holman Jones, Tony E. Adams and Carolyn Ellis, 84–106. Walnut Creek, CA: Left Coast Press, 2013.

Carter, Shelly. "How Much Subjectivity is Needed to Understand Our Lives Objectively?" *Qualitative Health Research* 12, no. 9 (2002): 1184–201.

Calafell, Bernadette Marie. "(I)dentities: Considering Accountability, Reflexivity, and Intersectionality in the I and the We." *Liminalities: A Journal of Performance Studies* 9, no. 2 (2013): 6–13. Accessed June 1, 2013. http://liminalities.net/9-2/calafell.pdf

Chang, Heewon. *Autoethnography as Method*. Walnut Creek, CA: Left Coast Press, 2008.

Chang, Heewon, Faith Wambura Ngunjiri, and Kathy-Ann C. Hernandez. *Collaborative Autoethnography*. Walnut Creek, CA: Left Coast Press, 2013.

Clair, Robin Patric., ed. *Expressions of Ethnography: Novel Approaches to Qualitative Methods*. Albany: State University of New York Press, 2003.

Denzin, Norman K. *Interpretive Autoethnography*. Thousand Oaks, CA: Sage, 2014.

Ellis, Carolyn. *The Ethnographic I: A Methodological Novel About Autoethnography*. Walnut Creek, CA: AltaMira Press, 2004.

Ellis, Carolyn, and Arthur P. Bochner, eds. *Composing Ethnography: Alternative Forms of Qualitative Writing*. Walnut Creek, CA: AltaMira Press, 1996.

———. "Autoethnography, Personal Narrative, Reflexivity." In *Handbook of Qualitative Research*, 2nd ed., edited by Norman K. Denzin and Yvonna S. Lincoln, 733–68. Thousand Oaks, CA: Sage, 2000.

Ellis, Carolyn, Tony E. Adams, and Arthur P. Bochner. "Autoethnography: An Overview." *Forum: Qualitative Social Research* 12, no. 1 (2011).

Ellis, Carolyn, and Michael G. Flaherty, eds. *Investigating Subjectivity: Research on Lived Experience*. Newbury Park, CA: Sage, 1992.

Ellis, Carolyn, Christine E. Kiesinger, and Lisa M. Tillmann-Healy. "Interactive Interviewing: Talking About Emotional Experience." In *Reflexivity and Voice*, edited by Rosanna Hertz, 119–49. Thousand Oaks, CA: Sage, 1997.

Ellis, Carolyn, and Jerry Rawicki. "Collaborative Witnessing of Survival During the Holocaust: An Exemplar of Relational Autoethnography." *Qualitative Inquiry* 19, no. 5 (2013): 366–80.

Gingrich-Philbrook, Craig. "Autoethnography's Family Values: Easy Access to Compulsory Experiences." *Text and Performance Quarterly* 25, no. 4 (2005): 297–314.

———. "Evaluating (Evaluations of) Autoethnography." In *Handbook of Autoethnography*, edited by Stacy Holman Jones, Tony E. Adams and Carolyn Ellis, 609–26. Walnut Creek, CA: Left Coast Press, 2013.

Goodall, H. L. *Writing the New Ethnography*. Walnut Creek, CA: AltaMira Press, 2000.

Hayano, David M. "Auto-Ethnography: Paradigms, Problems, and Prospects." *Human Organization* 38, no. 1 (1979): 99–104.

Hayler, Mike. *Autoethnography, Self-narrative and Teacher Education*. Rotterdam, Netherlands: Sense Publishers, 2011.

Holman Jones, Stacy. "Autoethnography: Making the Personal Political." In *Handbook of Qualitative Research*, edited by Norman K. Denzin and Yvonna S. Lincoln, 763–91. Thousand Oaks, CA: Sage, 2005.

Holman Jones, Stacy, and Tony E. Adams. "Autoethnography and Queer Theory: Making Possibilities." In *Qualitative Inquiry and Human Rights*, edited by Norman K. Denzin and Michael G. Giardina, 136–57. Walnut Creek, CA: Left Coast Press, 2010.

Holman Jones, Stacy, Tony E. Adams, and Carolyn Ellis, eds. *Handbook of Autoethnography*, Walnut Creek, CA: Left Coast Press, 2013.

Langellier, Kristin M. "Personal Narrative, Performance, Performativity: Two or Three Things I Know for Sure." *Text and Performance Quarterly* 19, no. 2 (1999): 125–44.

Leavy, Patricia. *Fiction as Research Practice: Short Stories, Novellas, and Novels*. Walnut Creek, CA: Left Coast Press, 2013.

Madison, D. Soyini. *Critical Ethnography: Method, Ethics, Performance*. 2nd ed. Thousand Oaks, CA: Sage, 2012.

Muncey, Tessa. *Creating Autoethnographies*. Thousand Oaks, CA: Sage, 2010.

Mykhalovskiy, Eric. "Reconsidering Table Talk: Critical Thoughts on the Relationship between Sociology, Autobiography and Self-Indulgence." *Qualitative Sociology* 19, no. 1 (1996): 131–51.

Reed-Danahay, Deborah, ed. *Auto/Ethnography*. New York: Berg, 1997.
Richardson, Laurel. "Narrative and Sociology." *Journal of Contemporary Ethnography* 19, no. 1 (1990): 116–35.
Sikes, Pat, ed. *Autoethnography*. Thousand Oaks, CA: Sage, 2013.
Scott, Julie-Ann. "Problematizing a Researcher's Performance of 'Insider Status': An Autoethnography of 'Designer Disabled' Identity." *Qualitative Inquiry* 19, no. 2 (2013): 101–15.
Spry, Tami. "Performing Autoethnography: An Embodied Methodological Praxis." *Qualitative Inquiry* 7, no. 6 (2001): 706–32.
———. *Body, Paper, Stage: Writing and Performing Autoethnography*. Walnut Creek, CA: Left Coast Press, 2011.
Tillmann-Healy, Lisa M. "Friendship as Method." *Qualitative Inquiry* 9, no. 5 (2003): 729–49.
Toyosaki, Satoshi, and Sandy L. Pensoneau-Conway. "Autoethnography as a Praxis of Social Justice." In *Handbook of Autoethnography*, edited by Stacy Holman Jones, Tony E. Adams and Carolyn Ellis, 557–75. Walnut Creek, CA: Left Coast Press, 2013.
Tullis Owen, Jillian A., Chris McRae, Tony E. Adams, and Alisha Vitale. "truth Troubles." *Qualitative Inquiry* 15, no. 1 (2009): 178–200.
Wall, Sarah. "An Autoethnography on Learning About Autoethnography." *International Journal of Qualitative Methods* 5, no. 2 (2006).
———. "Easier Said Than Done: Writing an Autoethnography." *International Journal of Qualitative Methods* 7, no. 1 (2008).
Wolcott, Harry F. *Ethnography Lessons: A Primer*. Walnut Creek, CA: Left Coast Press, 2010.

Autoethnographic Exemplars

Adams, Tony E. "Seeking Father: Relationally Reframing a Troubled Love Story." *Qualitative Inquiry* 12, no. 4 (2006): 704–23.
———. "Mothers, Faggots, and Witnessing (Un)Contestable Experience." *Cultural Studies <=> Critical Methodologies* 9, no. 5 (2009): 619–26.
———. *Narrating the Closet: An Autoethnography of Same-Sex Attraction*. Walnut Creek, CA: Left Coast Press, 2011.
———. "Missing Each Other." *Qualitative Inquiry* 18, no. 2 (2012): 193–96.
———. "Post-Coming out Complications." In *Critical Autoethnography: Intersecting Cultural Identities in Everyday Life*, edited by Robin M. Boylorn and Mark P. Orbe, 62–80. Walnut Creek, CA: Left Coast Press, 2014.
Alexander, Bryant Keith. *Performing Black Masculinity: Race, Culture, and Queer Identity*. Lanham, MD: AltaMira Press, 2006.
Bartleet, Brydie-Leigh, and Carolyn Ellis, eds. *Music Autoethnographies: Making Autoethnography Sing/Making Music Personal*. Bowen Hills: QLD Australian Academic Press, 2009.
Barthes, Roland. *A Lover's Discourse: Fragments*. Translated by Richard Howard. New York: Hill and Wang, 1978.

Benson, Thomas W. "Another Shooting in Cowtown." *Quarterly Journal of Speech* 67, no. 4 (1981): 347–406.

Berry, Keith. "Embracing the Catastrophe: Gay Body Seeks Acceptance." *Qualitative Inquiry* 13, no. 2 (2007): 259–81.

Bochner, Arthur P. *Coming to Narrative: A Personal History of Paradigm Change in the Human Sciences.* Walnut Creek, CA: Left Coast Press, 2014.

Bochner, Arthur P., and Carolyn Ellis, eds. *Ethnographically Speaking: Autoethnography, Literature, and Aesthetics.* Walnut Creek, CA: AltaMira Press, 2002.

Bolen, Derek M. "After Dinners, In the Garage, Out of Doors, and Climbing on Rocks." In *On (Writing) Families: Autoethnographies of Presence and Absence, Love and Loss,* edited by Jonathan Wyatt and Tony E. Adams, Rotterdam, Netherlands: Sense Publishers, 2014, 141–147.

Boylorn, Robin M. "Black Kids' (B.K.) Stories: Ta(L)King (About) Race Outside of the Classroom." *Cultural Studies <=> Critical Methodologies* 11, no. 1 (2011): 59–70.

———. "Gray or for Colored Girls Who Are Tired of Chasing Rainbows: Race and Reflexivity." *Cultural Studies <=> Critical Methodologies* 11, no. 2 (2011): 178–86.

———. *Sweetwater: Black Women and Narratives of Resistance.* New York: Peter Lang, 2013.

———. "'Sit with Your Legs Closed!' And Other Sayin's from My Childhood." In *Handbook of Autoethnography,* edited by Stacy Holman Jones, Tony E. Adams and Carolyn Ellis, 173–85. Walnut Creek, CA: Left Coast Press, 2013.

———. "Blackgirl Blogs, Auto/ethnography, and Crunk Feminism." *Liminalities: A Journal of Performance Studies* 9, no. 2 (2013): 73–82. Accessed June 1, 2013. http://liminalities.net/9-2/boylorn.pdf.

———. "My Daddy is Slick, Brown, and Cool Like Ice Water." In *On (Writing) Families: Autoethnographies of Presence and Absence, Love and Loss,* edited by Jonathan Wyatt and Tony E. Adams. Rotterdam, Netherlands: Sense Publishers, 2014, 85–93.

Boylorn, Robin M., and Mark P. Orbe, eds. *Critical Autoethnography: Intersecting Cultural Identities in Everyday Life.* Walnut Creek, CA: Left Coast Press, 2014.

Crawley, Sara L. "'They Still Don't Understand Why I Hate Wearing Dresses!' An Autoethnographic Rant on Dresses, Boats, and Butchness." *Cultural Studies <=> Critical Methodologies* 2, no. 1 (2002): 69–92.

Chawla, Devika. "Walk, Walking, Talking, Home." In *Handbook of Autoethnography,* edited by Stacy Holman Jones, Tony E. Adams and Carolyn Ellis, 162–72. Walnut Creek, CA: Left Coast Press, 2013.

Corey, Frederick C., and Thomas K. Nakayama. "Sextext." *Text and Performance Quarterly* 17, no. 1 (1997): 58–68.

Crawford, Lyall. "Personal Ethnography." *Communication Monographs* 63, no. 2 (1996): 158–70.

Crawley, Rex. "Favor: An Autoethnography of Survival." In *Critical Autoethnography: Intersecting Cultural Identities in Everyday Life,* edited by

Robin M. Boylorn and Mark P. Orbe, 222–33. Walnut Creek, CA: Left Coast Press, 2014.

Diversi, Marcelo, and Claudio Moreira. *Betweener Talk: Decolonizing Knowledge Production, Pedagogy, and Praxis*. Walnut Creek, CA: Left Coast Press, 2010.

Dykins Callahan, Sara B. "Academic Outings." *Symbolic Interaction* 31, no. 4 (2008): 351–75.

Ellis, Carolyn. "Sociological Introspection and Emotional Experience." *Symbolic Interaction* 14, no. 1 (1991): 23–50.

Ellis, Carolyn. "'There Are Survivors': Telling a Story of a Sudden Death." *The Sociological Quarterly* 34, no. 4 (1993): 711–30.

———. *Final Negotiations: A Story of Love, Loss, and Chronic Illness*. Philadelphia, PA: Temple University Press, 1995.

———. "'I Hate My Voice': Coming to Terms with Minor Bodily Stigmas." *The Sociological Quarterly* 39, no. 4 (1998): 517–37.

———. *Revision: Autoethnographic Reflections on Life and Work*. Walnut Creek, CA: Left Coast Press, 2009.

Fox, Ragan. "Re-Membering Daddy: Autoethnographic Reflections of My Father and Alzheimer's Disease." *Text and Performance Quarterly* 30, no. 1 (2010): 3–20.

———. "Tales of a Fighting Bobcat: An 'Auto-archaeology' of Gay Identity Formation and Maintenance," *Text and Performance Quarterly* 30, no. 2 (2010): 122–42.

Gannon, Susanne. "Sketching Subjectivities." In *Handbook of Autoethnography*, edited by Stacy Holman Jones, Tony E. Adams and Carolyn Ellis, 228–43. Walnut Creek, CA: Left Coast Press, 2013.

Glave, Thomas. *Words to Our Now: Imagination and Dissent*. Minneapolis, MN: University of Minneapolis Press, 2005.

Goodall, H. L. *Casing a Promised Land*. Carbondale: Southern Illinois University Press, 1994.

———. *A Need to Know: The Clandestine History of a CIA Family*. Walnut Creek, CA: Left Coast Press, 2006.

Griffin, Rachel Alicia. "I AM an Angry Black Woman: Black Feminist Autoethnography, Voice, and Resistance." *Women's Studies in Communication* 35, no. 2 (2012): 138–57.

Harris, Anne M. "Ghost-Child." In *On (Writing) Families: Autoethnographies of Presence and Absence, Love and Loss*, edited by Jonathan Wyatt and Tony E. Adams. Rotterdam, Netherlands: Sense Publishers, 2014, 69–75.

Holman Jones, Stacy. *Kaleidoscope Notes: Writing Women's Music and Organizational Culture*. Walnut Creek, CA: AltraMira Press, 1998.

———. "(M)othering Loss: Telling Adoption Stories, Telling Performativity." *Text and Performance Quarterly* 25, no. 2 (2005): 113–35.

———. *Torch Singing: Performing Resistance and Desire from Billie Holiday to Edith Piaf*. Lanham, MD; AltaMira Press. 2007.

———. "Crimes Against Experience." *Cultural Studies <=> Critical Methodologies* 9, no. 5 (2009): 608–18.

———. "Lost and Found." *Text and Performance Quarterly* 31, no. 4 (2011): 322–41.

———. "Always Strange." In *On (Writing) Families: Autoethnographies of Presence and Absence, Love and Loss*, edited by Jonathan Wyatt and Tony E. Adams. Rotterdam, Netherlands: Sense Publishers, 2014, 13–21.

Holman Jones, Stacy, and Tony E. Adams. "Undoing the Alphabet: A Queer Fugue on Grief and Forgiveness." *Cultural Studies <=> Critical Methodologies*, 14, no. 2 (2014): 102–10.

Jago, Barbara J. "Chronicling an Academic Depression." *Journal of Contemporary Ethnography* 31, no. 6 (2002): 729–57.

Marvasti, Amir. "Being Middle Eastern American: Identity Negotiation in the Context of the War on Terror." *Symbolic Interaction* 28, no. 4 (2006): 525–47.

Metta, Marilyn. *Writing Against, Alongside and Beyond Memory: Lifewriting as Reflexive, Poststructuralist Feminist Research Practice*. New York: Peter Lang, 2010.

Mingé, Jeanine, and Amber Lynn Zimmerman. *Concrete and Dust: Mapping the Sexual Terrains of Los Angeles*. New York: Routledge, 2013.

Pacanowsky, Michael. "Slouching Towards Chicago." *Quarterly Journal of Speech* 74, no. 4 (1988): 453–67.

Pelias, Ronald J. "The Critical Life." *Communication Education* 49, no. 3 (2000): 220–28.

———. *A Methodology of the Heart: Evoking Academic and Daily Life*. Walnut Creek, CA: AltaMira Press, 2004.

———. "Jarheads, Girly Men, and the Pleasures of Violence." *Qualitative Inquiry* 13, no. 7 (2007): 945–59.

———. *Leaning: A Poetics of Personal Relations*. Walnut Creek, CA: Left Coast Press, 2011.

Pineau, Elyse. "*Nursing Mother* and Articulating Absence." *Text and Performance Quarterly* 20, no. 1 (2000): 1–19.

Poulos, Christopher N., *Accidental Ethnography: An Inquiry into Family Secrecy*. Walnut Creek, CA: Left Coast Press, 2009.

Rambo, Carol. "Impressions of Grandmother: An Autoethnographic Portrait." *Journal of Contemporary Ethnography* 34, no. 5 (2005): 560–85.

———. "Twitch: A Performance of Chronic Liminality." In *Handbook of Autoethnography*, edited by Stacy Holman Jones, Tony E. Adams and Carolyn Ellis, 627–38. Walnut Creek, CA: Left Coast Press, 2013.

Richardson, Laurel. *Fields of Play: Constructing an Academic Life*. New Brunswick, NJ: Rutgers University Press, 1997.

Ronai, Carol Rambo. "Multiple Reflections of Child Sex Abuse." *Journal of Contemporary Ethnography* 23, no. 4 (1995): 395–426.

Sedgwick, Eve Kosofsky. *A Dialogue on Love*. Boston, MA: Beacon Press, 2000.

Smith, Phil, ed. *Both Sides of the Table: Autoethnographies of Educators Learning and Teaching With/In [Dis]ability*. New York: Peter Lang, 2013.

Stewart, Kathleen. *Ordinary Affects*. Durham, NC: Duke University Press, 2007.

Tamas, Sophie. *Life after Leaving: The Remains of Spousal Abuse*. Walnut Creek, CA: Left Coast Press, 2011.

———. "Who's There? A Week Subject." In *Handbook of Autoethnography*, edited by Stacy Holman Jones, Tony E. Adams and Carolyn Ellis, 186–201. Walnut Creek, CA: Left Coast Press, 2013.

Tillmann-Healy, Lisa M. "A Secret Life in a Culture of Thinness: Reflections on Body, Food, and Bulimia." In *Composing Ethnography: Alternative Forms of Qualitative Writing*, edited by Carolyn Ellis and Arthur P. Bochner, 76–108. Walnut Creek, CA: AltaMira Press, 1996.

——. *Between Gay and Straight: Understanding Friendship across Sexual Orientation*. Walnut Creek, CA: AltaMira Press, 2001.

Tomaselli, Keyan G. ed. *Writing in the San/d: Autoethnography Among Indigenous Southern Africans*. Lanham, MD: AltaMira Press, 2007.

Trujillo, Nick. *In Search of Naunny's Grave: Age, Class, Gender, and Ethnicity in an American Family*. Lanham, MD: Altamira Press, 2004.

Tuck, Eve, and C. Ree. "A Glossary of Haunting." In *Handbook of Autoethnography*, edited by Stacy Holman Jones, Tony E. Adams and Carolyn Ellis, 639–58. Walnut Creek, CA: Left Coast Press, 2013.

Visweswaran, Kamala. *Fictions of Feminist Ethnography*. Minneapolis: University of Minnesota Press, 1997.

Wyatt, Jonathan, and Tony E. Adams, eds. *On (Writing) Families: Autoethnographies of Presence and Absence, Love and Loss*. Rotterdam, Netherlands: Sense Publishers, 2014.

Wolf, Stacy. "Desire in Evidence." *Text and Performance Quarterly* 17 (1997): 343–51.

Special Journal Issues On/About Autoethnography

Adams, Tony E., and Stacy Holman Jones. "Special Issue: On Studying Ourselves and Others." *Liminalities: A Journal of Performance Studies* 9, no. 2 (2013). Accessed June 1, 2013. http://liminalities.net/9-2/

Adams, Tony E., and Jonathan Wyatt. "Special Issue: On (Writing) Fathers." *Qualitative Inquiry* 18, no. 2 (2012): 119–209.

Alexander, Bryant Keith. "Special Issue: Iconography of the West: Autoethnographic Representations of the West(erns)." *Cultural Studies <=> Critical Methodologies* 14, no. 3 (2014): 223–290.

Berry, Keith. "Special Issue: Queering Family/Home/Love/Loss." *Cultural Studies <=> Critical Methodologies* 14, no. 2 (2014): 91–173.

Berry, Keith, and Robin P. Clair. "Special Issue: The Call of Ethnographic Reflexivity: Narrating the Self's Presence in Ethnography." *Cultural Studies <=> Critical Methodologies* 11, no. 2 (2011): 95–209.

Boyle, Maree, and Ken Parry. "Special Issue on Organizational Autoethnography." *Culture and Organization* 3, no. 3 (2007): 185–266.

Ellis, Carolyn, and Arthur P. Bochner, eds. "Special Issue: Taking Ethnography into the Twenty-first Century." *Journal of Contemporary Ethnography* 25, no. 1 (1996): 3–166.

Gingrich-Philbrook, Craig, ed. "Special Issue: The Personal and Political in Solo Performance." *Text and Performance Quarterly* 20, no. 1 (2000): 1–114.

Hunt, Scott A., and Natalia Ruiz Junco, eds. "Two Thematic Issues: Defective Memory and Analytical Autoethnography." *Journal of Contemporary Ethnography* 35, no. 4 (2006): 71–372.

Myers, W. Benjamin, ed. "Special Issue: Writing Autoethnographic Joy."
    Qualitative Communication Research 1, no. 2 (2012): 157–252.
Ngunjiri, Faith W., Kathy-Ann Hernandez, and Heewon Chang. "Special
    Issue: Autoethnography as Research Practice." *Journal of Research Practice*
    6, no. 1 (2010). http://jrp.icaap.org/index.php/jrp/issue/view/13
Poulos, Christopher N., ed. "Special Issue: Autoethnography." *Iowa Journal of
    Communication* 40, no. 1 (2008): i–140.
Warren, John T., and Keith Berry, eds. "Special Issue: The Evidence of
    Experience, Cultural Studies, and Personal(ized) Scholarship." *Cultural
    Studies <=> Critical Methodologies* 9, no. 5 (2009): 595–695.

Resources on Autoethnography and Ethics

Adams, Tony E. "A Review of Narrative Ethics." *Qualitative Inquiry* 14, no. 2
    (2008): 175–94.
Alcoff, Linda. "The Problem of Speaking for Others." *Cultural Critique* 20
    (1991/1992): 5–32.
Barton, Bernadette. "My Auto/Ethnographic Dilemma: Who Owns the Story?"
    Qualitative Sociology 34 (2011): 431–45.
Berry, Keith. "Implicated Audience Member Seeks Understanding: Reexamining
    the 'Gift' of Autoethnography." *International Journal of Qualitative Methods*
    5, no. 3 (2006): 1–12.
Chatham-Carpenter, April. "'Do Thyself No Harm': Protecting Ourselves as
    Autoethnographers." *Journal of Research Practice* 6, no. 1 (2010), Accessed
    March 1, 2013, http://jrp.icaap.org/index.php/jrp/article/view/213/183
Conquergood, Dwight. "Performing as a Moral Act: Ethical Dimensions
    of the Ethnography of Performance." *Literature in Performance* 5, no. 2
    (1985): 1–13.
Ellis, Carolyn. "With Mother/With Child: A True Story." *Qualitative Inquiry* 7,
    no. 5 (2001): 598–616.
———. "Telling Secrets, Revealing Lives: Relational Ethics in Research with
    Intimate Others." *Qualitative Inquiry* 13, no. 1 (2007): 3–29.
Etherington, Kim. "Ethical Research in Reflexive Relationships." *Qualitative
    Inquiry* 13, no. 5 (2007): 599–616.
Irwin, Katherine. "Into the Dark Heart of Ethnography: The Lived Ethics
    and Inequality of Intimate Field Relationships." *Qualitative Sociology* 29
    (2006): 155–75.
Medford, Kristina. "Caught with a Fake ID: Ethical Questions About *Slippage*
    in Autoethnography." *Qualitative Inquiry* 12, no. 5 (2006): 853–64.
Stein, Arlene. "Sex, Truths, and Audiotape: Anonymity and the Ethics of
    Exposure in Public Ethnography." *Journal of Contemporary Ethnography* 39,
    no. 5 (2010): 554–68.
Tamas, Sophie. "Writing and Righting Trauma: Troubling the
    Autoethnographic Voice." *Forum: Qualitative Social Research* 10, no. 1

(2009). Accessed June 1, 2013. http://www.qualitative-research.net/index. php/fqs/article/viewArticle/1211

Tullis, Jillian A. "Self and Others: Ethics in Autoethnographic Research." In *Handbook of Autoethnography*, edited by Stacy Holman Jones, Tony E. Adams and Carolyn Ellis, 244–61. Walnut Creek, CA: Left Coast Press, 2013.

Wyatt, Jonathan. "Psychic Distance, Consent, and Other Ethical Issues." *Qualitative Inquiry* 12, no. 4 (2006): 813–18.

Resources on Autoethnographic Representation and Writing

Abu-Lughod, Lila. "Can There be a Feminist Ethnography?" *Woman and Performance: A Journal of Feminist Theory* 5, no. 1 (1990): 7–27.

Barry, Lynda. *What It Is*. Montreal: Drawn & Quarterly, 2008.

Clifford, James, and George Marcus, eds. *Writing Culture: The Poetics and Politics of Ethnography*, Berkeley: University of California Press, 1986.

Carver, Raymond. "On Writing." In *Fires: Essays, Stories, Poems*, 22–27. New York: Vintage, 1989.

Coles, Robert. *The Call of Stories*. Boston, MA: Houghton Mifflin, 1989.

Colyar, Julia. "Becoming Writing, Becoming Writers." *Qualitative Inquiry* 15, no. 2 (2009): 421–36.

———. "Reflections on Writing and Autoethnography." In *Handbook of Autoethnography*, edited by Stacy Holman Jones, Tony E. Adams and Carolyn Ellis, 363–83. Walnut Creek, CA: Left Coast Press, 2013.

Couser, G. Thomas. *Recovering Bodies: Illness, Disability, and Life Writing*. Madison: University of Wisconsin Press, 1997.

Frank, Arthur W. *The Wounded Storyteller*. Chicago, IL: University of Chicago Press, 1995.

Freeman, Mark. *Hindsight: The Promise and Peril of Looking Back*. New York: Oxford University Press, 2010.

Faulkner, Sandra L. *Poetry as Method: Reporting Research Through Verse*. Walnut Creek, CA: Left Coast Press, 2009.

Hill Collins, Patricia. *Black Feminist Thought: Knowledge, Consciousness, and the Politics of Empowerment*. Boston, MA: Unwin Hyman, 1990.

Keller, Evelyn Fox. *Reflections on Gender and Science*. New Haven, CT: Yale University Press, 1985.

Kilgard, Amy K. "Collage: A Paradigm for Performance Studies." *Liminalities: A Journal of Performance Studies* 5 (2009): 1–19. Accessed June 1, 2013. http://liminalities.net/5-3/collage.pdf

King, Stephen. *On Writing: A Memoir of the Craft*. New York: Scribner, 2000.

Lamott, Anne. *Bird by Bird: Some Instructions on Writing and Life*. New York: Anchor, 1994.

Pollock, Della. "Performing Writing." In *The Ends of Performance*, edited by Peggy Phelan and Jill Lane, 73–103. New York: New York University Press, 1998.

Reinharz, Shulamit. *On Becoming a Social Scientist*. New Brunswick, NJ: Transaction, 1984.

Richardson, Laurel. "Writing: A Method of Inquiry." In *Handbook of Qualitative Research*, edited by Norman K. Denzin and Yvonna S. Lincoln, 516–29. Thousand Oaks, CA: Sage, 1994.

Sedgwick, Eve Kosofsky. "Teaching 'Experimental Critical Writing.'" In *The Ends of Performance*, edited by Peggy Phelan and Jill Lane, 104–15. New York: New York University Press, 1998.

Shields, David. *Reality Hunger: A Manifesto*. New York: Alfred A. Knopf, 2010.

Spivak, Gayatri Chakravorty. "Can the Subaltern Speak?" In *Marxism and the Interpretation of Culture*, edited by Cary Nelson and Lawrence Grossberg, 271–313. Champaign: University of Illinois Press, 1988.

Taussig, Michael. *I Swear I Saw This: Drawings in Fieldwork Notebooks, Namely My Own*. Chicago, IL: The University of Chicago Press, 2011.

Van Maanen, John. *Tales of the Field: On Writing Ethnography*. Chicago, IL: University of Chicago Press, 1988.

Journals That Welcome Autoethnographic Work

Biography: An Interdisciplinary Quarterly
Communication, Culture, and Critique
Creative Approaches to Research
Cultural Studies <=> Critical Methodologies
Culture and Organization
Departures in Critical Qualitative Research
Emotion, Space, and Society
Ethnography
Forum: Qualitative Social Research
Health Communication
Illness, Crisis, and Loss
International Journal of Collaborative Practices
International Journal of Multicultural Education
International Journal of Qualitative Methods
International Journal of Qualitative Studies in Education
International Review of Qualitative Research
Journal of Contemporary Ethnography
Journal of Ethnographic and Qualitative Research
Journal of Loss and Trauma
Journal of Research Practice
Kaleidoscope: A Graduate Journal of Qualitative Communication Research
Life Writing
Liminalities
Methodological Innovations
Narrative Inquiry
Narrative Inquiry in Bioethics: A Journal of Qualitative Research
Power and Education

Public Voices
Qualitative Health Research
Qualitative Inquiry
Qualitative Research
Qualitative Research in Sport and Exercise
Qualitative Sociology
Sexualities
Sexuality & Culture
Storytelling, Self, Society: An Interdisciplinary Journal of Storytelling Studies
Symbolic Interaction
Text and Performance Quarterly
The Professional Geographer
The Qualitative Report
Women and Language
Women's Studies in Communication

Book Series That Publish Autoethnographic Monographs

Black Studies and Critical Thinking (Peter Lang)
Contemporary Ethnography (University of Pennsylvania Press)
Critical Cultural Studies in Global Health Communication (Left Coast Press)
Cultural Critique (Peter Lang)
Innovative Ethnographies (Routledge)
Interactionist Currents (Ashgate)
Qualitative Inquiry and Social Justice (Left Coast Press)
Social Fictions (Sense)
Writing Lives (Left Coast Press)

Organizations and Conferences That Support Autoethnography

Advances in Qualitative Methods
American Educational Research Association
Association for Qualitative Research
Centre for Qualitative Research (Bournemouth University)
Doing Autoethnography Conference
Ethnographic and Qualitative Research
International Congress of Qualitative Inquiry
National Communication Association
Organization for the Study of Communication, Language, and Gender
ResearchTalk Inc.
Society for the Study of Symbolic Interaction
The Qualitative Report

NOTES

Chapter 1

1. Joan Didion, *The White Album* (New York: Simon & Schuster, 1979): 11.
2. Jacqueline Allen-Collinson characterizes autoethnography as an engagement of self "in relation to others, to culture, to politics, and the engagement of selves in relation to future possibilities for research." Jacquelyn Allen-Collinson, "Autoethnography as the Engagement of Self/Other, Self/Culture, Self/Politics, and Selves/Futures," in *Handbook of Autoethnography*, ed. Stacy Holman Jones, Tony E. Adams, and Carolyn Ellis (Walnut Creek, CA: Left Coast Press, 2013): 282.
3. Deborah Reed-Danahay, "Anthropologists, Education, and Autoethnography," *Reviews in Anthropology* 38, no. 1 (2009): 32.
4. See Carolyn Ellis, *The Ethnographic I: A Methodological Novel About Autoethnography* (Walnut Creek, CA: AltaMira Press, 2004); Carolyn Ellis, *Revision: Autoethnographic Reflections on Life and Work* (Walnut Creek, CA: Left Coast Press, 2009); Carolyn Ellis, Tony E. Adams, and Arthur P. Bochner, "Autoethnography: An Overview," *Forum: Qualitative Social Research* 12, no. 1 (2011); Stacy Holman Jones, Tony E. Adams, Carolyn Ellis, "Introduction: Coming to Know Autoethnography as More Than a Method," in *Handbook of Autoethnography*, eds. Stacy Holman Jones, Tony E. Adams, and Carolyn Ellis (Walnut Creek, CA: Left Coast Press, 2013): 17–47.
5. Examples of autoethnographers who foreground discussions about their relationships to/with others include Tony E. Adams, "A Review of Narrative Ethics," *Qualitative Inquiry* 14, no. 2 (2008): 175–94; Bernadette Barton, "My Auto/Ethnographic Dilemma: Who Owns the Story?" *Qualitative Sociology*

34 (2011): 431–45; Carolyn Ellis, "Telling Secrets, Revealing Lives: Relational Ethics in Research with Intimate Others," *Qualitative Inquiry* 13, no. 1 (2007): 3–29; Kathy-Ann C. Hernandez and Faith Wambura Ngunjiri, "Relationships and Communities in Autoethnography," in *Handbook of Autoethnography*, eds. Stacy Holman Jones, Tony E. Adams and Carolyn Ellis (Walnut Creek, CA: Left Coast Press, 2013): 262–80; Kristina Medford, "Caught with a Fake ID: Ethical Questions About Slippage in Autoethnography," *Qualitative Inquiry* 12, no. 5 (2006): 853–64; Lisa M. Tillmann-Healy, "Friendship as Method," *Qualitative Inquiry* 9, no. 5 (2003): 729–49.

6. Keith Berry and Robin Clair edited a comprehensive collection of essays about reflexivity, each of which illuminates and interrogates the intersections between self and society, the particular and the general, the personal and the political. Keith Berry and Robin P. Clair, "Special Issue: The Call of Ethnographic Reflexivity: Narrating the Self's Presence in Ethnography," *Cultural Studies <=> Critical Methodologies* 11, no. 2 (2011): 95–209.

7. Arthur P. Bochner and Carolyn Ellis, "Communication as Autoethnography," in *Communication As…Perspectives on Theory*, eds. Gregory J. Shepherd, Jeffrey St. John, and Ted Striphas (Thousand Oaks, CA: Sage, 2006): 111.

8. Arthur P. Bochner and Carolyn Ellis, "Which Way to Turn?" *Journal of Contemporary Ethnography* 28, no. 5 (1999): 485–99; Carolyn Ellis, "Sociological Introspection and Emotional Experience," *Symbolic Interaction* 14, no. 1 (1991): 23–50.

9. Examples of autoethnographers who foreground discussions about social justice, critical research, and making life better include Tony E. Adams, "The Joys of Autoethnography: Possibilities for Communication Research," *Qualitative Communication Research* 1, no. 2 (2012): 181–94; Bernadette Marie Calafell, "(I)dentities: Considering Accountability, Reflexivity, and Intersectionality in the I and the We," *Liminalities: A Journal of Performance Studies* 9, no. 2 (2013): 6–13, accessed June 1, 2013, http://liminalities.net/9-2/calafell.pdf; Norman K. Denzin, *Interpretive Autoethnography*, (Thousand Oaks, CA: Sage, 2014); Stacy Holman Jones, "Autoethnography: Making the Personal Political," in *Handbook of Qualitative Research*, 3rd ed., eds. Norman K. Denzin and Yvonna S. Lincoln (Thousand Oaks, CA: Sage, 2005): 763–91.

10. We included similar versions of these stories in our introduction to the *Handbook of Autoethnography*. See Holman Jones, Adams, and Ellis, "Introduction."

11. Carolyn Ellis, " 'There are Survivors': Telling a Story of Sudden Death," *The Sociological Quarterly* 34, no. 4 (1993): 711–30; Carolyn Ellis, *Final Negotiations: A Story of Love, Loss, and Chronic Illness* (Philadelphia, PA: Temple University Press, 1995).

12. Carolyn Ellis, "Revisioning an Ethnographic Life: Integrating a Communicative Heart with a Sociological Eye," *Studies in Symbolic Interaction* 38 (2012): 123–51.

13. Arthur P. Bochner and Carolyn Ellis, *Ethnographically Speaking: Autoethnography, Literature, and Aesthetics* (Walnut Creek, CA: AltaMira Press, 2002); Carolyn Ellis and Arthur P. Bochner, *Composing Ethnography: Alternative Forms of Qualitative Writing* (Walnut Creek, CA: AltaMira Press, 1996); Carolyn Ellis and Arthur P. Bochner, "Autoethnography, Personal Narrative, Reflexivity," in *Handbook of Qualitative Research*, 2nd ed., eds. Norman K. Denzin and Yvonna S. Lincoln (Thousand Oaks, CA: Sage, 2000): 733–68.

14. Carolyn Ellis and Jerry Rawicki, "More than Mazel? Luck and Agency in Surviving the Holocaust," *Journal of Loss and Trauma* 19, no. 2 (2014); 99–120; Carolyn Ellis and Jerry Rawicki, "Collaborative Witnessing of Survival During the Holocaust: An Exemplar of Relational Autoethnography," *Qualitative Inquiry* 19, no. 5 (2013): 366–80; Carolyn Ellis and Jerry Rawicki, "Collaborative Witnessing and Sharing Authority in Conversations with Holocaust Survivors," in *Beyond Testimony and Trauma*, ed. Stephen High (Vancouver: University of British Columbia Press, in press); Jerry Rawicki and Carolyn Ellis, "Lechem Hara (Bad Bread) Lechem Tov (Good Bread): Survival and Sacrifice During the Holocaust," *Qualitative Inquiry* 17, no. 2 (2011): 155–57.

15. See Communication Studies 298, "Fragments of Self at the Postmodern Bar," *Journal of Contemporary Ethnography* 26, no. 3 (1997): 251–92.

16. Holman Jones, "Making the Personal Political."

17. Holman Jones, "Making the Personal Political."

18. See Tony E. Adams and Stacy Holman Jones, "Autoethnography is Queer," in *Handbook of Critical and Indigenous Methodologies*, eds. Norman K. Denzin, Yvonna S. Lincoln and Linda Tuhiwai Smith (Thousand Oaks, CA: Sage, 2008): 373–90; Tony E. Adams and Stacy Holman Jones, "Telling Stories: Reflexivity, Queer Theory, and Autoethnography," *Cultural Studies <=> Critical Methodologies* 11, no. 2 (2011): 108–16; Stacy Holman Jones and Tony E. Adams, "Autoethnography and Queer Theory: Making Possibilities," in *Qualitative Inquiry and Human Rights*, eds. Norman K. Denzin and Michael G. Giardina (Walnut Creek, CA: Left Coast Press, 2010): 136–57; Stacy Holman Jones and Tony E. Adams, "Autoethnography Is a Queer Method," in *Queer Methods and Methodologies*, eds. Kath Browne and Catherine J. Nash (Burlington, VT: Ashgate, 2010): 195–214; Stacy Holman Jones and Tony E. Adams, "Undoing the Alphabet: A Queer Fugue on Grief and Forgiveness," *Cultural Studies <=> Critical Methodologies* 14, no. 2 (2014): 102–110.

19. Stacy Holman Jones, "Lost and Found," *Text and Performance Quarterly* 31, no. 4 (2011): 322–41.

20. Holman Jones, "Lost and Found," 333.

21. Tony E. Adams, "Seeking Father: Relationally Reframing a Troubled Love Story," *Qualitative Inquiry* 12, no. 4 (2006): 704–23.

22. Adams, "Narrative Ethics."

23. Tony E. Adams, *Narrating the Closet: An Autoethnography of Same-Sex Attraction* (Walnut Creek, CA: Left Coast Press, 2011).

24. Adams and Holman Jones, "Autoethnography is Queer"; Adams and Holman Jones, "Telling Stories"; Holman Jones and Adams, "Making

Possibilities"; Holman Jones and Adams, "Autoethnography is a Queer Method"; Holman Jones and Adams, "Undoing the Alphabet."

25. See Adams, *Narrating the Closet.*

26. Evelyn Fox Keller, *Reflections on Gender and Science* (New Haven, CT: Yale University Press, 1985); Ronald J. Pelias, *Leaning: A Poetics of Personal Relations* (Walnut Creek, CA: Left Coast Press, 2011).

27. Eric Mykhalovskiy, "Reconsidering Table Talk: Critical Thoughts on the Relationship between Sociology, Autobiography and Self-Indulgence," *Qualitative Sociology* 19, no. 1 (1996): 133.

28. Ruth Behar, *The Vulnerable Observer* (Boston, MA: Beacon Press, 1996): 13.

29. Deborah Reed-Danahay, "Turning Points and Textual Strategies in Ethnographic Writing," *Qualitative Studies in Education* 15, no. 4 (2002): 423.

30. Stacy Holman Jones, "Autoethnography," in *The Blackwell Encyclopedia of Sociology*, ed. George Ritzer (Malden, MA: Blackwell, 2007): 231; see also George E. Marcus and Michael M.J. Fischer, *Anthropology as Cultural Critique: An Experimental Moment in the Human Sciences* (Chicago, IL: University of Chicago Press, 1999).

31. Renato Rosaldo, *Culture and Truth: The Remaking of Social Analysis* (Boston, MA: Beacon Press, 1989): 37.

32. Researchers who questioned the ability and desire to seek universal Truths especially with regard to social relations include Jean-François Lyotard, *The Postmodern Condition: A Report on Knowledge*, trans. Geoff Bennington and Brian Massumi (Minneapolis: University of Minnesota Press, 1984); Laurel Richardson, "Narrative and Sociology," *Journal of Contemporary Ethnography* 19, no. 1 (1990): 116–35.

33. Researchers who questioned the ability and desire to make certain and stable knowledge claims about humans, experiences, relationships, and cultures include Arthur P. Bochner, "Forming Warm Ideas," in *Rigor and Imagination: Essays from the Legacy of Gregory Bateson*, ed. Carol Wilder-Mott and John H. Weakland (New York: Praeger, 1981): 65–81; Shulamit Reinharz, *On Becoming a Social Scientist* (New Brunswick, NJ: Transaction 1984).

34. Researchers who questioned the prohibition against stories and story-telling as ways of knowing include Jerome Bruner, "Life as Narrative," *Social Research* 54, no. 1 (1986): 11–32; Robert Coles, *The Call of Stories* (Boston, MA: Houghton Mifflin, 1989); Walter R. Fisher, "Narration as Human Communication Paradigm: The Case of Public Moral Argument," *Communication Monographs* 51, no. 1 (1984): 1–22.

35. Researchers who questioned the bias against affect and emotion include Ellis, "Sociological Introspection"; Arlie Hochschild, *The Managed Heart: Commercialization of Human Feeling* (Berkeley: University of California Press, 1983); Keller, *Reflections.*

36. Clifford Geertz, *Local Knowledge* (New York: Basic Books, 1983).

37. Researchers who acknowledged and questioned the influence of social identities (e.g., race, age, gender, class, sexuality) on the research process, as well as how identities can influence the interpretation and evaluation of research

texts include Patricia Hill Collins, *Black Feminist Thought: Knowledge, Consciousness, and the Politics of Empowerment* (Boston, MA: Unwin Hyman, 1990); Marilyn Frye, *The Politics of Reality: Essays in Feminist Theory* (Trumansburg, NY: Crossing Press, 1983); Keller, *Reflections on Gender and Science*; Audre Lorde, *Sister Outsider* (Berkeley, CA: The Crossing Press, 1984); Linda Alcoff, "The Problem of Speaking for Others," *Cultural Critique* 20 (1991/1992): 5–32.

38. Researchers who questioned colonialist and invasive ethnographic practices include Alcoff, "Speaking for Others"; Abraham P. DeLeon, "How Do I Begin to Tell a Story That Has Not Been Told? Anarchism, Autoethnography, and the Middle Ground," *Equity & Excellence in Education* 43, no. 4 (2010): 398–413; Shino Konishi, "Representing Aboriginal Masculinity in Howard's Australia," in *Global Masculinities and Manhood*, ed. Ronald L. Jackson II and Murali Balaji (Urbana, IL: University of Illinois Press, 2011): 161–85; Agnes Riedmann, *Science That Colonizes: A Critique of Fertility Studies in Africa* (Philadelphia, PA: Temple University Press, 1993); Gayatri Chakravorty Spivak, "Can the Subaltern Speak?" in *Marxism and the Interpretation of Culture*, ed. Cary Nelson and Lawrence Grossberg (Champaign: University of Illinois Press, 1988): 271–313.

39. Dwight Conquergood, "Rethinking Ethnography: Towards a Critical Cultural Politics," *Communication Monographs* 58, no. 2 (1991): 180.

40. Holman Jones, "Autoethnography," 231; see Rosaldo, *Culture and Truth*.

41. Laurel Richardson, "Evaluating Ethnography," *Qualitative Inquiry* 6, no. 2 (2000): 253.

42. Paul Atkinson, Amanda Coffey, and Sara Delamont, *Key Themes in Qualitative Research: Continuities and Change* (Walnut Creek, CA: AltaMira Press, 2003): 57. See also Yvonne Jewkes, "Autoethnography and Emotion as Intellectual Resources: Doing Prison Research Differently," *Qualitative Inquiry* 18, no. 1 (2011): 63–75; Katherine R. Allen and Fred P. Piercy, "Feminist Autoethnography," in *Research Methods in Family Therapy*, eds. Douglas H. Sprenkle and Fred P. Piercy (New York: The Guilford Press, 2005): 155–69.

43. Atkinson, Coffey, and Delamont, *Key Themes*, 63. As journalist Ben Montgomery says in an interview with *Creative Nonfiction*: "I'm the one doing the telling. I'm the one asking the questions. I'm the one deciding where we go, what we witness. I think it's intellectually dishonest to pretend that's not the case or to try to trick readers into believing that you're an emotionless robot." Matt Tullis, "Journalism Equals Facts While Creative Nonfiction Equals Truth? Maybe It's Not That Simple. A Roundtable Discussion with Chris Jones, Thomas Lake, and Ben Montgomery," *Creative Nonfiction* 47 (2013): 70.

44. Holman Jones, "Making the Personal Political." See also Lila Abu-Lughod, "Can There be a Feminist Ethnography?" *Woman and Performance: A Journal of Feminist Theory* 5, no. 1 (1990): 7–27; Avery Gordon, *Ghostly Matters: Haunting and the Sociological Imagination* (Minneapolis: University of Minnesota Press, 1988); Barbara Tedlock,

"Ethnography and Ethnographic Representation," in *Handbook of Qualitative Research*, eds. Norman K. Denzin and Yvonna S. Lincoln (Thousand Oaks, CA: Sage, 2000): 455–86; Kamala Visweswaran, *Fictions of Feminist Ethnography* (Minneapolis: University of Minnesota Press, 1997).

45. Behar, *The Vulnerable Observer*; Marianne Paget, "Performing the Text," *Journal of Contemporary Ethnography* 19, no. 1 (1990): 136–55; Margery Wolf, *A Thrice Told Tale: Feminism, Postmodernism, and Ethnographic Responsibility* (Palo Alto, CA: Stanford University Press, 1992); Renato Rosaldo, *Culture and Truth*.

46. Ellis, "Sociological Introspection"; Ellis, *Final Negotiations*; Carolyn Ellis and Michael G. Flaherty, eds. *Investigating Subjectivity: Research on Lived Experience* (Newbury Park, CA: Sage, 1992); Jewkes, "Autoethnography and Emotion."

47. Tami Spry, *Body, Paper, Stage: Writing and Performing Autoethnography* (Walnut Creek, CA: Left Coast Press, 2011): 111.

48. Kathleen M. Blee, "Studying the Enemy," in *Our Studies, Ourselves: Sociologists' Lives and Work*, eds. Barry Glassner and Rosanna Hertz (New York: Oxford University Press, 2003): 22.

49. Conquergood, "Rethinking Ethnography"; Paul Stoller, *Sensuous Scholarship* (Philadelphia: University of Pennsylvania Press, 1997).

50. Carolyn Ellis, "Touching Back/Receiving Gifts," *Studies in Symbolic Interaction* 28 (2005): 35–41; Arthur W. Frank, *The Wounded Storyteller* (Chicago, IL: University of Chicago Press, 1995); Ronald J. Pelias, "Confessions of Apprehensive Performer," *Text and Performance Quarterly* 17, no. 1 (1997): 25–32. See also Nancy Mairs, *Remembering the Bone House* (Boston, MA: Beacon, 1995).

51. For instance, given that I (Tony) do research about gay male sexuality, I often read about a subculture of men who enjoy and advocate for unprotected sex, and some of whom do so in order to acquire HIV—often known as "bug chasers." See Timothy Dean, *Unlimited Intimacy: Reflections on the Subculture of Barebacking* (Chicago, IL: University of Chicago Press, 2009). I also have written about men who enjoy gaining weight and who help others gain weight. See Tony E. Adams and Keith Berry, "Size Matters: Performing (Il)Logical Male Bodies on *Fatclub.Com*," *Text and Performance Quarterly* 33, no. 4 (2013): 308–25. In all my research, I frequently assess my right to critique others who are exercising choice and freedom in how they live. I may be unfamiliar with or bothered by their practices, but if I put forth suggestions and criticisms about why these men should change their behaviors I need to do so without coming across as arrogant, patronizing, and uninformed. For more about the constraints of choice and critique in research, see Orit Avishai, Lynne Gerber, and Jennifer Randles, "The Feminist Ethnographer's Dilemma: Reconciling Progressive Research Agendas with Fieldwork Realities," *Journal of Contemporary Ethnography* 42, no. 4 (2012): 394–426; Rachel Anderson Droogsma, "Redefining Hijab: American Muslim Women's Standpoints on Veiling," *Journal of Applied Communication Research* 35, no. 3 (2007): 294–319; David A. Gerber, "The 'Careers' of People Exhibited in Freak

Shows: The Problem of Volition and Valorization," in *Freakery: Cultural Spectacles of the Extraordinary Body*, ed. Rosemarie Garland Thomson (New York: New York University Press, 1996): 38–54.

52. Stanley Milgram, "Behavioral Study of Obedience," *Journal of Abnormal and Social Psychology* 67, no. 4 (1963): 375. See also Diana Baumrind, "Some Thoughts on Ethics of Research: After Reading Milgram's 'Behavioral Study of Obedience,'" *American Psychologist* 19, no. 6 (1964): 421–23; Stanley Milgram, "Issues in the Study of Obedience: A Reply to Baumrind," *American Psychologist* 19 (1964): 848–52.

53. John Heller, cited in Stephen B. Thomas and Sandra Crouse Quinn, "The Tuskegee Syphilis Study, 1932 to 1972: Implications for HIV Education and AIDS Risk Education Programs in the Black Community," *American Journal of Public Health* 81, no. 11 (1991): 1501.

54. Rebecca Skloot, *The Immortal Live of Henrietta Lacks* (New York: Crown, 2010).

55. Thomas and Quinn, "Tuskegee Syphilis," 1500.

56. Dwight Conquergood, "Poetics, Play, Process, and Power: The Performative Turn in Anthropology," *Text and Performance Quarterly* 1, no. 1 (1989): 84.

57. Jewkes, "Autoethnography and Emotion," 71–72.

58. Sam Joshi, "Homo Sutra: Disrobing Desire in the Adult Cinema," *Journal of Creative Work* 1, no. 2 (2007), accessed October 1, 2012, http://www.scientificjournals.org/journals2007/articles/1188.pdf. Lyall Crawford makes a similar observation: "For me, what is most problematic about fieldwork, what may make it wrong in some way, is the deliberate interference it entails. We go into the field. We place ourselves in some social setting. We may even ask the 'natives' to take us in or, better yet, be invited without asking. I am skeptical about this. Even though I am deeply intrigued with human behavior and thoroughly enjoy reading ethnographic accounts, I am uneasy about the inherently intrusive nature of fieldwork." Lyall Crawford, "Personal Ethnography," *Communication Monographs* 63, no. 2 (1996): 163.

59. Dwight Conquergood, "Performing as a Moral Act: Ethical Dimensions of the Ethnography of Performance," *Literature in Performance* 5, no. 2 (1985): 5–7.

60. Conquergood, "Performing as a Moral Act," 9.

61. Reed-Danahay, "Turning Points," 423.

62. Tony E. Adams and Stacy Holman Jones, "Performing Identity, Critical Reflexivity, and Community: The Hopeful Work of Studying Ourselves and Others," *Liminalities: A Journal of Performance Studies* 9, no. 2 (2013): 1, accessed June 1, 2013, http://liminalities.net/9-2/introduction.pdf.

63. Adams and Holman Jones, "Performing Identity."

64. Behar, *The Vulnerable Observer*, 13.

65. bell hooks, "Theory as Liberatory Practice," *Yale Journal of Law and Feminism* 4, no. 1 (1991/1992): 1–12.

66. Lorde, *Sister Outsider*, 116.

67. Carole Blair, Julie R. Brown, and Leslie A. Baxter, "Disciplining the Feminine," *Quarterly Journal of Speech* 80, no. 4 (1994): 383–409; Katherine

Grace Hendrix, "An Invitation to Dialogue: Do Communication Journal Reviewers Mute the Race-Related Research of Scholars of Color?" *Southern Communication Journal* 70, no. 4 (2005): 329–45.

68. Frye, *The Politics of Reality*; Elissa Foster, "Commitment, Communication, and Contending with Heteronormativity: An Invitation to Greater Reflexivity in Interpersonal Research," *Southern Communication Journal* 73, no. 1 (2008): 84–101; Thomas Glave, *Words to Our Now: Imagination and Dissent* (Minneapolis, MN: University of Minneapolis Press, 2005): 116–29; Emily Martin, "The Egg and the Sperm: How Science Has Constructed a Romance Based on Stereotypical Male-Female Roles," *Signs: Journal of Women in Culture* 16, no. 3 (1991): 485–501; Lindsy Van Gelder, "Marriage as a Restricted Club," in *Against the Current*, eds. Pamela J. Annas and Robert C. Rosen (Upper Saddle River, NJ: Prentice Hall, 1998): 294–97; Kath Weston, *Families We Choose: Lesbians, Gays, Kinship* (New York: Columbia University Press, 1991).

69. Riedmann, *Science that Colonizes*; Spivak, "Subaltern."

70. Robin Patric Clair, "The Changing Story of Ethnography," in *Expressions of Ethnography*, ed. Robin Patric Clair (Albany: State University of New York Press, 2003): 3. For recent concerns about speaking for others, see Alcoff, "Speaking for Others"; Marcelo Diversi and Claudio Moreira, *Betweener Talk: Decolonizing Knowledge Production, Pedagogy, and Praxis* (Walnut Creek, CA: Left Coast Press, 2010); Linda Tuhiwai Smith, *Decolonizing Methodologies: Research and Indigenous Species* (New York: Zed Books, 1999); Keyan G. Tomaselli, Lauren Dyll-Myklebust, and Sjoerd van Grootheest, "Personal/Political Interventions Via Autoethnography: Dualisms, Knowledge, Power, and Performativity in Research Relations," in *Handbook of Autoethnography*, eds. Stacy Holman Jones, Tony E. Adams and Carolyn Ellis (Walnut Creek, CA: Left Coast Press, 2013): 576–94. For recent discussions about excluding others from particular communities or activities, see Jacqueline Alemany, "Military Readies to Integrate Women into Combat," *CBSNEWS*, accessed November 1, 2013, http://www.cbsnews.com/news/military-readies-to-integrate-women-into-combat/; John Eligon, "New Neighbor's Agenda: White Power Takeover," *The New York Times*, accessed November 1, 2013, http://www.nytimes.com/2013/08/30/us/white-supremacists-plan-angers-a-north-dakota-town.html?_r=0; Donna Riley, "Hidden in Plain View: Feminists Doing Engineering Ethics, Engineers Doing Feminist Ethics," *Science and Engineering Ethics* 19, no. 1 (2013): 1–18.

71. Critiques of invasive and oppressive—colonialist—research practices also contributed to the recognition of sovereign identities of cultural others and the emergence of identity politics. For example, Stephen Thomas and Sandra Quinn argue that the end of the Tuskegee Syphilis study was heavily influenced by the rise of the Civil Rights and Black Power movements—movements tied to, and made possible by, particular racial identities. See Thomas and Quinn, "Tuskegee Syphilis."

72. Karl G. Heider, "What Do People Do? Dani Auto-Ethnography," *Journal of Anthropological Research* 31, no. 1 (1975): 3–17.

73. Walter Goldschmidt, "Anthropology and the Coming Crisis: An Autoethnographic Appraisal," *American Anthropologist* 79, no. 2 (1977): 294.

74. David M. Hayano, "Auto-Ethnography: Paradigms, Problems, and Prospects," *Human Organization* 38, no. 1 (1979): 99.

75. See Thomas W. Benson, "Another Shooting in Cowtown," *Quarterly Journal of Speech* 67, no. 4 (1981): 347–406; Coles, *The Call of Stories*; Dwight Conquergood, "Between Experience and Meaning: Performance as a Paradigm for Meaningful Action," in *Renewal and Revision: The Future of Interpretation*, ed. Ted Colson (Denton, TX: NB Omega Publication, 1986): 26–59; James Clifford and George Marcus, eds. *Writing Culture: The Poetics and Politics of Ethnography* (Berkeley: University of California Press, 1986); Vincent Crapanzano, *Tuhami: Portrait of a Moroccan* (Chicago, IL: University of Chicago Press, 1980); Norman K. Denzin, *Interpretive Biography* (Newbury Park, CA: Sage, 1989); Fisher, "Narration"; Keller, *Reflections on Gender and Science*; Ann Oakley, "Interviewing Women: A Contradiction in Terms," in *Doing Feminist Research*, ed. Helen Roberts (New York: Routledge, 1981): 30–61; Michael Pacanowsky, "Slouching Towards Chicago," *Quarterly Journal of Speech* 74, no. 4 (1988): 453–67; Reinharz, *On Becoming a Social Scientist*; Carol Rambo Ronai and Carolyn Ellis, "Turn-Ons for Money: Interactional Strategies of the Table Dancer," *Journal of Contemporary Ethnography* 18, no. 3 (1989): 271–98; Marjorie Shostak, *Nisa: The Life and Words of a!Kung Woman* (Cambridge, MA: Harvard University Press, 1981); John Van Maanen, *Tales of the Field: On Writing Ethnography* (Chicago, IL: University of Chicago Press, 1988); Irving Kenneth Zola, *Missing Pieces: A Chronicle of Living with a Disability* (Philadelphia, PA: Temple University Press, 1982).

76. Alice A. Deck, "Autoethnography: Zora Neale Hurston, Noni Jabavu, and CrossDisciplinary Discourse," *Black American Literature Forum* 24, no. 2 (1990): 237–56; Françoise Lionnet, "Autoethnography: The An-archic Style of *Dust Tracks on a Road*," in *Autobiographical Voices: Race, Gender, Self-portraiture*, ed. Françoise Lionnet (Ithaca, NY: Cornell University Press, 1989): 97–129.

77. See Ellis, "Sociological Introspection"; Ellis and Flaherty, *Investigating Subjectivity*; Ellis, "There are Survivors"; Ellis, *Final Negotiations*; Ellis and Bochner, *Composing Ethnography*.

78. Arthur P. Bochner, "Perspectives on Inquiry II: Theories and Stories," in *Handbook of Interpersonal Communication*, eds. Mark L. Knapp and Gerald R. Miller (Thousand Oaks, CA: Sage, 1994): 21–41; Arthur P. Bochner, "It's About Time: Narrative and the Divided Self," *Qualitative Inquiry* 3, no. 4 (1997): 418–38; Arthur P. Bochner, "Narrative's Virtues," *Qualitative Inquiry* 7, no. 2 (2001): 131–57; Arthur P. Bochner, "Perspectives on Inquiry III: The Moral of Stories," in *Handbook of Interpersonal Communication*, eds. Mark L. Knapp and John A. Daly (Thousand Oaks, CA: Sage, 2002): 73–101.

79. Stacy Holman Jones, *Kaleidoscope Notes: Writing Women's Music and Organizational Culture* (Walnut Creek, CA: AltraMira Press, 1998).

80. Influential essays (1990–1999) about or related to autoethnography include Dwight Conquergood, "Rethinking Ethnography"; Frederick C. Corey and Thomas K. Nakayama, "Sextext," *Text and Performance Quarterly* 17, no. 1 (1997): 58–68; Carolyn Ellis, Christine E. Kiesinger, and Lisa M. Tillmann-Healy, "Interactive Interviewing: Talking About Emotional Experience," in *Reflexivity and Voice*, ed. Rosanna Hertz (Thousand Oaks, CA: Sage, 1997): 119–49; bell hooks, "Theory as Liberatory Practice"; Lyall Crawford, "Personal Ethnography"; and Eric Mykhalovskiy, "Reconsidering Table Talk"; Mark Neumann, "Collecting Ourselves at the End of the Century," in *Composing Ethnography: Alternative Forms of Qualitative Writing*, eds. Carolyn Ellis and Arthur P. Bochner (Walnut Creek, CA: AltaMira Press, 1996): 172–98; Carol Rambo Ronai, "The Reflexive Self through Narrative: A Night in the Life of an Erotic Dancer/ Researcher," in *Investigating Subjectivity: Research on Lived Experience*, eds. Carolyn Ellis and Michael G. Flaherty (Newbury Park, CA: Sage, 1992): 102–24; Carol Rambo Ronai, "Multiple Reflections of Child Sex Abuse," *Journal of Contemporary Ethnography* 23, no. 4 (1995): 395–426; Carol Rambo Ronai, "My Mother Is Mentally Retarded," in *Composing Ethnography: Alternative Forms of Qualitative Writing*, eds. Carolyn Ellis and Arthur P. Bochner (Walnut Creek, CA: AltaMira, 1996): 109–31.

81. Influential books (1990–1999) about or related to autoethnography include Ruth Behar, *The Vulnerable Observer*; Sheron J Dailey, ed. *The Future of Performance Studies: Visions & Revisions* (Annandale, VA: National Communication Association, 1998); H. L. Goodall, *Casing a Promised Land* (Carbondale: Southern Illinois University Press, 1994); Ronald J. Pelias, *Writing Performance: Poeticizing the Researcher's Body* (Carbondale: Southern Illinois University Press, 1999); Deborah Reed-Danahay, ed. *Auto/Ethnography* (New York: Berg, 1997); Laurel Richardson, *Fields of Play: Constructing an Academic Life* (New Brunswick, NJ: Rutgers University Press, 1997); Linda Tuhiwai Smith, *Decolonizing Methodologies*.

82. Norman K. Denzin and Yvonna S. Lincoln, eds. *Handbook of Qualitative Research* (Thousand Oaks, CA: Sage, 1994).

83. Jean D. Clandinin and Michael F. Connelly, "Personal Experience Methods," in *Handbook of Qualitative Research*, eds. Norman K. Denzin and Yvonna S. Lincoln (Thousand Oaks, CA: Sage, 1994): 413–27.

84. Laurel Richardson, "Writing: A Method of Inquiry," in *Handbook of Qualitative Research*, eds. Norman K. Denzin and Yvonna S. Lincoln (Thousand Oaks, CA: Sage): 516–29.

85. See Norman K. Denzin and Yvonna S. Lincoln, eds. *Handbook of Qualitative Research*. 2nd ed. (Thousand Oaks, CA: Sage, 2000); Norman K. Denzin and Yvonna S. Lincoln, eds. *Handbook of Qualitative Research*. 3rd ed. (Thousand Oaks, CA: Sage, 2005); Ellis and Bochner, "Autoethnography, Personal Narrative, Reflexivity"; Holman Jones, "Making the Personal Political."

86. Brydie-Leigh Bartleet and Carolyn Ellis, eds. *Music Autoethnographies: Making Autoethnography Sing/Making Music Personal* (Bowen Hills,

QLD Australian Academic Press); Bochner and Ellis, *Ethnographically Speaking*; Ellis, *The Ethnographic I*; Ellis, *Revision*.

87. Stacy Holman Jones, *Torch Singing: Performing Resistance and Desire from Billie Holiday to Edith Piaf* (Lanham, MD; AltaMira Press, 2007). See also Holman Jones, "The Way We Were, Are, and Might Be: Torch Singing as Autoethnography," in *Ethnographically Speaking: Autoethnography, Literature, and Aesthetics*, ed. Arthur P. Bochner and Carolyn Ellis (Walnut Creek, CA: AltaMira, 2001): 44–56; Holman Jones, "Emotional Space: Performing the Resistive Possibilities of Torch Singing," *Qualitative Inquiry* 8, no. 6 (2002): 738–59; Holman Jones, "Crimes Against Experience," *Cultural Studies <=> Critical Methodologies* 9, no. 5 (2009): 608–18.

88. Influential books (2000–2009) about or related to autoethnography include Bryant Keith Alexander, *Performing Black Masculinity: Race, Culture, and Queer Identity* (Lanham, MD: AltaMira Press, 2006); Heewon Chang, *Autoethnography as Method* (Walnut Creek, CA: Left Coast Press, 2008); Robin Patric Clair, ed. *Expressions of Ethnography: Novel Approaches to Qualitative Methods* (Albany: State University of New York Press, 2003); H. L. Goodall, *Writing the New Ethnography* (Walnut Creek, CA: AltaMira Press, 2000); H. L. Goodall, *A Need to Know: The Clandestine History of a CIA Family* (Walnut Creek, CA: Left Coast Press, 2006); Ronald J. Pelias, *A Methodology of the Heart: Evoking Academic and Daily Life* (Walnut Creek, CA: AltaMira Press, 2004); Christopher N. Poulos, *Accidental Ethnography: An Inquiry into Family Secrecy* (Walnut Creek, CA: Left Coast Press, 2009); Lisa M. Tillmann-Healy, *Between Gay and Straight: Understanding Friendship across Sexual Orientation* (Walnut Creek, CA: AltaMira Press, 2001); Keyan G. Tomaselli, ed. *Writing in the San/d: Autoethnography Among Indigenous Southern Africans* (Lanham, MD: AltaMira Press, 2007); Jonathan Wyatt and Ken Gale, *Between the Two: A Nomadic Inquiry into Collaborative Writing and Subjectivity* (Newcastle upon Tyne: Cambridge Scholars Publishing, 2009).

Influential essays (2000–2009) about or related to autoethnography include Adams, "Seeking Father"; Adams, "Narrative Ethics"; Adams and Holman Jones, "Autoethnography is Queer"; Leon Anderson, "Analytic Autoethnography," *Journal of Contemporary Ethnography* 35, no. 4 (2006): 373–95; Keith Berry, "Implicated Audience Member Seeks Understanding: Reexamining the 'Gift' of Autoethnography," *International Journal of Qualitative Methods* 5, no. 3 (2006): 1–12; Keith Berry, "Embracing the Catastrophe: Gay Body Seeks Acceptance," *Qualitative Inquiry* 13, no. 2 (2007): 259–81; Keith Berry, "Promise in Peril: Ellis and Pelias and the Subjective Dimensions of Ethnography," *Review of Communication* 8, no. 2 (2008): 154–73; Robin M. Boylorn, "E Pluribus Unum (Out of Many, One)," *Qualitative Inquiry* 12, no. 4 (2006): 651–80; Robin M. Boylorn, "As Seen on TV: An Autoethnographic Reflection on Race and Reality Television," *Critical Studies in Media Communication* 25, no. 4 (2008): 413–33; Sara L. Crawley, "'They Still Don't Understand Why I Hate Wearing Dresses!' An Autoethnographic Rant on Dresses, Boats, and Butchness," *Cultural Studies <=> Critical Methodologies* 2, no. 1

(2002): 69–92; Craig Gingrich-Philbrook, "Autoethnography's Family Values: Easy Access to Compulsory Experiences," *Text and Performance Quarterly* 25, no. 4 (2005): 297–314; Barbara J. Jago, "Chronicling an Academic Depression," *Journal of Contemporary Ethnography* 31, no. 6 (2002): 729–57; Stacy Holman Jones, "(M)othering Loss: Telling Adoption Stories, Telling Performativity," *Text and Performance Quarterly* 25, no. 2 (2005): 113–35; Ronald J. Pelias, "The Critical Life," *Communication Education* 49, no. 3 (2000): 220–28; Elyse Pineau, "*Nursing Mother* and Articulating Absence," *Text and Performance Quarterly* 20, no. 1 (2000): 1–19; Tami Spry, "Performing Autoethnography: An Embodied Methodological Praxis," *Qualitative Inquiry* 7, no. 6 (2001): 706–32; Lisa M. Tillmann, "Body and Bulimia Revisited: Reflections on 'a Secret Life,'" *Journal of Applied Communication Research* 37, no. 1 (2009): 98–112; Jillian A. Tullis Owen, Chris McRae, Tony E. Adams, and Alisha Vitale, "truth Troubles," *Qualitative Inquiry* 15, no. 1 (2009): 178–200; Sarah Wall, "An Autoethnography on Learning About Autoethnography," *International Journal of Qualitative Methods* 5, no. 2 (2006); Sarah Wall, "Easier Said Than Done: Writing an Autoethnography," *International Journal of Qualitative Methods* 7, no. 1 (2008); Jonathan Wyatt, "Psychic Distance, Consent, and Other Ethical Issues," *Qualitative Inquiry* 12, no. 4 (2006): 813–18.

Influential journal issues (2000–2009) about or related to autoethnography from the 2000s include Maree Boyle and Ken Parry, "Special Issue on Organizational Autoethnography," *Culture and Organization* 3, no. 3 (2007): 185–266; Carolyn Ellis and Arthur P. Bochner, eds. "Special Issue: Taking Ethnography into the Twenty-first Century," *Journal of Contemporary Ethnography* 25, no. 1 (1996): 3–166; Scott A. Hunt and Natalia Ruiz Junco, eds. "Two Thematic Issues: Defective Memory and Analytical Autoethnography," *Journal of Contemporary Ethnography* 35, no. 4 (2006): 71–372; Christopher N. Poulos, ed. "Special Issue: Autoethnography," *Iowa Journal of Communication* 40, no. 1 (2008): i–140; John T. Warren and Keith Berry, eds. "Special Issue: The Evidence of Experience, Cultural Studies, and Personal(ized) Scholarship," *Cultural Studies <=> Critical Methodologies* 9, no. 5 (2009): 595–695.

89. Recent (2010–2014) books about autoethnography include Adams, *Narrating the Closet*; Robin M. Boylorn, *Sweetwater: Black Women and Narratives of Resistance* (New York: Peter Lang, 2013); Robin M. Boylorn and Mark P. Orbe, eds. *Critical Autoethnography: Intersecting Cultural Identities in Everyday Life* (Walnut Creek, CA: Left Coast Press, 2014); Heewon Chang and Drick Boyd, eds. *Spirituality in Higher Education: Autoethnographies* (Walnut Creek, CA: Left Coast Press, 2011); Heewon Chang, Faith Wambura Ngunjiri, and Kathy-Ann C. Hernandez, *Collaborative Autoethnography* (Walnut Creek, CA: Left Coast Press, 2013); Norman K. Denzin, *Interpretive Autoethnography* (Thousand Oaks, CA: Sage, 2014); Mike Hayler, *Autoethnography, Self-narrative and Teacher Education* (Rotterdam, Netherlands: Sense Publishers, 2011); Jeanine Mingé and Amber Lynn Zimmerman, *Concrete and Dust: Mapping the Sexual Terrains of Los Angeles* (New York: Routledge,

2013); Tessa Muncey *Creating Autoethnographies* (Thousand Oaks, CA: Sage, 2010); Ronald J. Pelias, *Leaning: A Poetics of Personal Relations* (Walnut Creek, CA: Left Coast Press, 2011); Cynthia Cole Robinson and Pauline Clardy, eds. *Tedious Journeys: Autoethnography by Women of Color in Academe* (New York: Peter Lang, 2010); Nigel P. Short, Lydia Turner, and Alec Grant, eds. *Contemporary British Autoethnography* (Rotterdam, Netherlands: Sense Publishers, 2013); Phil Smith, ed. *Both Sides of the Table: Autoethnographies of Educators Learning and Teaching With/In [Dis]ability* (New York: Peter Lang, 2013); Spry, *Body, Paper, Stage*; Sophie Tamas, *Life After Leaving* (Walnut Creek, CA: Left Coast Press, 2011); Jonathan Wyatt and Tony E. Adams, eds. *On (Writing) Families: Autoethnographies of Presence and Absence, Love and Loss* (Rotterdam, Netherlands: Sense Publishers, 2014).

    Recent (2010–2014) journal issues about autoethnography include Tony E. Adams and Stacy Holman Jones, "Special Issue: On Studying Ourselves and Others," *Liminalities: A Journal of Performance Studies* 9, no. 2 (2013), accessed June 1, 2013, http://liminalities.net/9-2/; Tony E. Adams and Jonathan Wyatt, "Special issue: On (Writing) Fathers," *Qualitative Inquiry* 18, no. 2 (2012): 119–209; Berry and Clair, "Ethnographic Reflexivity"; W. Benjamin Myers, "Special Issue: Writing Autoethnographic Joy," *Qualitative Communication Research* 1, no. 2 (2012): 157–252; Faith W. Ngunjiri, Kathy-Ann Hernandez, and Heewon Chang, "Special Issue: Autoethnography as Research Practice," *Journal of Research Practice* 6, no. 1 (2010). http://jrp.icaap.org/index.php/jrp/issue/view/13.

90. Examples of autoethnography in Anthropology: Keyan G. Tomaselli, "Visualizing Different Kinds of Writing: Auto-ethnography, Social Science," *Visual Anthropology* 26, no. 2 (2013): 165–180; Tomaselli, Dyll-Myklebust, and van Grootheest, "Personal/Political Interventions." An example of autoethnography in Art and Design: Thommy Eriksson, "Being Native: Distance, Closeness and Doing Auto/Self-ethnography," *ArtMonitor* 8 (2010): 91–100. Examples of autoethnography in Business: Clair Doloriert and Sally Sambrook, "Accommodating an Autoethnographic PhD: The Tale of the Thesis, the Viva Voce, and the Traditional Business School," *Journal of Contemporary Ethnography* 40, no. 5 (2011): 582–615; Mark Learmonth and Michael Humphreys, "Autoethnography and Academic Identity: Glimpsing Business School Doppelgängers," *Organization* 19, no. 1 (2012): 99–117. Examples of autoethnography in Communication: Ragan Fox, "'You Are Not Allowed to Talk About Production': Narratization on (and Off) the Set of CBS's *Big Brother*," *Critical Studies in Media Communication* 30, no. 3 (2013): 189–208; Rachel Alicia Griffin, "I AM an Angry Black Woman: Black Feminist Autoethnography, Voice, and Resistance," *Women's Studies in Communication* 35, no. 2 (2012): 138–57; Boylorn, *Sweetwater*; Boylorn and Orbe, *Critical Autoethnography*. An example of autoethnography in Criminology: Jewkes, "Autoethnography and Emotion." Examples of autoethnography in Education: Margot Duncan, "Going Native: Autoethnography as a Design Tool," in *Handbook of Design in Educational Technology*, eds. Rosemary Luckin, Sadhana

Puntambekar, Peter Goodyear, Barbara Grabowski, Joshua Underwood and Niall Winters (New York: Routledge, 2013): 201–10; Sherick Hughes, Julie L. Pennington, and Sara Makris, "Translating Autoethnography across the AERA Standards: Toward Understanding Autoethnographic Scholarship as Empirical Research," *Educational Researcher* 41, no. 6 (2012): 209–19; Royel M. Johnson, "Black and Male on Campus: An Autoethnographic Account," *Journal of African American Males in Education* 4, no. 2 (2013): 25–45; Robinson and Clardy, *Tedious Journeys*; Smith, *Both Sides of the Table*. An example of autoethnography in Geography: David Butz, "Autoethnography as Sensibility," in *The Sage Handbook of Qualitative Geography*, eds. Dydia DeLyser, Steve Herbert, Stuart Aitken, Mike Crang, and Linda McDowell (Thousand Oaks, CA: Sage, 2010): 138–55. An example of autoethnography in Music: Bartleet and Ellis, *Music Autoethnographies*. Examples of autoethnography in Nursing: Kim Foster, Margaret McAllister, and Louise O'Brien, "Extending the Boundaries: Autoethnography as an Emergent Method in Mental Health Nursing Research," *International Journal of Mental Health Nursing* 15, no. 1 (2006): 44–53; Patricia Ann Sealy, "Autoethnography: Reflective Journaling and Meditation to Cope With Life-Threatening Breast Cancer," *Clinical Journal of Oncology Nursing* 16, no. 1 (2012): 38–41. Examples of autoethnography in Psychology: David Carless and Kitrina Douglas, "A History of Autoethnographic Inquiry," in *Handbook of Autoethnography*, eds. Stacy Holman Jones, Tony E. Adams and Carolyn Ellis (Walnut Creek, CA: Left Coast Press, 2013): 84–106; Mark Freeman, "From Absence to Presence: Finding Mother, Ever Again," in *On (Writing) Families: Autoethnographies of Presence and Absence, Love and Loss*, eds. Jonathan Wyatt and Tony E. Adams (Rotterdam, Netherlands: Sense Publishers, 2014). An example of autoethnography in Social Work: Paige Averett and Danielle Soper, "Sometimes I Am Afraid: An Autoethnography of Resistance and Compliance," *The Qualitative Report* 16, no. 2 (2011): 358–76; Examples of autoethnography in Sociology: Leon Anderson and Bonnie Glass-Coffin, "I Learn by Going: Autoethnographic Modes of Inquiry," in *Handbook of Autoethnography*, eds. Stacy Holman Jones, Tony E. Adams and Carolyn Ellis (Walnut Creek, CA: Left Coast Press, 2013): 57–83; Barton, "My Auto/ Ethnographic Dilemma"; Crawley, "Wearing Dresses"; Sara L. Crawley, "Autoethnography as Feminist Self-Interview," in *The SAGE Handbook of Interview Research*, 2nd ed., eds. Jaber F. Gubrium, James A. Holstein, Amir B. Marvasti, and Karyn D. McKinney (Thousand Oaks, CA: Sage, 2012): 143–60; Denzin, *Interpretive Autoethnography*; Laurel Richardson, "Sentimental Journey," in *Handbook of Autoethnography*, eds. Stacy Holman Jones, Tony E. Adams and Carolyn Ellis (Walnut Creek, CA: Left Coast Press, 2013): 339–56.

91. See Norman K. Denzin and Yvonna S. Lincoln, eds. *The SAGE Handbook of Qualitative Research*. 4th ed. (Thousand Oaks, CA: Sage, 2011); Stephen D. Lapan, MaryLynn T. Quartaroli, and Frances J. Riemer, eds. *Qualitative Research: An Introduction to Methods and Designs* (San Francisco, CA: John Wiley & Sons, 2011); Patricia Leavy, ed. *Oxford Handbook of Qualitative*

Research (Oxford: Oxford University Press, 2014); Ieva Zaķe and Michael DeCesare, eds. *New Directions in Sociology: Essays on Theory and Methodology in the 21st Century* (Jefferson, NC: McFarland & Company, 2011).

92. Pat Sikes, ed. *Autoethnography* (Thousand Oaks, CA: Sage, 2013).
93. Stacy Holman Jones, Tony E. Adams, and Carolyn Ellis, eds. *Handbook of Autoethnography* (Walnut Creek, CA: Left Coast Press, 2013).
94. Smaro Kamboureli, "The Politics of the Beyond: 43 Theses on Autoethnography and Complicity," in *Asian Canadian Writing Beyond Autoethnography*, eds. Eleanor Ty and Christl Verduyn (Waterloo: Wilfrid Laurier University Press, 2008): 31–54.
95. Richardson, "Evaluating Ethnography," 254. See also Alcoff, "Speaking for Others."
96. Lorde, *Sister Outsider*, 37.

Chapter 2

1. Ronai, "Multiple Reflections," 421.
2. Holman Jones, "Making the Personal Political"; Holman Jones, "Lost and Found."
3. Dwight Conquergood, "Performance Studies: Interventions and Radical Research," *The Drama Review* 46, no. 2 (2002): 146.
4. Conquergood, "Interventions and Radical Research," 149.
5. As Kristin Langellier writes, stories create a "two-way" contract: "'let me tell you a story' promises a performance and constitutes an audience; and 'a story about what happened to me' re-presents personal experience." Langellier continues: "In a word, personal experience stories are *made*, not found, by either narrators or researchers." Kristin M. Langellier, "Personal Narrative, Performance, Performativity: Two or Three Things I Know for Sure," *Text and Performance Quarterly* 19, no. 2 (1999): 128. See also Ronai, "Reflexive Self"; Ronai, "Multiple Reflections"; Adams, "Narrative Ethics"; Boylorn, "E Pluribus Unum"; Boylorn, "As Seen on TV"; Mary Weems, "Fire: A Year in Poems," in *Handbook of Autoethnography*, eds. Stacy Holman Jones, Tony E. Adams and Carolyn Ellis (Walnut Creek, CA: Left Coast Press, 2013): 313–20.
6. Gingrich-Philbrook, "Family Values."
7. See, for example, Brydie-Leigh Bartleet, "Artful and Embodied Methods, Modes of Inquiry, and Forms of Representation," in *Handbook of Autoethnography*, eds. Stacy Holman Jones, Tony E. Adams and Carolyn Ellis (Walnut Creek, CA: Left Coast Press, 2013): 443–64; David Carless and Kitrina Douglas, "Songwriting and the Creation of Knowledge," in *Music Autoethnographies: Making Autoethnography Sing/Making Music Personal*, eds. Brydie-Leigh Bartleet and Carolyn Ellis (Bowen Hills, QLD Australian Academic Press): 23–38; Marilyn Metta, "Putting the Body on the Line: Embodied Writing and Recovery through Domestic Violence," in *Handbook of Autoethnography*, eds. Stacy Holman Jones, Tony E. Adams

and Carolyn Ellis (Walnut Creek, CA: Left Coast Press, 2013): 486–509; Jeanine Marie Mingé, "The Stained Body: A Fusion of Embodied Art on Rape and Love," *Journal of Contemporary Ethnography* 36, no. 3 (2007): 252–80; Mingé & Zimmerman, *Concrete and Dust*; Pelias, *Leaning*; Pineau, "Nursing Mother"; Spry, *Body, Paper, Stage*.

8. See, for example, James Merrill, *The Inner Room* (New York: Knopf, 1988); Eve Kosofsky Sedgwick, "Teaching 'Experimental Critical Writing,'" in *The Ends of Performance*, eds. Peggy Phelan and Jill Lane (New York: New York University Press, 1998): 104–15; Sara Lundquist, "The Aesthetics of Enclosure: James Merrill's Inner Rooms," *English Studies in Canada* 31, no. 1 (2005): 31–53.

9. My (Stacy's) wording references Timothy Materer's and Sara Lundquist's analyses of James Merrill's *The Inner Room*. See Timothy Materer, "James Merrill's Late Poetry: AIDS and the 'Stripping Process,'" *Arizona Quarterly* 64, no 2 (2006): 125–26; Lundquist, "The Aesthetics of Enclosure," 31–32.

10. Merrill, *Inner*, 57.

11. I (Stacy) first read about Merrill's "Prose of Departure" in Sedgwick's essay, "Teaching 'Experimental Critical Writing.'" Sedgwick offers Merrill's poetry as a prompt for lessons on "pluralizing voices" and "modularity." The lesson on pluralizing voices focuses on how differences in form (moving between poetry and prose) can be felt in how we hear writing; how the time and space of a text might change; and how the mode of address, as well as "the expectation of just who might be listening, and how," might be understood as a *relation* among readers and writers, identities and expectations. The lesson on modularity focuses on the "effects involved when more or less discrete units of the same form (sonnet, haiku) keep happening again and again." In the longer version of the essay, I use pluralized voices—differences in form and mode of exchange and address—to show how identities and lives are performed *in relation* to others. I also show how modularity happens again and again not only in accounts of our lives, but also in our identities and relationships. Sedgwick, "Teaching 'Experimental Critical Writing,'" 111–13.

12. Materer takes up this criticism of Merrill's poetry—its lack of emotion, its control and impersonal tone, its pleasurable wordplay, and its superficiality—arguing that these criticisms mistake Merrill's restraint and desire for an affirmative (if not happy) ending as shallowness while overlooking the "deeply emotional and nearly despairing poems" that he wrote in the 1980s until his death in 1995. Materer, "James Merrill's Late Poetry," 124.

13. My (Stacy's) wording is drawn from Lundquist's observation that Merrill's poetry holds together opposites "in a knot that tightens toward the centre, allowing logic to leap the space between two worlds, two opposites." Lundquist also writes that the haiku in Merrill's prose poems create "inner rooms" (also the title of the collection in which "Prose of Departure" is included) that summon an "incantatory, momentary magic" within the "surrounding, louder prose of imminent departure." In these haiku, within the inner rooms they create, we are "still in touch," "still linked by love." Lundquist, "The Aesthetics of Enclosure," 32, 44–5.

14. Eve Kosofsky Sedgwick, *A Dialogue on Love* (Boston, MA: Beacon Press, 2000): 42.

15. Holman Jones, "Lost and Found," 323–24.

16. Jillian A. Tullis, "Self and Others: Ethics in Autoethnographic Research," in *Handbook of Autoethnography*, eds. Stacy Holman Jones, Tony E. Adams and Carolyn Ellis (Walnut Creek, CA: Left Coast Press, 2013): 244–61.

17. See Ellis, "Relational Ethics"; Tillmann-Healy, "Friendship as Method"; Katherine Irwin, "Into the Dark Heart of Ethnography: The Lived Ethics and Inequality of Intimate Field Relationships," *Qualitative Sociology* 29 (2006): 155–75.

18. Adams, *Narrating the Closet*; Mohan J. Dutta and Ambar Basu, "Negotiating Our Postcolonial Selves," in *Handbook of Autoethnography*, eds. Stacy Holman Jones, Tony E. Adams and Carolyn Ellis (Walnut Creek, CA: Left Coast Press, 2013): 143–61; Holman Jones, *Kaleidoscope Notes*; Holman Jones, *Torch Singing*; Tomaselli, Dyll-Myklebust, and van Grootheest, "Personal/Political Interventions"; Antonio C. La Pastina, "The Implications of an Ethnographer's Sexuality," *Qualitative Inquiry* 12, no. 4 (2006): 724–35.

19. See, for example, Rex Crawley, "Favor: An Autoethnography of Survival," in *Critical Autoethnography: Intersecting Cultural Identities in Everyday Life*, eds. Robin M. Boylorn and Mark P. Orbe (Walnut Creek, CA: Left Coast Press, 2014): 222–33; Nicole L. Defenbaugh, *Dirty Tale: A Narrative Journey of the IBD Body* (Cresskill, NJ: Hampton Press, 2011); Foster, "Commitment"; H. L. Goodall, *The Daily Narrative* (blog), accessed June 1, 2013, http://www.hlgoodall.com/blog.html; Metta, "Embodied Writing"; Pineau, "Nursing Mother"; Elyse Pineau, "The Kindness of [Medical] Strangers: An Ethnopoetic Account of Embodiment, Empathy, and Engagement," in *Writings of Healing and Resistance*, ed. Mary Weems (New York: Peter Lang, 2013): 63–9; Richardson, "Sentimental Journey"; Tamas, *Life After Leaving*.

20. See, for example, Tony E. Adams, "Post-Coming out Complications," in *Critical Autoethnography: Intersecting Cultural Identities in Everyday Life*, eds. Robin M. Boylorn and Mark P. Orbe (Walnut Creek, CA: Left Coast Press, 2014): 62–80; Barton, "My Auto/Ethnographic Dilemma"; Robin M. Boylorn, "Black Kids' (B.K.) Stories: Ta(L)King (About) Race Outside of the Classroom," *Cultural Studies <=> Critical Methodologies* 11, no. 1 (2011): 59–70; Robin M. Boylorn, "Gray or for Colored Girls Who Are Tired of Chasing Rainbows: Race and Reflexivity," *Cultural Studies <=> Critical Methodologies* 11, no. 2 (2011): 178–86; Boylorn, *Sweetwater*; Robin M. Boylorn, "'Sit with Your Legs Closed!' And Other Sayin's from My Childhood," in *Handbook of Autoethnography*, eds. Stacy Holman Jones, Tony E. Adams and Carolyn Ellis (Walnut Creek, CA: Left Coast Press, 2013): 173–85; Sara B. Dykins Callahan, "Academic Outings," *Symbolic Interaction* 31, no. 4 (2008): 351–75; Carolyn Ellis, "Maternal Connections," in *Composing Ethnography: Alternative Forms of Qualitative Writing*, eds. Carolyn Ellis and Arthur P. Bochner (Walnut Creek, CA: AltaMira Press, 1996): 240–43; Carolyn Ellis, "'I Hate My Voice': Coming to Terms with

Minor Bodily Stigmas," *The Sociological Quarterly* 39, no. 4 (1998): 517–37; Carolyn Ellis, "With Mother/With Child: A True Story," *Qualitative Inquiry* 7, no. 5 (2001): 598–616; Carolyn Ellis, "No Longer Hip: Losing My Balance and Adapting to What Ails Me," *Qualitative Research in Sport, Exercise and Health* 6, no. 1 (2014): 1–19; Griffin, "Black Feminist Autoethnography"; Holman Jones, "Lost and Found"; Stacy Holman Jones, "Always Strange," in *On (Writing) Families: Autoethnographies of Presence and Absence, Love and Loss*, eds. Jonathan Wyatt and Tony E. Adams (Rotterdam, Netherlands: Sense Publishers, 2014); Blake A. Paxton, "Transforming Minor Bodily Stigmas Through Holding onto Grief: A 'Hair' Raising Possibility," *Qualitative Inquiry* 19, no. 5 (2013): 355–65; Dale Rivera, "A Mother's Son," *Cultural Studies <=> Critical Methodologies* 13, no. 2 (2013): 88–94.

21. Denzin, *Interpretive Autoethnography.*

22. Autoethnographers who have explicitly written about epiphanies include Adams, *Narrating the Closet*; Carolyn Ellis and Arthur P. Bochner, "Telling and Performing Personal Stories: The Constraints of Choice in Abortion," in *Investigating Subjectivity: Research on Lived Experience*, eds. Carolyn Ellis and Michael G. Flaherty (Newbury Park, CA: Sage, 1992): 79–101; Christopher N. Poulos, "Spirited Accidents: An Autoethnography of Possibility," *Qualitative Inquiry* 16, no. 1 (2010): 49–56; Sealy, "Reflective Journaling."

23. Carolyn Ellis, "'At Home With 'Real Americans': Communicating Across the Urban/Rural and Black/White Divides in the 2008 Presidential Election," *Cultural Studies <=> Critical Methodologies* 9, no. 6 (2009): 721–33.

24. Ellis, "'Real Americans,'" 729–30.

25. Elissa Foster, "My Eyes Cry without Me: Illusions of Choice in the Transition to Motherhood," in *Contemplating Maternity in an Era of Choice: Explorations into Discourses of Reproduction*, eds. Sara Hayden and D. Lynn O'Brien Hallstein (Lanham, MD: Lexington, 2010): 139–58.

26. Robin M. Boylorn, "My Daddy is Slick, Brown, and Cool like Ice Water," in *On (Writing) Families: Autoethnographies of Presence and Absence, Love and Loss*, eds. Jonathan Wyatt and Tony E. Adams (Rotterdam, Netherlands: Sense Publishers, 2014): 85–93.

27. Goodall, *The Daily Narrative.*

28. Keith Berry, "Spinning Autoethnographic Reflexivity, Cultural Critique, and Negotiating Selves," in *Handbook of Autoethnography*, eds. Stacy Holman Jones, Tony E. Adams and Carolyn Ellis (Walnut Creek, CA: Left Coast Press, 2013): 212.

29. Calafell, "Considering Accountability."

30. Peggy McIntosh, "White Privilege and Male Privilege: A Personal Account of Coming to See Correspondences Through Work in Women's Studies," in *Understanding Diversity: Readings, Cases, and Exercises*, eds. Carol P. Harvey and M. June Allard (New York: HarperCollins, 1995): 130–139.

31. Sara Ahmed, *Queer Phenomenology: Orientations, Objects, Others* (Durham, NC: Duke University Press, 2006).

32. Tony E. Adams, "Mothers, Faggots, and Witnessing (Un)Contestable Experience," *Cultural Studies <=> Critical Methodologies* 9, no. 5 (2009): 619–26; Adams, *Narrating the Closet.*

33. Kristin M. Langellier and Eric E. Peterson, "Shifting Contexts in Personal Narrative Performance," in *The SAGE Handbook of Performance Studies*, ed. D. Soyini Madison and Judith Hamera (Thousand Oaks, CA, Sage, 2005): 155.

34. Goodall, *The New Ethnography*; Harry F. Wolcott, *Ethnography Lessons: A Primer* (Walnut Creek, CA: Left Coast Press, 2010).

35. Shulamit Reinharz, *Feminist Methods in Social Research* (Oxford: Oxford University Press, 1992): 260.

36. This is a revised account from Adams, "The Joys of Autoethnography."

37. Carolyn Ellis, "Negotiating Terminal Illness: Communication, Collusion, and Coalition in Caregiving," in *Loss and Trauma: General and Close Relationship Perspectives*, eds. John H. Harvey and Eric D. Miller (Philadelphia, PA: Brunner-Routledge, 2000): 284–304.

38. Lisa M. Tillmann-Healy, "A Secret Life in a Culture of Thinness: Reflections on Body, Food, and Bulimia," in *Composing Ethnography: Alternative Forms of Qualitative Writing*, eds. Carolyn Ellis and Arthur P. Bochner (Walnut Creek, CA: AltaMira Press, 1996): 80. See also Tillmann, "Body and Bulimia Revisited."

39. Clifford Geertz, *The Interpretation of Cultures* (New York: Basic Books, 1973): 10. For examples of autoethnographies that effectively use "thick description," see Boylorn, *Sweetwater*; Devika Chawla, "Walk, Walking, Talking, Home," in *Handbook of Autoethnography*, eds. Stacy Holman Jones, Tony E. Adams and Carolyn Ellis (Walnut Creek, CA: Left Coast Press, 2013): 162–72; Ellis, "Maternal Connections"; Goodall, *A Need to Know*; Richardson, "Sentimental Journey."

40. Jim Thomas's definition of critical ethnography nicely summarizes the essence of critical autoethnography: Critical autoethnography is a method that facilitates "social consciousness and societal change," aids "emancipatory goals," and negates "repressive" cultural influences. Jim Thomas, *Doing Critical Ethnography* (Newbury Park, CA: Sage, 1993): 4. See also DeLeon, "Anarchism"; Norman K. Denzin, Yvonna S. Lincoln and Linda Tuhiwai Smith, eds. *Handbook of Critical and Indigenous Methodologies* (Thousand Oaks, CA: Sage, 2008); D. Soyini Madison, *Critical Ethnography: Method, Ethics, Performance*. 2nd ed. (Thousand Oaks, CA: Sage, 2012). Critical autoethnography explicitly rubs against Martyn Hammersley's belief that social research should not advocate on behalf of cultural change. See Martyn Hammersley, *Methodology: Who Needs It?* (Thousand Oaks, CA: Sage, 2011).

41. This section is based on my (Stacy's) reading of adoption stories, including Tonya Bishoff and Jo Rankin, eds. *Seeds from a Silent Tree: An Anthology* (San Diego, CA: Pandal Press, 1997); Susan Soon-Keum Cox, *Voices from Another Place: A Collection of Works from a Generation Born in Korea and Adopted to other Countries* (St. Paul, MN: Yeong & Yeong, 1999); Jane Jeong Trenka, *The Language of Blood: A Memoir* (St. Paul, MN: Borealis Books, 2003); Jane Jeong Trenka, *Fugitive Visions: An Adoptee's Return to Korea* (St. Paul, MN: Graywolf Press, 2009); Jane Jeong Trenka, Julia Chinyere Oparah, and Sun Yung Shin, eds. *Outsiders Within: Writing on Transracial Adoption* (Cambridge, MA: South End Press, 2006).

42. Trenka, *Fugitive Visions*, 196.
43. Trenka *Fugitive Visions*, 91–94.
44. Jacqueline Taylor, *Waiting for the Call: From Preacher's Daughter to Lesbian Mom* (Ann Arbor: University of Michigan Press, 2007): 212.
45. Holman Jones, "Lost and Found," 325–26.
46. Calafell, "Considering Accountability."
47. Ellis, "Relational Ethics"; Holman Jones, "Making the Personal Political"; Spry, *Body, Paper, Stage*.
48. Glenn D. Hinson, "'You've got to Include an Invitation': Engaged Reciprocity and Negotiated Purpose in Collaborative Ethnography" (presentation, Annual Convention of the American Anthropological Association, Chicago, Illinois, April 15–18, 1999); Jacqueline Adams, "The Wrongs of Reciprocity: Fieldwork among Chilean Working-Class Women," *Journal of Contemporary Ethnography* 27, no. 2 (1998): 219–41.
49. Harry J. Elam Jr., *Taking It to the Streets: The Social Protest Theater of Luis Valdez and Amiri Baraka* (Ann Arbor: University of Michigan Press, 1997); bell hooks, "Performance Practice as a Site of Opposition," in *Let's Get It On: The Politics of Black Performance*, ed. Catherine Ugwu (Seattle, WA: Bay, 1995): 210–21.
50. Ellis and Rawicki, "More than Mazel?"
51. This is a revised account from Ellis and Rawicki, "More than Mazel?" See also Ellis and Rawicki, "Relational Autoethnography"; Carolyn Ellis and Chris J. Patti, "With Heart: Compassionate Interviewing and Storytelling with Holocaust Survivors," *Storytelling, Self, Society* (in press); Rawicki and Ellis, "Sharing Authority."
52. See, for example, Tony E. Adams, "Paradoxes of Sexuality, Gay Identity, and the Closet," *Symbolic Interaction* 33, no. 2 (2010): 234–56; Amir Marvasti, "Being Middle Eastern American: Identity Negotiation in the Context of the War on Terror," *Symbolic Interaction* 28, no. 4 (2006): 525–47.
53. Marilyn Metta, *Writing Against, Alongside and Beyond Memory: Lifewriting as Reflexive, Poststructuralist Feminist Research Practice* (New York: Peter Lang, 2010); Mingé & Zimmerman, *Concrete and Dust*; Lisa M. Tillmann, "Wedding Album: An Anti-Heterosexist Performance Text," in *Handbook of Autoethnography*, eds. Stacy Holman Jones, Tony E. Adams and Carolyn Ellis (Walnut Creek: Left Coast Press, 2013); Sophie Tamas, "Who's There? A Week Subject," in *Handbook of Autoethnography*, eds. Stacy Holman Jones, Tony E. Adams and Carolyn Ellis (Walnut Creek, CA: Left Coast Press, 2013): 186–201; Eve Tuck and C. Ree, "A Glossary of Haunting," in *Handbook of Autoethnography*, eds. Stacy Holman Jones, Tony E. Adams and Carolyn Ellis (Walnut Creek, CA: Left Coast Press, 2013): 639–58.
54. Holman Jones, "Always Strange," 16–17.
55. Butler writes, "When we recognize another, or when we ask for recognition for ourselves, we are not asking for an Other to see us as we are, as we already are, as we always have been, as we were constituted prior to the encounter itself." Judith Butler, *Giving an Account of Oneself* (New York: Fordham University Press, 2005): 44.
56. Butler writes, "Instead, in the asking, in the petition, we have already become something new.... To ask for recognition, or to offer it, is precisely

not to ask for recognition for what one already is. It is to solicit a becoming, to instigate a transformation, to petition the future always in relation to the other." Butler, *Giving an Account*, 44.

57. Chawla, "Walking"; Ellis, "Maternal Connections"; Pelias, "The Critical Life"; Weems, "Fire."

58. Ellis, "Maternal Connections."

59. Rawicki and Ellis, "Sharing Authority."

60. Adams, *Narrating the Closet*, 27.

61. Adams, "Paradoxes."

62. Some autoethnographers do not explicitly identify or include research questions, often because a research question is unknown at the beginning of a project and/or because a question would disrupt the flow of the text/story. See, for example, Ellis, "Maternal Connections"; Holman Jones, "Lost and Found"; Tamas, "A Week Subject." Research questions also might be included in an article's abstract, or they might be left to readers to determine.

63. hooks, "Theory as Liberatory Practice"; Richardson, "Evaluating Ethnography."

64. Ellis, *The Ethnographic I*, 33.

65. Adams, "Seeking Father"; Tony E. Adams, "Missing Each Other," *Qualitative Inquiry* 18, no. 2 (2012): 193–96.

66. Kenneth Burke, *The Philosophy of Literary Form: Studies in Symbolic Action*. 3rd ed. (Berkeley: University of California Press, 1974).

67. Coles, *The Call of Stories*; Bochner, "It's About Time."

68. Ellis, *The Ethnographic I*, 34. See also Adams, "Mothers, Faggots"; Ruth Behar, "A Sixth Memo for the Millennium: Vulnerability," accessed August 15, 2013, http://www.mit.edu/~bhdavis/BeharLec.html; Spry, *Body, Paper, Stage*.

69. Holman Jones, Adams, and Ellis, "Coming to Know," 24.

70. Behar, *The Vulnerable Observer*, 14.

71. Adams, *Narrating the Closet*.

72. See, for example, April Chatham-Carpenter, "'Do Thyself No Harm': Protecting Ourselves as Autoethnographers," *Journal of Research Practice* 6, no. 1 (2010), accessed March 1, 2013, http://jrp.icaap.org/index.php/jrp/article/view/213/183; Hernandez and Ngunjiri, "Relationships and Communities"; Jago, "Academic Depression"; Barbara J. Jago, "Shacking Up: An Autoethnographic Tale of Cohabitation." *Qualitative Inquiry* 17, no. 2 (2011): 204–19; Metta, *Writing Against*; Tamas, *Life After Leaving*; Tillmann, "A Secret Life"; Tillmann-Healy, "Body and Bulimia"; Tullis, "Self and Others."

73. Spry, *Body, Paper, Stage*, 47.

74. Goodall, *The New Ethnography*.

75. Bochner, "Perspectives on Inquiry III"; Dutta and Basu, "Postcolonial Selves"; Archana A. Pathak, "Opening My Voice, Claiming My Space: Theorizing the Possibilities of Postcolonial Approaches to Autoethnography," *Journal of Research Practice* 6, no. 1 (2010), accessed June 14, 2012, http://jrp.icaap.org/index.php/jrp/article/view/231/191;

Tomaselli, Dyll-Myklebust, and van Grootheest, "Personal/Political Interventions."

76. Berry, "Autoethnographic Reflexivity"; Norman K. Denzin, "Interpretive Autoethnography," in *Handbook of Autoethnography*, eds. Stacy Holman Jones, Tony E. Adams and Carolyn Ellis (Walnut Creek, CA: Left Coast Press, 2013): 123–42; Griffin, "Black Feminist Autoethnography"; Tuck and Ree, "A Glossary of Haunting."

77. Adams, *Narrating the Closet*, 106–07.

78. Ellis, "Seeking My Brother's Voice: Holding onto Long-Term Grief through Photographs, Stories, and Reflections," in *Stories of Complicated Grief: A Critical Anthology*, ed. Eric Miller (Washington, DC: National Association of Social Workers Press, 2014): 3–21; Holman Jones and Adams, "Undoing the Alphabet." See also Lorraine Hedtke and John Winslade, *Re-membering Lives: Conversations with the Dying and the Bereaved* (Amityville, NY: Baywood Publishing Company, 2004).

79. See Dwight Conquergood, "Beyond the Text: Toward a Performative Cultural Politics," in *The Future of Performance Studies: Visions and Revisions*, ed. Sheron J. Dailey (Annandale, VA: National Communication Association, 1998): 25–36; Elyse Lamm Pineau, "Re-Casting Rehearsal: Making a Case for Production as Research," *Journal of the Illinois Speech and Theatre Association* 46 (1995): 43–52.

80. H. L. Goodall, "Narrative Ethnography as Applied Communication Research," *Journal of Applied Communication Research* 32, no. 3 (2004): 191.

81. Pelias, "The Critical Life," 223.

82. Robin M. Boylorn, "Blackgirl Blogs, Auto/ethnography, and Crunk Feminism," *Liminalities: A Journal of Performance Studies* 9, no. 2 (2013): 81, accessed June 1, 2013, http://liminalities.net/9-2/boylorn.pdf

83. Chimamanda Adichie, "The Danger of a Single Story," accessed October 1, 2013, http://dotsub.com/view/63ef5d28-6607-4fec-b906-aaae6cff7dbe/viewTranscript/eng

84. Adichie, "Danger." Other researchers also note the dangers of a single story (or too few) stories. For example, communication scholars Bernadette Calafell and Shane Moreman write, "While Latinas/os are the largest 'minority' group in the United States, little academic work in the Communication field has been attendant to our communities, thus neglecting how these communities are both adding to and changing the academy's theories and practices." Bernadette Marie Calafell and Shane T. Moreman, "Envisioning an Academic Readership: Latina/o Performativities per the Form of Publication," *Text and Performance Quarterly* 29, no. 2 (2009): 123. See also Blair, Brown, and Baxter, "Disciplining the Feminine"; Boylorn, "E Pluribus Unum"; Calafell, "Considering Accountability."

85. Fisher, "Narration."

86. See Frank, *The Wounded Storyteller*, 97–114.

87. For example, Marie Battiste notes, "Indigenous people's epistemology is derived from the immediate ecology; from peoples' experiences, perceptions, thoughts, and memory, including experiences shared with others; and from the spiritual world discovered in dreams, visions, inspirations,

and signs interpreted with the guidance of healers or elders. Most Indigenous peoples hold various forms of literacies in holistic ideographic systems, which act as partial knowledge meant to interact with the oral traditions." Marie Battiste, "Research Ethics for Protecting Indigenous Knowledge and Heritage," in *Handbook of Critical and Indigenous Methodologies*, eds. Norman K. Denzin, Yvonna S. Lincoln and Linda Tuhwai Smith (Thousand Oaks, CA: Sage, 2008): 499. See also Tomaselli, Dyll-Myklebust, and van Grootheest, "Personal/Political Interventions."

88. Keyan G. Tomaselli, "Stories to Tell, Stories to Sell: Resisting Textualization," *Cultural Studies* 17, no. 6 (2003): 859. See also Konishi, "Aboriginal Masculinity."

89. See, for example, Bartleet, "Artful and Embodied Methods"; Carolyn Ellis, *Behind the Wall*, digital video, directed by Carolyn Ellis, featuring Jerry Rawicki (Warsaw, Poland: Total Film, 2013); Anne Harris and Rebecca Long, "Smart Bitch: Talking Back in Unity," *Liminalities* 9, no. 3 (2013), accessed December 2, 2013, http://liminalities.net/9-3/smart.html; Metta, "Embodied Writing"; Jeanine M. Mingé, "Mindful Autoethnography, Local Knowledges," in *Handbook of Autoethnography*, eds. Stacy Holman Jones, Tony E. Adams and Carolyn Ellis (Walnut Creek, CA: Left Coast Press, 2013): 425–42.

90. Harris and Long, "Smart Bitch."

91. Tomaselli, "Resisting Textualization," 863.

92. See Boylorn, "E Pluribus Unum"; Calafell, "Considering Accountability"; Sara L. Crawley and Nadzeya Husakouskaya, "How Global Is Queer? A Co-Autoethnography of Politics, Pedagogy, and Theory in Drag," in *Handbook of Autoethnography*, eds. Stacy Holman Jones, Tony E. Adams and Carolyn Ellis (Walnut Creek, CA: Left Coast Press, 2013): 321–38; Satoshi Toyosaki and Sandy L. Pensoneau-Conway, "Autoethnography as a Praxis of Social Justice," in *Handbook of Autoethnography*, eds. Stacy Holman Jones, Tony E. Adams and Carolyn Ellis (Walnut Creek, CA: Left Coast Press, 2013): 557–75.

93. See Adams, "The Joy of Autoethnography"; Boylorn, "Blackgirl Blogs."

94. Andreas G. Philaretou and Katherine R. Allen, "Researching Sensitive Topics through Autoethnographic Means," *The Journal of Men's Studies* 14, no. 1 (2006): 75.

95. Lorde, *Sister Outsider*.

Chapter 3

1. Holman Jones, "The Way We Were"; Ellis and Bochner, "Autoethnography, Personal Narrative, Reflexivity."

2. Norman Denzin, *Interpretive Ethnography: Ethnographic Practices for the 21st Century* (Thousand Oaks, CA: Sage, 1996).

3. Holman Jones, "Making the Personal Political."

4. Anne M. Harris, "Ghost-child," in *On (Writing) Families: Autoethnographies of Presence and Absence, Love and Loss*, eds. Jonathan Wyatt and Tony E. Adams (Rotterdam, Netherlands: Sense Publishers, 2014): 69–75.

5. Ellis, *The Ethnographic I.*
6. Denzin, *Interpretive Autoethnography*; Ellis, Adams, and Bochner, "Autoethnography: An Overview"; Ellis and Bochner, "Telling and Performing"; Poulos, "Spirited Accidents."
7. Arthur P. Bochner, "The Functions of Human Communication in Interpersonal Bonding," in *Handbook of Rhetorical and Communication Theory*, eds. Carroll C. Arnold and John Waite Bowers (Boston: Allyn and Bacon, 1984): 595.
8. Holman Jones, "Lost and Found," 336; Deborah D. Gray, *Attaching in Adoption: Practical Tool's for Today's Parents* (Indianapolis, IN: Perspectives Press, 2002): 103.
9. Adams, *Narrating the Closet.*
10. Derek M. Bolen, "After Dinners, In the Garage, Out of Doors, and Climbing on Rocks," in *On (Writing) Families: Autoethnographies of Presence and Absence, Love and Loss*, eds. Jonathan Wyatt and Tony E. Adams (Rotterdam, Netherlands: Sense Publishers, 2014): 142.
11. Madison, *Critical Ethnography*, 21.
12. Madison, *Critical Ethnography*, 22.
13. Goodall, *The New Ethnography*, 51.
14. Goodall, *The New Ethnography*, 58. Examples of autoethnographies that address "gaps" in existing research include Keith Berry, "Un(covering) the Gay Interculturalist," in *Identity Research and Communication: Intercultural Reflections and Future Directions*, eds. Nilanjana Bardhan and Mark P. Orbe (Lanham, MD: Lexington Books, 2012): 223–37; Foster, "Commitment"; Griffin, "Black Feminist Autoethnography"; Ronai, "My Mother is Mentally Retarded."
15. Ragan Fox, "Tales of a Fighting Bobcat: An 'Auto-archaeology' of Gay Identity Formation and Maintenance," *Text and Performance Quarterly* 30, no. 2 (2010): 124. Other autoethnographers who have also found compelling storylines in the examination of personal and cultural texts and artifacts include Boylorn, "As Seen on TV"; Susanne Gannon, "Sketching Subjectivities," in *Handbook of Autoethnography*, eds. Stacy Holman Jones, Tony E. Adams and Carolyn Ellis (Walnut Creek, CA: Left Coast Press, 2013): 228–43; Goodall, *A Need to Know*; Andrew F. Herrmann, "My Father's Ghost: Interrogating Family Photos," *Journal of Loss and Trauma* 10, no. 4 (2005): 337–46.
16. Ilja Maso, "Phenomenology and Ethnography," in *Handbook of Ethnography*, eds. Paul Atkinson, Amanda Coffey, Sara Delamont, John Lofland and Lyn Lofland (Thousand Oaks, CA: Sage, 2001): 136–44.
17. Conquergood, "Interventions and Radical Research," 146.
18. See, for example, Adams, *Narrating the Closet*; Holman Jones, "Lost and Found."
19. See, for example, Berry, "Embracing the Catastrophe"; Boylorn, *Sweetwater*; Mingé and Zimmerman, *Concrete and Dust.*
20. Lisa M. Tillmann, "Don't Ask, Don't Tell: Coming Out in an Alcoholic Family," *Journal of Contemporary Ethnography* 38, no. 6 (2009): 677–712; Lisa M. Tillmann, "Coming Out and Going Home: A Family Ethnography," *Qualitative Inquiry* 16, no. 2 (2010): 116–29.

21. Sherryl Kleinman, "Feminist Fieldworker: Connecting Research, Teaching, and Memoir," in *Our Studies, Ourselves: Sociologists' Lives and Work*, eds. Barry Glassner and Rosanna Hertz (New York: Oxford University Press, 2003): 230.

22. Madison, *Critical Ethnography*, 25.

23. Madison, *Critical Ethnography*, 25–27.

24. Adams and Berry, "Size Matters."

25. Goodall, *The New Ethnography*, 24.

26. Goodall, *The New Ethnography*, 24.

27. Poulos, *Accidental Ethnography*, 47.

28. Mark Freeman, "Data are Everywhere: Narrative Criticism in the Literature of Experience," in *Narrative Analysis: Studying the Development of Individuals in Society*, eds. Colette Daiute and Cynthia Lightfoot (Thousand Oaks, CA: Sage, 2004): 73.

29. Freeman, "Data are Everywhere," 73.

30. Della Pollock, "Memory, Remembering, and Histories of Change," in *The SAGE Handbook of Performance Studies*, eds. D. Soyini Madison and Judith Hamera (Thousand Oaks, CA: Sage, 2006): 90.

31. Pollock, "Memory," 88.

32. Pollock, "Memory," 90.

33. Pollock, "Memory," 93.

34. Madison, *Critical Ethnography*.

35. James P. Spradley, *The Ethnographic Interview* (New York: Holt, Rinehart & Winston, 1979).

36. Kusenbach, Margaret, "Street Phenomenology: The Go-Along as Ethnographic Research Tool," *Ethnography* 4, no. 3 (2003): 455–85; Lyndsay Brown and Kevin Durrheim, "Different Kinds of Knowing: Generating Qualitative Data Through Mobile Interviewing, *Qualitative Inquiry* 15, no. 5 (2009): 911–30; Kristin Lozanski and Melanie Beres, "Temporary Transience and Qualitative Research: Methodological Lessons from Fieldwork with Independent Travelers and Seasonal Workers," *International Journal of Qualitative Methods* 6, no. 2 (2007): 911–30.

37. Daniel Makagon and Mark Neumann, *Recording Culture: Audio Documentary and the Ethnographic Experience* (Thousand Oaks, CA: Sage, 2009); Sarah Pink, *Doing Sensory Ethnography* (Thousand Oaks, CA: Sage, 2009).

38. Douglas Harper, "Talking About Pictures: A Case for Photo Elicitations," *Visual Studies* 17, no. 1 (2002): 13–26; Jane Jorgenson and Tracy Sullivan, "Accessing Children's Perspectives through Participatory Photo Interviews," *Forum: Qualitative Social Research*, 11, no. 1 (2009), accessed December 2, 2013, http://www.qualitative-research.net/index.php/fqs/article/view/447; Alan Radley and Diane Taylor, "Images of Recovery: A Photo Elicitation Study on the Hospital Ward," *Qualitative Health Research* 13, no. 1 (2003): 177–99.

39. Ellis, *The Ethnographic I*; Ellis, *Revision*; Ellis, Kiesinger, and Tillmann-Healy, "Interactive Interviewing."

40. Marvasti, "Being Middle Eastern American," 526.

41. Ellis and Rawicki, "Relational Autoethnography."
42. Frank, *The Wounded Storyteller*, 144.
43. Ellis and Rawicki, "Relational Autoethnography," 378.
44. Michael Jackson, *At Home in the World* (Durham, NC: Duke University Press): 163.
45. Frank, *The Wounded Storyteller*, 158.
46. Ellis and Rawicki, "Relational Autoethnography," 378.
47. Adams, "Seeking Father," 720. See also Ellis, "Relational Ethics."
48. Tullis, "Self and Others."
49. Some universities have developed ethical guidelines that address autoethnography specifically. See, for example, Ryerson University's guidelines at http://www.ryerson.ca/content/dam/about/vpresearch/autoethnography.pdf. If you are a member of a university community and want to conduct an autoethnographic project, we encourage you to consult with your IRB before proceeding with your work in order to determine whether your project is considered research and whether you are exempt from IRB approval.
50. Department of Health, Education, and Welfare (United States), "The Belmont Report," accessed December 2, 2013, http://www.hhs.gov/ohrp/humansubjects/guidance/belmont.html.
51. As Tomaselli, Dyll, and Francis observe, "The requirement by ethics committees that even illiterate informants sign release forms bureaucratize and alienate the condition of 'being there' and strip the organic nature of observation and the encounter of its spontaneity." Keyan G. Tomaselli, Lauren Dyll, and Michael Francis, "'Self' and 'Other': Auto-Reflexive and Indigenous Ethnography," in *Handbook of Critical and Indigenous Methodologies*, eds. Norman K. Denzin, Yvonna S. Lincoln and Linda Tuhwai Smith (Thousand Oaks, CA: Sage, 2008): 350. See also Battiste, "Research Ethics"; Ellis, "Relational Ethics."
52. Ellis and Rawicki, "Relational Autoethnography."
53. Kim Etherington, "Ethical Research in Reflexive Relationships," *Qualitative Inquiry* 13, no. 5 (2007): 607; Tullis, "Self and Others."
54. Ellis and Rawicki, "Relational Autoethnography," 376–77.
55. See, for example, Carolyn Ellis, "Emotional and Ethical Quagmires in Returning to the Field," *Journal of Contemporary Ethnography* 24, no. 1 (1995): 68–98; Tamas, *Life After Leaving*.
56. Ellis, "Maternal Connections."
57. Ellis, "With Mother/With Child."
58. Ellis, "With Mother/With Child"; Ellis, *Revision*.
59. My work is typically available only on password-protected databases, though sometimes it becomes more widely available when others post files of my work. In the past, I have written to those who have posted these works and asked them to remove the works in an effort to protect my child's privacy. Still, publishing the work means that it is accessible—and that I want it to be accessed and read—by others, including people who may know my child.
60. Arlene Stein, "Sex, Truths, and Audiotape: Anonymity and the Ethics of Exposure in Public Ethnography," *Journal of Contemporary Ethnography* 39, no. 5 (2010): 554–68.

61. See Adams, *Narrating the Closet*; Bernadette Barton, *Pray the Gay Away: The Extraordinary Lives of Bible Belt Gays* (New York: New York University Press, 2012).

62. Michalina Maliszewska, "An Autoethnographic Examination of International Student Experiences in the United States" (Master's thesis, Northeastern Illinois University, 2009).

63. Ellis, *The Ethnographic I*.

64. Ellis, "Relational Ethics."

65. Ellis, "Relational Ethics," 4.

66. Tillmann-Healy, "Friendship as Method."

67. Ellis and Rawicki, "Relational Autoethnography," 377.

68. Ellis, "Relational Ethics," 13; Jewkes, "Autoethnography and Emotion"; Irwin, "Dark Heart of Ethnography."

69. Ellis, "Relational Ethics;" Tamas, *Life After Leaving*.

70. See, for example, Michael V. Angrosino, *Opportunity House: Ethnographic Stories of Mental Retardation* (Walnut Creek, CA: AltaMira Press, 1988); Boylorn, *Sweetwater*; Ellis, *The Ethnographic I*.

71. See, for example, Chang, Ngunjiri, and Hernandez, *Collaborative Autoethnography*; Dutta and Basu, "Postcolonial Selves"; Patricia Geist-Martin, Lisa Gates, Liesbeth Wiering, Erika Kirby, Renee Houston, Anne Lilly, and Juan Moreno. "Exemplifying Collaborative Autoethnographic Practice via Shared Stories of Mothering," *Journal of Research Practice* 6, no. 1 (2010), accessed October 3, 2013, http://jrp.icaap.org/index.php/jrp/article/view/209; Tomaselli, Dyll-Myklebust and van Grootheest, Personal/Political Interventions"; Satoshi Toyosaki, Sandra L. Pensoneau-Conway, Nathan A. Wendt, and Kyle Leathers, "Community Autoethnography: Compiling the Personal and Resituating Whiteness," *Cultural Studies <=> Critical Methodologies* 9, no. 1 (2009): 56–83.

72. Shelly Carter, "How Much Subjectivity is Needed to Understand Our Lives Objectively?" *Qualitative Health Research* 12, no. 9 (2002): 1184–201.

73. Ellis, "Maternal Connections."

74. Adams, "Seeking Father"; Adams, "Narrative Ethics"; Adams, *Narrating the Closet*.

75. Ellis, *Revision*, 317.

76. Ellis, *Final Negotiations*, 15–16.

77. See, for example, Berry, "Implicated Audience Member"; Ayanna F. Brown and Lisa William-White, "'We are Not the Same Minority': The Narratives of Two Sisters Navigating Identity and Discourse at Public and Private White Institutions," in *Tedious Journeys: Autoethnography by Women of Color in Academe*, eds. Cynthia Cole Robinson and Pauline Clardy (New York: Peter Lang, 2010): 149–75; Ellis, "Relational Ethics"; Craig Gingrich-Philbrook, "Evaluating (Evaluations of) Autoethnography," in *Handbook of Autoethnography*, eds. Stacy Holman Jones, Tony E. Adams and Carolyn Ellis (Walnut Creek, CA: Left Coast Press, 2013): 609–26.

78. Chatham-Carpenter, "Protecting Ourselves," section 2.1.

79. See also Tillmann, "Body and Bulimia Revisited"; Tillmann-Healy, "A Secret Life."

80. Sophie Tamas, "Writing and Righting Trauma: Troubling the Autoethnographic Voice," *Forum: Qualitative Social Research*, vol. 10, no. 1 (2009), accessed June 1, 2013, http://www.qualitative-research.net/index.php/fqs/article/viewArticle/1211

81. Tamas, "A Week Subject," 200.

82. Jago, "Academic Depression, 738.

83. Brown and William-White, "Navigating Identity."

84. Lisa William-White, "Dare I Write about Oppression on Sacred Ground [Emphasis Mine]," *Cultural Studies <=> Critical Methodologies* 11, no. 3 (2011): 236–42.

85. See also Berry, "Autoethnographic Reflexivity"; Metta, *Writing Against*; Metta, "Embodied Writing"; Gannon, "Sketching Subjectivities"; Carol Rambo, "Twitch: A Performance of Chronic Liminality," in *Handbook of Autoethnography*, eds. Stacy Holman Jones, Tony E. Adams and Carolyn Ellis (Walnut Creek, CA: Left Coast Press, 2013): 627–38; Ronai, "Multiple Reflections"; Tuck and Ree, "A Glossary of Haunting."

86. Hernandez and Ngunjiri, "Relationships and Communities," 274.

87. See Conquergood, "Rethinking Ethnography"; Crawford, "Personal Ethnography."

88. Ellis and Bochner, "Telling and Performing."

89. Ellis, "Relational Ethics," 22.

90. Patricia Leavy, "Fiction and the Feminist Academic Novel," *Qualitative Inquiry* 18, no. 6 (2012): 519.

91. Barton, "My Auto/Ethnographic Dilemma."

92. Madison, *Critical Ethnography*, 43.

93. Goodall, *The New Ethnography*, 121.

94. See Chang, *Autoethnography*; Ellis, *The Ethnographic I*; Thomas R. Lindlof and Bryan C. Taylor, *Qualitative Communication Research Methods*. 3rd ed. (Thousand Oaks, CA: Sage, 2010); Madison, *Critical Ethnography*; Sarah J. Tracy, *Qualitative Research Methods: Collecting Evidence, Crafting Analysis, Communicating Impact* (Malden, MA: Blackwell, 2013).

95. Goodall, *The New Ethnography*, 121.

96. Ellis, "Minor Bodily Stigmas," 535.

97. Lynn Miller, "Saved by Stein: Or the Life You Perform May Become Your Own," *Text and Performance Quarterly* 32, no. 2 (2012): 184.

Chapter 4

1. Richardson, "A Method of Inquiry"; Julia Colyar, "Becoming Writing, Becoming Writers," *Qualitative Inquiry* 15, no. 2 (2009): 421–36; Julia E. Colyar, "Reflections on Writing and Autoethnography," in *Handbook of Autoethnography*, eds. Stacy Holman Jones, Tony E. Adams and Carolyn Ellis (Walnut Creek, CA: Left Coast Press, 2013): 363–83.

2. Denzin, "Interpretive Autoethnography"; Berry, "Autoethnographic Reflexivity"; Ellis, "No Longer Hip"; Holman Jones and Adams, "Undoing the Alphabet"; Jeanine M. Mingé and John Burton Sterner, "The Transitory Radical: Making Place with Cancer," in *Critical*

Autoethnography: Intersecting Cultural Identities in Everyday Life, eds. Robin M. Boylorn and Mark P. Orbe (Walnut Creek, CA: Left Coast Press, 2014): 33–46; Poulos, *Accidental Ethnography*.

3. Spry, *Body, Paper, Stage*, 36.

4. Bolen, "After Dinners," 142.

5. See, for example, Allen-Collinson, "Autoethnography"; Boylorn, *Sweetwater*; Chawla, "Walking"; Sandra L. Faulkner, "That Baby Will Cost You: An Intended Ambivalent Pregnancy," *Qualitative Inquiry* 18, no. 4 (2012): 333–40; Richardson, "Sentimental Journey"; Tillmann-Healy, *Between Gay and Straight*.

6. Ellis, *The Ethnographic I*, 331–332.

7. Stephen King, *On Writing: A Memoir of the Craft* (New York: Scribner, 2000): 151; see Anne Lamott, *Bird by Bird: Some Instructions on Writing and Life* (New York: Anchor, 1994).

8. Aimee Bender, "Why the Best Way to Get Creative Is to Make Some Rules," accessed July 17, 2013, http://www.oprah.com/spirit/Writing-Every-Day-Writers-Rules-Aimee-Bender

9. Goodall, *The New Ethnography*, 22.

10. Playwright Charles Mee's (2002) advice for actors resembles my (Stacy's) advice for writers: "I think actors should throw themselves into the ocean of the text in the same way that I throw myself into this ocean of material that comes into my plays, and just somehow trust that their instincts and thoughts will sort it all out for them. If you try to apply any one set of standards to understanding it, that's reductionist; you'll probably work against it. If you try to work intellectually, you'll lose; if you try to understand it psychologically, you'll lose; if you try to understand it as a political argument, you'll lose. But if you throw yourself into the middle of all those things that are at play, then your intelligence—which includes your head and your heart and sometimes your neurons and your cells—will work it through for you." Erin B. Mee, "Shattered and Fucked up and Full of Wreckage: The Words and Works of Charles L. Mee," *The Drama Review* 46, no. 3 (2002): 90.

11. Goodall, *The New Ethnography*.

12. Holman Jones, "Lost and Found."

13. Lisa Fittko, quoted in Michael Taussig, *I Swear I Saw This: Drawings in Fieldwork Notebooks, Namely My Own* (Chicago, IL: The University of Chicago Press, 2011): 9. Fittko took Walter Benjamin over the French-Spanish border. Her story of this journey is told in her autobiography *Escape Through the Pyrenees*. Though, as Yates points out in his "Invent/Story" of the briefcase and missing manuscript and the proliferation of "Benjaminiana and Benjamin-themed texts and objects" (par. 6) the briefcase and manuscript have inspired, Fittko's account of the journey, the case, the missing manuscript, and their import and relation to Benjamin's work and life have been subject to multiple revisions. Julian Yates, "The Briefcase of Walter Benjamin/Benjamin Walter's Briefcase: An Invent/Story," *Rhizomes* 20 (2010), accessed March 3, 2013, http://www.rhizomes.net/issue20/yates/.

14. Taussig, *I Swear I Saw This*, 9.
15. Yates recounts the inventory and activity of Benjamin's stay at the Hotel de Francia, which included four phone calls, one letter, and five sodas with lemon, and of course his purported suicide by an overdose of morphine (par. 12).
16. Yates writes that the letter was a farewell addressed to Theodor Adorno. Benjamin gave the letter to a fellow traveler, Mrs. Henry Gurland, who later wrote that she destroyed the letter, but recounted its content from memory (par. 66).
17. This line references writing about several types of calls: Taylor's interweaving of being "called" to surrender to God and the "call" bearing news of a child that prospective adoptive parents wait to receive (*Waiting*), Craig Gingrich-Philbrook's "death-call" ("Family Values," 305), Robert Coles's *The Call of Stories*, and Yates's "Invent/Story" of the call to writing in absence and in search of possibility.
18. Stephen Dunning and William Stafford, "Getting the Knack: 20 Poetry Writing Exercises," 1992, accessed July 17, 2013, http://www.readwrite-think.org/professional-development/professional-library/getting-kn ack-poetry-writing-30358.html/.
19. See Sandra L. Faulkner, *Poetry as Method: Reporting Research Through Verse* (Walnut Creek, CA: Left Coast Press, 2009); Sedgwick, "Teaching 'Experimental Critical Writing'"; Spry, *Body, Paper, Stage*. Poet Rita Dove argues that poetry "can use the visual and use the oral to orchestrate our breathing, so that it becomes a consciously physical act to read a poem: aloud or to yourself." Sharon Olds adds that the left margin is the backbone of a poem, a "column of strength," whereas the right margin, with its uneven line breaks, is a pine tree, with pine-cone nouns hanging off staggered lines, surprising the reader with the dance of the branches. Rita Dove, Ron Padgett, and Sharon Olds, "Breaking the Line, Breaking the Narrative," 2011, accessed July 17, 2013, http://www.poets.org/viewmedia.php/prmMID/23060.
20. Haiku are, typically, three-line poems that conform to a 17-syllable structure—lines one and three are composed of five syllables and line two is composed of seven syllables.
21. Sedgwick, *A Dialogue on Love*, 194.
22. Lynda Barry, *What It Is* (Montreal: Drawn & Quarterly, 2008); Taussig, *I Swear I Saw This*.
23. Barry, *What It Is*, 143–46.
24. Goodall, *The New Ethnography*, 84–5.
25. Goodall, *The New Ethnography*; Margarete Sandelowski, "Writing a Good Read: Strategies for Re-Presenting Qualitative Data," *Research in Nursing & Health* 21 (1998): 375–82.
26. Tamas, "Writing and Righting."
27. Goodall, *The New Ethnography*, 135–36.
28. Goodall, *The New Ethnography*, 136.
29. See James Buzard, "'Anywhere's Nowhere': Bleak House as Autoethnography," *The Yale Journal of Criticism* 12, no. 1 (1999): 7–39; Ellis, Adams, and Bochner, "Autoethnography: An Overview"; Arthur P. Bochner, "Bird on the Wire: Freeing the Father within Me," *Qualitative Inquiry* 18, no. 2 (2012): 168–73.

30. Darrel N. Caulley, "Making Qualitative Research Reports Less Boring: The Techniques of Writing Creative Nonfiction," *Qualitative Inquiry* 14, no. 3 (2008): 442. See also Ellis, *The Ethnographic I.*
31. Jackson, *At Home*; Bochner, "Freeing the Father."
32. See, for example, Holman Jones, "Lost and Found"; Adams and Holman Jones, "Telling Stories"; Pelias, "The Critical Life"; Glave, *Words to Our Now*, 116–29.
33. Adams, *Narrating the Closet*, 63–83.
34. Caulley, "Qualitative Research."
35. Buzard, "Bleak House," 18.
36. Adams, *Narrating the Closet*; Buzard, "Bleak House"; Satoshi Toyosaki, "Communication Sensei's Storytelling: Projecting Identity into Critical Pedagogy," *Cultural Studies <=> Critical Methodologies* 7, no. 1 (2007): 48–73.
37. Goodall, *The New Ethnography*, 139.
38. Lamott, *Bird by Bird*, 47.
39. King, *On Writing*, 178–79.
40. King, *On Writing*, 181–82.
41. King, *On Writing*, 188.
42. King, *On Writing*, 117.
43. Adams, *Narrating the Closet*, 17.
44. King, *On Writing*, 121.
45. Goodall, *The New Ethnography*.
46. Lamott, *Bird by Bird*, 54–55.
47. Goodall, *The New Ethnography*, 127.
48. Ellis, *The Ethnographic I*, 337–38.
49. See, for example, Patricia Leavy, *Fiction as Research Practice: Short Stories, Novellas, and Novels* (Walnut Creek, CA: Left Coast Press, 2013); Boylorn, *Sweetwater*; Faulkner, *Poetry as Method*; Bartleet and Ellis, *Music Autoethnographies*; Bartleet, "Artful and Embodied Methods."
50. However, some autoethnographic texts do adopt more of a social scientific form for presenting research through the use of an "Introduction-Literature Review-Method-Findings-Discussion-Conclusion" structure (e.g., Adams, "Paradoxes"; Marvasti, "Being Middle Eastern American"). In autoethnographies that use this form, the "data" or discoveries made in fieldwork, the researcher's interests and experiences, and the interpretations, "findings," and understandings generated by the research are represented in distinct sections (Chang, *Autoethnography as Method*).
51. Van Maanen, *Tales of the Field.*
52. We include Van Maanen's three types of tales within this typology; realist and impressionist tales are included in the discussion of those art movements, while confessional tales are included in the discussion of expressionism. For a general overview of realism, impressionism, expressionism, and conceptualism in the arts, see http://www.theartstory.org/section_movements.htm
53. Geertz, *The Interpretation of Cultures*, 10.
54. See, for example, Philip Burnard, "Seeing the Psychiatrist: An Autoethnographic Account," *Journal of Psychiatric and Mental Health Nursing* 14 (2007): 808–13; La Pastina, "Ethnographer's Sexuality"; Julie

Lindquist, *A Place to Stand: Politics and Persuasion in a Working-Class Bar* (Oxford: Oxford University Press, 2002); Marvasti, "Being Middle Eastern American"; Robert Mizzi, "Unraveling Researcher Subjectivity through Multivocality in Autoethnography," *Journal of Research Practice* 6, no. 1 (2010), accessed June 1, 2013, http://jrp.icaap.org/index.php/jrp/article/view/201/185; Toyosaki, "Sensei's Storytelling."

55. See, for example, Anderson, "Analytic Autoethnography"; Kevin D. Vryan, "Expanding Analytic Autoethnography and Enhancing Its Potential," *Journal of Contemporary Ethnography* 35, no. 4 (2006): 405–09.

56. See, for example, Johnny Saldaña, ed. *Ethnodrama: An Anthology of Reality Theatre* (Walnut Creek, CA: Altamira Press, 2005).

57. See, for example, Adams, "Seeking Father"; Adams, "Missing Each Other"; Dykins Callahan, "Academic Outings"; Jago, "Academic Depression"; Jago, "Shacking Up"; Ronai, "Reflexive Self"; Ronai, "Multiple Reflections"; Ronai, "My Mother is Mentally Retarded"; Carol Rambo, "Impressions of Grandmother: An Autoethnographic Portrait," *Journal of Contemporary Ethnography* 34, no. 5 (2005): 560–85; Rambo, "Twitch."

58. See, for example, Boylorn, "Sayin's"; Boylorn, *Sweetwater*; Chawla, "Walking"; Andrew F. Herrmann, "How Did We Get This Far Apart? Disengagement, Relational Dialectics, and Narrative Control," *Qualitative Inquiry* 13, no. 7 (2007): 989–1007; Ronald J. Pelias, "Jarheads, Girly Men, and the Pleasures of Violence," *Qualitative Inquiry* 13, no. 7 (2007): 945–59; Spry, *Body, Paper, Stage*; Tillmann, "Body and Bulimia Revisited"; Tillmann-Healy, "A Secret Life."

59. See, for example, Berry, "Catastrophe"; Denise Elmer, "Silent Sermons and the Identity Gap: The Communication of Gender Identity in Place and Space," *Iowa Journal of Communication* 40, no. 1 (2008): 45–63; Mingé and Zimmerman, *Concrete and Dust*; Neumann, "Collecting Ourselves."

60. See, for example, Ellis et al., "Interactive Interviewing"; Carolyn Ellis and Leigh Berger, "Their Story/My Story/Our Story," in *Handbook of Interview Research*, eds. Jaber F. Gubrium and James A. Holstein (Thousand Oaks, CA: Sage, 2001): 849–75; Steven W. Schoen and David S. Spangler, "Making Sense under a Midnight Sun: Transdisciplinary Art, Documentary Film, and Cultural Exchange," *Cultural Studies <=> Critical Methodologies* 11, no. 5 (2011): 423–33.

61. See, for example, Bryant Keith Alexander, Claudio Moreira, and hari stephen kumar, "Resisting (Resistance) Stories: A Tri-Autoethnographic Exploration of Father Narratives across Shades of Difference," *Qualitative Inquiry* 18, no. 2 (2012): 121–33; Arthur P. Bochner and Carolyn Ellis, "Telling and Living: Narrative Co-Construction and the Practices of Interpersonal Relationships," in *Social Approaches to Communication*, ed. Wendy Leeds-Hurwitz (New York: Guilford, 1995): 201–13; Colette N. Cann and Eric J. DeMeulenaere, "Critical Co-Constructed Autoethnography," *Cultural Studies <=> Critical Methodologies* 12, no. 2 (2012): 146–58; Ellis and Berger, "Their Story/My Story/Our Story"; Theon E. Hill and Isaac Clarke Holyoak, "Dialoguing Different in Joint Ethnographic Research: Reflections on Religion, Sexuality, and Race," *Cultural Studies <=> Critical Methodologies* 11, no. 2 (2011): 187–94; Hernandez and Ngunjiri, "Relationships and

Communities"; Wyatt and Gale, *Between the Two*; Jonathan Wyatt and Ken Gale, "Getting Out of Selves: An Assemblage/Ethnography?" in *Handbook of Autoethnography*, eds. Stacy Holman Jones, Tony E. Adams and Carolyn Ellis (Walnut Creek, CA: Left Coast Press, 2013): 300–12.

62. See, for example, Van Maanen, *Tales of the Field*; Goodall, *Casing the Promised Land*; Holman Jones, *Kaleidoscope Notes*; Ellis, *The Ethnographic I*.

63. See, for example, Ellis and Rawicki, "More than Mazel?"; Ellis and Rawicki, "Relational Autoethnography"; Rawicki and Ellis, "Sharing Authority."

64. See, for example, Berry, "Autoethnographic Reflexivity"; Boylorn, *Sweetwater*; Ellis, *The Ethnographic I*; Jago, "Academic Depression"; Christopher N. Poulos, "Writing My Way Through: Memory, Autoethnography, Identity, Hope," in *Handbook of Autoethnography*, eds. Stacy Holman Jones, Tony E. Adams and Carolyn Ellis (Walnut Creek, CA: Left Coast Press, 2013): 465–77; Tamas, "A Week Subject"; Leah R. Vande Berg and Nick Trujillo, *Cancer and Death: A Love Story in Two Voices* (Creskill, NJ: Hampton Press, 2008).

65. See, for example, Chang and Boyd, *Spirituality in Higher Education*; Ellis, "Negotiating Terminal Illness"; Ellis, "With Mother/With Child"; Holman Jones and Adams, "Undoing the Alphabet"; Nick Trujillo, *In Search of Naunny's Grave: Age, Class, Gender, and Ethnicity in an American Family* (Lanham, MD: Altamira Press, 2004).

66. Sol LeWitt, "Paragraphs on Conceptual Art," par. 2, accessed July 17, 2013, http://www.tufts.edu/programs/mma/fah188/sol_lewitt/paragraphs%20 on%20conceptual%20art.htm

67. Della Pollock, "Performing Writing," in *The Ends of Performance*, ed. Peggy Phelan and Jill Lane (New York, NY: New York University Press, 1998): 175.

68. See, for example, Wilfredo Alvarez, "Finding 'Home' in/through Latinidad Ethnography: Experiencing Community in the Field with 'My People,'" *Liminalities: A Journal of Performance Studies* 9, no. 2 (2013): 49–58, accessed June 1, 2013, http://liminalities.net/9-2/alvarez.pdf; Battiste, "Research Ethics"; Diversi and Moreira, *Betweener Talk*; Patricia Pierce Erikson, "'Defining Ourselves through Baskets': Museum Autoethnography and the Makah Cultural and Research Center," in *Coming to Shore: Northwest Coast Ethnology, Traditions, and Visions*, eds. Marie Mauzé, Michael E. Harkin and Sergei Kan (Lincoln: University of Nebraska Press, 2004): 346; Griffin, "Black Feminist Autoethnography"; Julie-Ann Scott, "Problematizing a Researcher's Performance of 'Insider Status': An Autoethnography of 'Designer Disabled' Identity," *Qualitative Inquiry* 19, no. 2 (2013): 101–15.

69. Madison, *Critical Ethnography*.

70. Bryant Keith Alexander, "Teaching Autoethnography and Autoethnographic Pedagogy," in *Handbook of Autoethnography*, eds. Stacy Holman Jones, Tony E. Adams and Carolyn Ellis (Walnut Creek, CA: Left Coast Press, 2013): 538–56; Boylorn and Orbe, *Critical Autoethnography*; Calafell, "Considering Accountability"; John T. Warren, "Reflexive Teaching: Toward Critical Autoethnographic Practices of/in/on Pedagogy," *Cultural Studies <=> Critical Methodologies* 11, no. 2 (2011): 139–44.

71. Toyosaki, Pensoneau-Conway, Wendt and Leathers, "Community Autoethnography"; Dutta and Basu, "Postcolonial Selves"; Archana

A. Pathak, "Musings on Postcolonial Autoethnography," in *Handbook of Autoethnography*, eds. Stacy Holman Jones, Tony E. Adams and Carolyn Ellis (Walnut Creek, CA: Left Coast Press, 2013): 595–608; Tomaselli, Dyll-Myklebust and van Grootheest, "Personal/Political Interventions."

72. Holman Jones and Adams, "Autoethnography is a Queer Method."

73. Bochner, "It's About Time"; Bochner, "Narrative's Virtues."

74. Craig Gingrich-Philbrook, "Autobiographical Performance Scripts: Refreshment," *Text and Performance Quarterly* 17, no. 4 (1997): 352–60; Holman Jones and Adams, "Autoethnography is a Queer Method."

75. Burke, *The Philosophy of Literary Form*.

76. Coles, *The Call of Stories*; Bochner, "It's About Time."

77. Boylorn, "Race and Reflexivity."

78. Bochner, "It's About Time"; Bochner, "Narrative's Virtues"; Bochner, "Freeing the Father."

79. Ronai, "Reflexive Self"; Ronai, "Multiple Reflections"; Ronai, "My Mother is Mentally Retarded."

80. Ellis, *Final Negotiations*.

81. See, for example, Adams, *Narrating the Closet*; Adams, "Post-Coming Out Complications"; Ellis et al., "Interactive Interviewing"; Andrew F. Herrmann, "'Losing Things Was Nothing New': A Family's Stories of Foreclosure," *Journal of Loss and Trauma* 16, no. 6 (2011): 497–510; Chris J. Patti, "Split-Shadows: Myths of a Lost Father and Son," *Qualitative Inquiry*, 18, no. 2 (2012): 153–61; Tillmann, "Body and Bulimia Revisited"; Tillmann-Healy, "A Secret Life."

82. Judith Butler, *Excitable Speech: A Politics of the Performative* (New York: Routledge, 1997): 145.

83. See Roland Barthes, *A Lover's Discourse: Fragments*, trans. Richard Howard (New York: Hill and Wang, 1978); Walter Benjamin, *Illuminations*, trans. Harry Zohn (New York: Schocken Books, 1969); Judith Butler, *Giving an Account of Oneself* (New York: Fordham University Press, 2005); Jacques Derrida, *Writing and Difference*, trans. Alan Bass (Chicago, IL: University of Chicago Press, 1978); Julia Kristeva, "Stabat Mater," in *The Portable Kristeva*, ed. Kelly Oliver (New York: Columbia University Press, 1987): 308–31; Kathleen Stewart, *Ordinary Affects* (Durham, NC: Duke University Press, 2007); Michael Taussig, *I Swear I Saw This*.

84. Holman Jones, "Lost and Found," 334.

85. Taussig writes that it is a "memorial, too, a type of monument, to slow down and think." Taussig, *I Swear I Saw This*, 29.

86. I (Stacy) borrow this wording from Kathleen Stewart's *Ordinary Affects*, which "tries to slow the quick jump to representational thinking and evaluative critique long enough to find ways of approaching the complex and uncertain objects that fascinate because they literally hit us or exert a pull on us." For Stewart, slowing this quick jump means signaling an "ordinary world whose forms of living are now being composed and suffered, rather than seeking the closure or clarity of a book's interiority or riding a great rush of signs to a satisfying end." Stewart, *Ordinary Affects*, 4–5.

87. Stewart, *Ordinary Affects*, 127.

88. See Gingrich-Philbrook, Family Values"; Wyatt and Gale, "Assemblage/ Ethnography"; Spry, *Body, Paper, Stage*; Stacy Wolf, "Desire in Evidence," *Text and Performance Quarterly* 17 (1997): 343–51; Tamas, "A Week Subject."

89. Adams, "Mothers, Faggots," 619.

90. Inspiring examples of writing in/as reverie and following lines of flight can also be found in Craig Gingrich-Philbrook, "Love's Excluded Subjects: Staging Irigaray's Heteronormative Essentialism," *Cultural Studies* 15, no. 2 (2001): 222–28; Judith Halberstam, *The Queer Art of Failure* (Durham, NC: Duke University Press, 2011); Rebecca Solnit, *A Field Guide to Getting Lost* (New York: Penguin, 2006); Stewart, *Ordinary Affects*; Taussig, *I Swear I Saw This*; Jonathan Wyatt, Ken Gale, Susanne Gannon, and Bronwyn Davies, *Deleuze and Collaborative Writing: An Immanent Plane of Composition* (New York: Peter Lang, 2011).

91. Julia Kristeva's split text ("Stabat Mater") of semiotic and symbolic narratives of Christianity on motherhood and her experience in/of motherhood is a well-known example of juxtaposition. Kristeva, *The Portable Kirsteva*; See also Carter, "Subjectivity."

92. Laing, R. D. *Knots* (New York: Random House, 1970): n.p.

93. Laing, *Knots*, 41.

94. Tuck and Ree, "A Glossary of Haunting."

95. Mingé and Zimmerman, *Concrete and Dust*.

96. Amy K. Kilgard, "Collage: A Paradigm for Performance Studies," *Liminalities: A Journal of Performance Studies* 5 (2009): 1–19, accessed June 1, 2013. http://liminalities.net/5-3/collage.pdf.

97. Fisher, "Narration," 349.

98. Fisher, "Narration," 349–50.

99. Fisher, "Narration," 349–50.

100. See Arthur P. Bochner, *Coming to Narrative: A Personal History of Paradigm Change in the Human Sciences* (Walnut Creek, CA: Left Coast Press, 2014); Ellis, *Revision*; Tullis Owen, McRae, Adams, and Vitale, "truth Troubles."

101. Ellis, "Relational Ethics."

102. Spry, *Body, Paper, Stage*, 136–37.

103. Ellis, *Revision*, 315–50.

104. King, *On Writing*, 210.

105. King, *On Writing*, 220.

106. Raymond Carver, "On Writing," in *Fires: Essays, Stories, Poems* (New York: Vintage): 24–5.

Chapter 5

1. See Gingrich-Philbrook, "Evaluating"; Karen Tracy and Eric Eisenberg, "Giving Criticism: A Multiple Goals Case Study," *Research on Language and Social Interaction* 24 (1990/1991): 37–70.

2. Paul Atkinson, "Narrative Turn or Blind Alley?" *Qualitative Health Research* 7, no. 3 (1997): 339.

3. Aslihan Agaogl, "Academic Writing: Why No 'Me' in PhD?" accessed October 1, 2013, http://www.theguardian.com/higher-education-network/blog/2013/apr/19/academic-writing-first-person-singular

4. David Shields, *Reality Hunger: A Manifesto* (New York: Alfred A. Knopf, 2010): 7.

5. Arlene Croce, "Discussing the Undiscussable," in *Writing in the Dark, Dancing in The New Yorker* (New York: Farrar, 2003): 708–19.

6. Croce, "Discussing," 709.

7. Croce, "Discussing," 710.

8. Marcia B. Siegel, "Virtual Criticism and the Dance of Death," *TDR: The Drama Review* 40, no. 2 (1996): 61.

9. Gingrich-Philbrook, "Evaluating," 618; Paul Bonin-Rodriguez, Jill Dolan and Jaclyn Pryor, "Colleague Criticism: Performance, Writing, and Queer Collegiality, *Liminalities: A Journal of Performance Studies* 5, no. 1 (2009), accessed June 1, 2013, http://liminalities.net/5-1/Colleague-Criticism.pdf

10. Gingrich-Philbrook, "Evaluating," 618.

11. Gingrich-Philbrook, "Evaluating," 618.

12. Gingrich-Philbrook, "Evaluating," 618.

13. Michael Quinn Patton, *Qualitative Research and Evaluation Methods*, 3rd ed. (Thousand Oaks, CA: Sage, 2002): 542.

14. Gingrich-Philbrook, "Evaluating."

15. Pollock, "Performing Writing," 79.

16. Arthur P. Bochner, "Criteria Against Ourselves." *Qualitative Inquiry* 6, no. 2 (2000): 266–72; Chang, *Autoethnography as Method*; Patricia Ticineto Clough, "Comments on Setting Criteria for Experimental Writing," *Qualitative Inquiry* 6, no. 2 (2000): 278–91; Norman K. Denzin, "Aesthetics and the Practices of Qualitative Inquiry," *Qualitative Inquiry* 6, no. 2 (2000): 256–65; Carolyn Ellis, "Creating Criteria: An Ethnographic Short Story," *Qualitative Inquiry* 6, no. 2 (2000): 273–77; Ellis, *The Ethnographic I*; Richardson, "Evaluating Ethnography"; Laurel Richardson, "Tales from the Crypt," *International Review of Qualitative Research* 2, no. 3 (2009): 345–50; Wall, "Writing an Autoethnography."

17. G. Thomas Couser, *Recovering Bodies: Illness, Disability, and Life Writing* (Madison: University of Wisconsin Press, 1997): 70.

18. Adams, *Narrating the Closet*, 40–1.

19. Adams, *Narrating the Closet*, 68–70.

20. Holman Jones, "Lost and Found," 326.

21. Ellis, "With Mother/With Child."

22. Ellis and Rawicki, "More than Mazel?" Ellis and Rawicki, "Relational Autoethnography"; Ellis and Chris J. Patti, "Compassionate Interviewing"; Rawicki and Ellis, "Sharing Authority."

23. See Atkinson, "Narrative Turn"; Paul Atkinson and Sara Delamont, "Can the Silenced Speak? A Dialogue for Two Unvoiced Actors," *International Review of Qualitative Research* 3, no. 1 (2010): 11–7; James Buzard, "On Auto-Ethnographic Authority," *The Yale Journal*

of Criticism 16, no. 1 (2003): 61–91; Sara Delamont, "The Only Honest Thing: Autoethnography, Reflexivity and Small Crises in Fieldwork," *Ethnography and Education* 4, no. 1 (2009): 51–63; Carolyn Ellis, "Fighting Back or Moving On: An Autoethnographic Response to Critics," *International Review of Qualitative Research* 2, no. 3 (2009): 371–78; Marvin M. Tolich, "A Critique of Current Practice: Ten Foundational Guidelines for Autoethnographers," *Qualitative Health Research* 20, no. 12 (2010): 1599–610.

24. Lamott, *Bird by Bird*, 208–21.
25. Derek M. Bolen, "Toward an Applied Communication Relational Inqueery: Autoethnography, Co-constructed Narrative, and Relational Futures," (doctoral dissertation, Wayne State University, 2012).

REFERENCES

Abu-Lughod, Lila. "Can There be a Feminist Ethnography?" *Woman and Performance: A Journal of Feminist Theory* 5, no. 1 (1990): 7–27.

Adams, Jacqueline. "The Wrongs of Reciprocity: Fieldwork Among Chilean Working-Class Women." *Journal of Contemporary Ethnography* 27, no. 2 (1998): 219–41.

Adams, Tony E. "Seeking Father: Relationally Reframing a Troubled Love Story." *Qualitative Inquiry* 12, no. 4 (2006): 704–23.

———. "A Review of Narrative Ethics." *Qualitative Inquiry* 14, no. 2 (2008): 175–94.

———. "Mothers, Faggots, and Witnessing (Un)Contestable Experience." *Cultural Studies <=> Critical Methodologies* 9, no. 5 (2009): 619–26.

———. "Paradoxes of Sexuality, Gay Identity, and the Closet." *Symbolic Interaction* 33, no. 2 (2010): 234–56.

———. *Narrating the Closet: An Autoethnography of Same-Sex Attraction*. Walnut Creek, CA: Left Coast Press, 2011.

———. "The Joys of Autoethnography: Possibilities for Communication Research." *Qualitative Communication Research* 1, no. 2 (2012): 181–94.

———. "Missing Each Other." *Qualitative Inquiry* 18, no. 2 (2012): 193–96.

———. "Post-Coming out Complications." In *Critical Autoethnography: Intersecting Cultural Identities in Everyday Life*, edited by Robin M. Boylorn and Mark P. Orbe, 62–80. Walnut Creek, CA: Left Coast Press, 2014.

Adams, Tony E., and Keith Berry. "Size Matters: Performing (Il)Logical Male Bodies on *Fatclub.Com*." *Text and Performance Quarterly* 33, no. 4 (2013): 308–25.

Adams, Tony E., and Stacy Holman Jones. "Autoethnography is Queer." In *Handbook of Critical and Indigenous Methodologies*, edited by Norman

K. Denzin, Yvonna S. Lincoln and Linda Tuhiwai Smith, 373–90. Thousand Oaks, CA: Sage, 2008.

———. "Telling Stories: Reflexivity, Queer Theory, and Autoethnography." *Cultural Studies <=> Critical Methodologies* 11, no. 2 (2011): 108–16.

———. eds. "Special Issue: On Studying Ourselves and Others." *Liminalities: A Journal of Performance Studies* 9, no. 2 (2013). Accessed June 1, 2013. http://liminalities.net/9-2/

———. "Performing Identity, Critical Reflexivity, and Community: The Hopeful Work of Studying Ourselves and Others." *Liminalities: A Journal of Performance Studies* 9, no. 2 (2013): 1–5. Accessed June 1, 2013. http://liminalities.net/9-2/introduction.pdf

Adams, Tony E., and Jonathan Wyatt. "Special issue: On (Writing) Fathers." *Qualitative Inquiry* 18, no. 2 (2012): 119–209.

Adichie, Chimamanda. "The Danger of a Single Story." Accessed October 1, 2013. http://dotsub.com/view/63ef5d28-6607-4fec-b906-aaae6cff7dbe/viewTranscript/eng

Agaogl, Aslihan. "Academic Writing: Why No 'Me' in PhD?" Accessed October 1, 2013. http://www.theguardian.com/higher-education-network/blog/2013/apr/19/academic-writing-first-person-singular

Ahmed, Sara. *Queer Phenomenology: Orientations, Objects, Others.* Durham, NC: Duke University Press, 2006.

Alcoff, Linda. "The Problem of Speaking for Others." *Cultural Critique* 20 (1991/1992): 5–32.

Alemany, Jacqueline. "Military Readies to Integrate Women into Combat." *CBSNEWS* (2013, June 29). Accessed November 1, 2013. http://www.cbsnews.com/news/military-readies-to-integrate-women-into-combat/

Alexander, Bryant Keith. *Performing Black Masculinity: Race, Culture, and Queer Identity.* Lanham, MD: AltaMira Press, 2006.

———. "Teaching Autoethnography and Autoethnographic Pedagogy." In *Handbook of Autoethnography*, edited by Stacy Holman Jones, Tony E. Adams and Carolyn Ellis, 538–56. Walnut Creek, CA: Left Coast Press, 2013.

Alexander, Bryant Keith, Claudio Moreira, and hari stephen kumar. "Resisting (Resistance) Stories: A Tri-Autoethnographic Exploration of Father Narratives Across Shades of Difference." *Qualitative Inquiry* 18, no. 2 (2012): 121–33.

Allen, Katherine R., and Fred P. Piercy. "Feminist Autoethnography." In *Research Methods in Family Therapy*, edited by Douglas H. Sprenkle and Fred P. Piercy, 155–69. New York: The Guilford Press, 2005.

Allen-Collinson, Jacquelyn. "Autoethnography as the Engagement of Self/Other, Self/Culture, Self/Politics, and Selves/Futures." In *Handbook of Autoethnography*, edited by Stacy Holman Jones, Tony E. Adams and Carolyn Ellis, 281–99. Walnut Creek, CA: Left Coast Press, 2013.

Alvarez, Wilfredo. "Finding "Home" in/through Latinidad Ethnography: Experiencing Community in the Field with 'My People.'" *Liminalities: A Journal of Performance Studies* 9, no. 2 (2013): 49–58. Accessed June 1, 2013. http://liminalities.net/9-2/alvarez.pdf

Anderson, Leon. "Analytic Autoethnography." *Journal of Contemporary Ethnography* 35, no. 4 (2006): 373–95.

Anderson, Leon, and Bonnie Glass-Coffin. "I Learn by Going: Autoethnographic Modes of Inquiry." In *Handbook of Autoethnography*, edited by Stacy Holman Jones, Tony E. Adams and Carolyn Ellis, 57–83. Walnut Creek, CA: Left Coast Press, 2013.

Angrosino, Michael V. *Opportunity House: Ethnographic Stories of Mental Retardation.* Walnut Creek, CA: AltaMira Press, 1988.

Atkinson, Paul. "Narrative Turn or Blind Alley?" *Qualitative Health Research* 7, no. 3 (1997): 325–44.

Atkinson, Paul, and Sara Delamont. "Can the Silenced Speak? A Dialogue for Two Unvoiced Actors." *International Review of Qualitative Research* 3, no. 1 (2010): 11–17.

Atkinson, Paul, Amanda Coffey, and Sara Delamont. *Key Themes in Qualitative Research: Continuities and Change.* Walnut Creek, CA: AltaMira Press, 2003.

Averett, Paige, and Danielle Soper. "Sometimes I Am Afraid: An Autoethnography of Resistance and Compliance." *The Qualitative Report* 16, no. 2 (2011): 358–76.

Avishai, Orit, Lynne Gerber, and Jennifer Randles. "The Feminist Ethnographer's Dilemma: Reconciling Progressive Research Agendas with Fieldwork Realities." *Journal of Contemporary Ethnography* 42, no. 4 (2012): 394–26.

Barry, Lynda. *What It Is.* Montreal: Drawn & Quarterly, 2008.

Barthes, Roland. *A Lover's Discourse: Fragments.* Translated by Richard Howard. New York: Hill and Wang, 1978.

Bartleet, Brydie-Leigh. "Artful and Embodied Methods, Modes of Inquiry, and Forms of Representation." In *Handbook of Autoethnography*, edited by Stacy Holman Jones, Tony E. Adams and Carolyn Ellis, 443–64. Walnut Creek, CA: Left Coast Press, 2013.

Bartleet, Brydie-Leigh and Carolyn Ellis, eds. *Music Autoethnographies: Making Autoethnography Sing/Making Music Personal.* Bowen Hills: QLD Australian Academic Press, 2009.

Barton, Bernadette. "My Auto/Ethnographic Dilemma: Who Owns the Story?" *Qualitative Sociology* 34 (2011): 431–45.

———. *Pray the Gay Away: The Extraordinary Lives of Bible Belt Gays.* New York: New York University Press, 2012.

Battiste, Marie. "Research Ethics for Protecting Indigenous Knowledge and Heritage." In *Handbook of Critical and Indigenous Methodologies*, edited by Norman K. Denzin, Yvonna S. Lincoln and Linda Tuhwai Smith, 497–09. Thousand Oaks, CA: Sage, 2008.

Baumrind, Diana. "Some Thoughts on Ethics of Research: After Reading Milgram's 'Behavioral Study of Obedience.'" *American Psychologist* 19, no. 6 (1964): 421–23.

Behar, Ruth. *The Vulnerable Observer.* Boston, MA: Beacon Press, 1996.

———. "A Sixth Memo for the Millennium: Vulnerability." 1998. Accessed August 15, 2013. http://www.mit.edu/~bhdavis/BeharLec.html

Bender, Aimee. "Why the Best Way to Get Creative Is to Make Some Rules." 2012. Accessed July 17, 2013. http://www.oprah.com/spirit/Writing-Every-Day-Writers-Rules-Aimee-Bender

Benjamin, Walter. *Illuminations*. Translated by Harry Zohn. New York: Schocken Books, 1969.

Benson, Thomas W. "Another Shooting in Cowtown." *Quarterly Journal of Speech* 67, no. 4 (1981): 347–406.

Berry, Keith. "Implicated Audience Member Seeks Understanding: Reexamining the 'Gift' of Autoethnography." *International Journal of Qualitative Methods* 5, no. 3 (2006): 1–12.

———. "Embracing the Catastrophe: Gay Body Seeks Acceptance." *Qualitative Inquiry* 13, no. 2 (2007): 259–81.

———. "Promise in Peril: Ellis and Pelias and the Subjective Dimensions of Ethnography." *Review of Communication* 8, no. 2 (2008): 154–73.

———. "Reconciling the Relational Echoes of Addiction: Holding On." *Qualitative Inquiry* 18, no. 2 (2012): 134–43.

———. "Un(covering) the Gay Interculturalist." In *Identity Research and Communication: Intercultural Reflections and Future Directions*, edited by Nilanjana Bardhan and Mark P. Orbe, 223–37. Lanham, MD: Lexington Books, 2012.

———. "Spinning Autoethnographic Reflexivity, Cultural Critique, and Negotiating Selves." In *Handbook of Autoethnography*, edited by Stacy Holman Jones, Tony E. Adams and Carolyn Ellis, 209–27. Walnut Creek, CA: Left Coast Press, 2013.

Berry, Keith, and Robin P. Clair. "Special Issue: The Call of Ethnographic Reflexivity: Narrating the Self's Presence in Ethnography." *Cultural Studies <=> Critical Methodologies* 11, no. 2 (2011): 95–209.

Bishoff, Tonya, and Jo Rankin, eds. *Seeds from a Silent Tree: An Anthology*. San Diego, CA: Pandal Press, 1997.

Blair, Carole, Julie R. Brown, and Leslie A. Baxter. "Disciplining the Feminine." *Quarterly Journal of Speech* 80, no. 4 (1994): 383–09.

Blee, Kathleen M. "Studying the Enemy." In *Our Studies, Ourselves: Sociologists' Lives and Work*, edited by Barry Glassner and Rosanna Hertz, 13–23. New York: Oxford University Press, 2003.

Bochner, Arthur P. "Forming Warm Ideas." In *Rigor and Imagination: Essays from the Legacy of Gregory Bateson*, edited by Carol Wilder-Mott and John H. Weakland, 65–81. New York: Praeger, 1981.

———. "The Functions of Human Communication in Interpersonal Bonding." In *Handbook of Rhetorical and Communication Theory*, edited by Carroll C. Arnold and John Waite Bowers, 544–21. Boston, MA: Allyn and Bacon, 1984.

———. "Perspectives on Inquiry II: Theories and Stories." In *Handbook of Interpersonal Communication*, edited by Mark L. Knapp and Gerald R. Miller, 21–41. Thousand Oaks, CA: Sage, 1994.

———. "It's About Time: Narrative and the Divided Self." *Qualitative Inquiry* 3, no. 4 (1997): 418–38.

———. "Criteria Against Ourselves." *Qualitative Inquiry* 6, no. 2 (2000): 266–72.

———. "Narrative's Virtues." *Qualitative Inquiry* 7, no. 2 (2001): 131–57.

———. "Perspectives on Inquiry III: The Moral of Stories." In *Handbook of Interpersonal Communication*, edited by Mark L. Knapp and John A. Daly, 73–101. Thousand Oaks, CA: Sage, 2002.

———. "Bird on the Wire: Freeing the Father within Me." *Qualitative Inquiry* 18, no. 2 (2012): 168–73.

———. *Coming to Narrative: A Personal History of Paradigm Change in the Human Sciences*. Walnut Creek, CA: Left Coast Press, 2014.

Bochner, Arthur P., and Carolyn Ellis. "Personal Narrative as a Social Approach to Interpersonal Communication." *Communication Theory* 2, no. 2 (1992): 165–72.

———. "Telling and Living: Narrative Co-Construction and the Practices of Interpersonal Relationships." In *Social Approaches to Communication*, edited by Wendy Leeds-Hurwitz, 201–13. New York: Guilford, 1995.

———. "Which Way to Turn?" *Journal of Contemporary Ethnography* 28, no. 5 (1999): 485–99.

———. eds. *Ethnographically Speaking: Autoethnography, Literature, and Aesthetics*. Walnut Creek, CA: AltaMira Press, 2002.

———. "Communication as Autoethnography." In *Communication As...Perspectives on Theory*, edited by Gregory J. Shepherd, Jeffrey St. John and Ted Striphas, 110–22. Thousand Oaks, CA: Sage, 2006.

Bolen, Derek M. (2012). "Toward an Applied Communication Relational Inqueery: Autoethnography, Co-constructed Narrative, and Relational Futures." Doctoral dissertation, Wayne State University, 2012.

———. "After Dinners, In the Garage, Out of Doors, and Climbing on Rocks." In *On (Writing) Families: Autoethnographies of Presence and Absence, Love and Loss*, edited by Jonathan Wyatt and Tony E. Adams, 141–7. Rotterdam, Netherlands: Sense Publishers, 2014.

Bonin-Rodriguez, Paul, Jill Dolan, and Jaclyn Pryor. "Colleague-Criticism: Performance, Writing, and Queer Collegiality." *Liminalities: A Journal of Performance Studies* 5, no. 1 (2009). Accessed June 1, 2013. http://liminalities.net/5-1/Colleague-Criticism.pdf

Boyle, Maree, and Ken Parry. "Special Issue on Organizational Autoethnography." *Culture and Organization* 3, no. 3 (2007): 185–266.

Boylorn, Robin M. "E Pluribus Unum (Out of Many, One)." *Qualitative Inquiry* 12, no. 4 (2006): 651–80.

———. "As Seen on TV: An Autoethnographic Reflection on Race and Reality Television." *Critical Studies in Media Communication* 25, no. 4 (2008): 413–33.

———. "Black Kids' (B.K.) Stories: Ta(L)King (About) Race Outside of the Classroom." *Cultural Studies <=> Critical Methodologies* 11, no. 1 (2011): 59–70.

———. "Gray or for Colored Girls Who Are Tired of Chasing Rainbows: Race and Reflexivity." *Cultural Studies <=> Critical Methodologies* 11, no. 2 (2011): 178–86.

———. *Sweetwater: Black Women and Narratives of Resistance*. New York: Peter Lang, 2013.

———."'Sit with Your Legs Closed!' And Other Sayin's from My Childhood." In *Handbook of Autoethnography*, edited by Stacy Holman Jones, Tony E. Adams and Carolyn Ellis, 173–85. Walnut Creek, CA: Left Coast Press, 2013.

———. "Blackgirl Blogs, Auto/ethnography, and Crunk Feminism." *Liminalities: A Journal of Performance Studies* 9, no. 2 (2013): 73–82. Accessed June 1, 2013. http://liminalities.net/9-2/boylorn.pdf.

———. "My Daddy is Slick, Brown, and Cool Like Ice Water." In *On (Writing) Families: Autoethnographies of Presence and Absence, Love and Loss*, edited by Jonathan Wyatt and Tony E. Adams, 85–93. Rotterdam, Netherlands: Sense Publishers, 2014.

Boylorn, Robin M., and Mark P. Orbe, eds. *Critical Autoethnography: Intersecting Cultural Identities in Everyday Life*. Walnut Creek, CA: Left Coast Press, 2014.

Brown, Lyndsay, and Kevin Durrheim. "Different Kinds of Knowing: Generating Qualitative Data Through Mobile Interviewing. *Qualitative Inquiry* 15, no. 5 (2009): 911–930.

Brown, Ayanna F., and Lisa William-White. "'We are Not the Same Minority': The Narratives of Two Sisters Navigating Identity and Discourse at Public and Private White Institutions." In *Tedious Journeys: Autoethnography by Women of Color in Academe*, edited by Cynthia Cole Robinson and Pauline Clardy, 149–175. New York: Peter Lang, 2010.

Bruner, Jerome. "Life as Narrative." *Social Research* 54, no. 1 (1986): 11–32.

Burke, Kenneth. *The Philosophy of Literary Form: Studies in Symbolic Action*. 3rd ed. Berkeley: University of California Press, 1974.

Burnard, Philip. "Seeing the Psychiatrist: An Autoethnographic Account." *Journal of Psychiatric and Mental Health Nursing* 14 (2007): 808–13.

Butler, Judith. *Excitable Speech: A Politics of the Performative*. New York: Routledge, 1997.

———. *Giving an Account of Oneself*. New York: Fordham University Press, 2005.

Butz, David. "Autoethnography as Sensibility." In *The SAGE Handbook of Qualitative Geography*, edited by Dydia Delyser, Steve Herbert, Stuart Aitken, Mike Crang and Linda McDowell, 138–155. Thousand Oaks, CA: Sage, 2010.

Buzard, James. "'Anywhere's Nowhere': Bleak House as Autoethnography." *The Yale Journal of Criticism* 12, no. 1 (1999): 7–39.

———. "On Auto-Ethnographic Authority." *The Yale Journal of Criticism* 16, no. 1 (2003): 61–91.

Calafell, Bernadette Marie. "(I)dentities: Considering Accountability, Reflexivity, and Intersectionality in the I and the We." *Liminalities: A Journal of Performance Studies* 9, no. 2 (2013): 6–13. Accessed June 1, 2013. http://liminalities.net/9-2/calafell.pdf

Calafell, Bernadette Marie, and Shane T. Moreman. "Envisioning an Academic Readership: Latina/o Performativities per the Form of Publication." *Text and Performance Quarterly* 29, no. 2 (2009): 123–30.

Cann, Colette N., and Eric J. DeMeulenaere. "Critical Co-Constructed Autoethnography." *Cultural Studies <=> Critical Methodologies* 12, no. 2 (2012): 146–58.

Carless, David, and Kitrina Douglas. "A History of Autoethnographic Inquiry." In *Handbook of Autoethnography*, edited by Stacy Holman Jones, Tony E. Adams and Carolyn Ellis, 84–106. Walnut Creek, CA: Left Coast Press, 2013.

Carter, Shelly. "How Much Subjectivity is Needed to Understand Our Lives Objectively?" *Qualitative Health Research* 12, no. 9 (2002): 1184–201.

Carver, Raymond. "On Writing." In *Fires: Essays, Stories, Poems,* 22–7. New York: Vintage, 1989.

Caulley, Darrel N. "Making Qualitative Research Reports Less Boring: The Techniques of Writing Creative Nonfiction." *Qualitative Inquiry* 14, no. 3 (2008): 424–49.

Chang, Heewon. *Autoethnography as Method.* Walnut Creek, CA: Left Coast Press, 2008.

Chang, Heewon, and Drick Boyd, eds. *Spirituality in Higher Education: Autoethnographies.* Walnut Creek, CA: Left Coast Press, 2011.

Chang, Heewon, Faith Wambura Ngunjiri, and Kathy-Ann C. Hernandez. *Collaborative Autoethnography.* Walnut Creek, CA: Left Coast Press, 2013.

Chatham-Carpenter, April. " 'Do Thyself No Harm': Protecting Ourselves as Autoethnographers." *Journal of Research Practice* 6, no. 1 (2010), accessed March 1, 2013, http://jrp.icaap.org/index.php/jrp/article/view/213/183

Chawla, Devika. "Walk, Walking, Talking, Home." In *Handbook of Autoethnography*, edited by Stacy Holman Jones, Tony E. Adams and Carolyn Ellis, 162–72. Walnut Creek, CA: Left Coast Press, 2013.

Clair, Robin Patric., ed. *Expression of Ethnography: Novel Approaches to Qualitative Methods* (Albany: State University of New York Press, 2003.

———. "The Changing Story of Ethnography." In *Expressions of Ethnography*, edited by Robin Patric Clair, 3–26. Albany: State University of New York Press, 2003.

Clandinin, Jean D., and Michael F. Connelly. "Personal Experience Methods." In *Handbook of Qualitative Research*, edited by Norman K. Denzin and Yvonna S. Lincoln, 413–27. Thousand Oaks, CA: Sage, 1994.

Clifford, James, and George Marcus, eds. *Writing Culture: The Poetics and Politics of Ethnography*, Berkeley: University of California Press, 1986.

Clough, Patricia Ticineto. "Comments on Setting Criteria for Experimental Writing." *Qualitative Inquiry* 6, no. 2 (2000): 278–91.

Coles, Robert. *The Call of Stories.* Boston, MA: Houghton Mifflin, 1989.

Colyar, Julia. "Becoming Writing, Becoming Writers." *Qualitative Inquiry* 15, no. 2 (2009): 421–36.

———. "Reflections on Writing and Autoethnography." In *Handbook of Autoethnography*, edited by Stacy Holman Jones, Tony E. Adams and Carolyn Ellis, 363–83. Walnut Creek, CA: Left Coast Press, 2013.

Communication Studies 298. "Fragments of Self at the Postmodern Bar." *Journal of Contemporary Ethnography* 26, no. 3 (1997): 251–92.

Conquergood, Dwight. "Performing as a Moral Act: Ethical Dimensions of the Ethnography of Performance." *Literature in Performance* 5, no. 2 (1985): 1–13.

———. "Between Experience and Meaning: Performance as a Paradigm for Meaningful Action." In *Renewal and Revision: The Future of Interpretation*, edited by Ted Colson, 26–59. Denton, TX: NB Omega Publication, 1986.

———. "Poetics, Play, Process, and Power: The Performative Turn in Anthropology." *Text and Performance Quarterly* 1, no. 1 (1989): 82–95.

———. "Rethinking Ethnography: Towards a Critical Cultural Politics." *Communication Monographs* 58, no. 2 (1991): 179–94.

———. "Beyond the Text: Toward a Performative Cultural Politics." In *The Future of Performance Studies: Visions and Revisions*, edited by Sheron J. Dailey, 25–36. Annandale, VA: National Communication Association, 1998.

———. "Performance Studies: Interventions and Radical Research." *The Drama Review* 46, no. 2 (2002): 145–56.

Corey, Frederick C., and Thomas K. Nakayama. "Sextext." *Text and Performance Quarterly* 17, no. 1 (1997): 58–68.

Couser, G. Thomas. *Recovering Bodies: Illness, Disability, and Life Writing.* Madison: University of Wisconsin Press, 1997.

Cox, Susan Soon-Keum. *Voices from Another Place: A Collection of Works from a Generation Born in Korea and Adopted to other Countries.* St. Paul, MN: Yeong & Yeong, 1999.

Crapanzano, Vincent. *Tuhami: Portrait of a Moroccan.* Chicago, IL: University of Chicago Press, 1980.

Crawford, Lyall. "Personal Ethnography." *Communication Monographs* 63, no. 2 (1996): 158–70.

Crawley, Rex. "Favor: An Autoethnography of Survival." In *Critical Autoethnography: Intersecting Cultural Identities in Everyday Life*, edited by Robin M. Boylorn and Mark P. Orbe, 222–33. Walnut Creek, CA: Left Coast Press, 2014.

Crawley, Sara L. "'They Still Don't Understand Why I Hate Wearing Dresses!' An Autoethnographic Rant on Dresses, Boats, and Butchness." *Cultural Studies <=> Critical Methodologies* 2, no. 1 (2002): 69–92.

———. "Autoethnography as Feminist Self-Interview." In *The SAGE Handbook of Interview Research.* 2nd ed. Edited by Jaber F. Gubrium, James A. Holstein, Amir B. Marvasti and Karyn D. McKinney, 143–60. Thousand Oaks, CA: Sage, 2012.

Crawley, Sara L., and Nadzeya Husakouskaya. "How Global Is Queer? A Co-Autoethnography of Politics, Pedagogy, and Theory in Drag." In *Handbook of Autoethnography*, edited by Stacy Holman Jones, Tony E. Adams and Carolyn Ellis, 321–38. Walnut Creek, CA: Left Coast Press, 2013.

Croce, Arlene. "Discussing the Undiscussable." In *Writing in the Dark, Dancing in The New Yorker* (New York: Farrar, 2003): 708–19.

Dailey, Sheron J., ed. *The Future of Performance Studies: Visions & Revisions.* Annandale, VA: National Communication Association, 1998.

Dean, Tim. *Unlimited Intimacy: Reflections on the Subculture of Barebacking.* Chicago, IL: University of Chicago Press, 2009.

Deck, Alice A. "Autoethnography: Zora Neale Hurston, Noni Jabavu, and CrossDisciplinary Discourse." *Black American Literature Forum* 24, no. 2 (1990): 237–256.

Defenbaugh, Nicole L. *Dirty Tale: A Narrative Journey of the IBD Body.* Cresskill, NJ: Hampton Press, 2011.

Delamont, Sara. "The Only Honest Thing: Autoethnography, Reflexivity and Small Crises in Fieldwork." *Ethnography and Education* 4, no. 1 (2009): 51–63.

DeLeon, Abraham P. "How Do I Begin to Tell a Story That Has Not Been Told? Anarchism, Autoethnography, and the Middle Ground." *Equity & Excellence in Education* 43, no. 4 (2010): 398–13.

Denzin, Norman K. *Interpretive Biography.* Newbury Park, CA: Sage, 1989.

———. *Interpretive Ethnography: Ethnographic Practices for the 21st Century.* Thousand Oaks, CA: Sage, 1996.

———. "Aesthetics and the Practices of Qualitative Inquiry." *Qualitative Inquiry* 6, no. 2 (2000): 256–65.

———. "Interpretive Autoethnography." In *Handbook of Autoethnography,* edited by Stacy Holman Jones, Tony E. Adams and Carolyn Ellis, 123–42. Walnut Creek, CA: Left Coast Press, 2013.

———. *Interpretive Autoethnography.* Thousand Oaks, CA: Sage, 2014.

Denzin, Norman K., and Yvonna S. Lincoln, eds. *Handbook of Qualitative Research.* Thousand Oaks, CA: Sage, 1994.

———. eds. *Handbook of Qualitative Research.* 2nd ed. Thousand Oaks, CA: Sage, 2000.

———. eds. *Handbook of Qualitative Research.* 3rd ed. Thousand Oaks, CA: Sage, 2005.

———. eds. *The SAGE Handbook of Qualitative Research.* 4th ed. Thousand Oaks, CA: Sage, 2011.

Denzin, Norman K., Yvonna S. Lincoln, and Linda Tuhiwai Smith, eds. *Handbook of Critical and Indigenous Methodologies.* Thousand Oaks, CA: Sage, 2008.

Department of Health, Education, and Welfare (United States). "The Belmont Report" (1979). Accessed December 2, 2013. http://www.hhs.gov/ohrp/humansubjects/guidance/belmont.html.

Derrida, Jacques. *Writing and Difference.* Translated by Alan Bass. Chicago, IL: University of Chicago Press, 1978.

Diversi, Marcelo, and Claudio Moreira. *Betweener Talk: Decolonizing Knowledge Production, Pedagogy, and Praxis.* Walnut Creek, CA: Left Coast Press, 2010.

Didion, Joan. *The White Album.* New York: Simon & Schuster, 1979.

Doloriert, Clair, and Sally Sambrook. "Accommodating an Autoethnographic PhD: The Tale of the Thesis, the Viva Voce, and the Traditional Business School." *Journal of Contemporary Ethnography* 40, no. 5 (2011): 582–15.

Dove, Rita, Ron Padgett, and Sharon Olds. "Breaking the Line, Breaking the Narrative." Accessed July 17, 2013. http://www.poets.org/viewmedia.php/prmMID/23060

Droogsma, Rachel Anderson. "Redefining Hijab: American Muslim Women's Standpoints on Veiling." *Journal of Applied Communication Research* 35, no. 3 (2007): 294–19.

Duncan, Margot. "Going Native: Autoethnography as a Design Tool." In *Handbook of Design in Educational Technology*, edited by Rosemary Luckin, Sadhana Puntambekar, Peter Goodyear, Barbara Grabowski, Joshua Underwood and Niall Winters, 201–10. New York: Routledge, 2013.

Dunning, Stephen, and William Stafford. "Getting the Knack: 20 Poetry Writing Exercises." Accessed July 17, 2013. http://www.readwrite-think.org/professional-development/professional-library/getting-kn ack-poetry-writing-30358.html/

Dutta, Mohan J., and Ambar Basu. "Negotiating Our Postcolonial Selves." In *Handbook of Autoethnography*, edited by Stacy Holman Jones, Tony E. Adams and Carolyn Ellis, 143–61. Walnut Creek, CA: Left Coast Press, 2013.

Dykins Callahan, Sara B. "Academic Outings." *Symbolic Interaction* 31, no. 4 (2008): 351–75.

Elam, Harry J. Jr., *Taking It to the Streets: The Social Protest Theater of Luis Valdez and Amiri Baraka*. Ann Arbor: University of Michigan Press, 1997.

Eligon, John. "New Neighbor's Agenda: White Power Takeover." *The New York Times* (2013, August 30). Accessed November 1, 2013. http://www.nytimes. com/2013/08/30/us/white-supremacists-plan-angers-a-north-dakota-town. html?_r=0;

Ellis, Carolyn. "Sociological Introspection and Emotional Experience." *Symbolic Interaction* 14, no. 1 (1991): 23–50.

———. "'There are Survivors': Telling a Story of a Sudden Death." *The Sociological Quarterly* 34, no. 4 (1993): 711–30.

———. *Final Negotiations: A Story of Love, Loss, and Chronic Illness*. Philadelphia, PA: Temple University Press, 1995.

———. "Emotional and Ethical Quagmires in Returning to the Field." *Journal of Contemporary Ethnography* 24, no. 1 (1995): 68–98.

———. "Maternal Connections." In *Composing Ethnography: Alternative Forms of Qualitative Writing*, edited by Carolyn Ellis and Arthur P. Bochner, 240–43. Walnut Creek, CA: AltaMira Press, 1996.

———. "'I Hate My Voice': Coming to Terms with Minor Bodily Stigmas." *The Sociological Quarterly* 39, no. 4 (1998): 517–37.

———. "Creating Criteria: An Ethnographic Short Story." *Qualitative Inquiry* 6, no. 2 (2000): 273–77.

———. "Negotiating Terminal Illness: Communication, Collusion, and Coalition in Caregiving." In *Loss and Trauma: General and Close Relationship Perspectives*, edited by John H. Harvey and Eric D. Miller, 284–304. Philadelphia, PA: Brunner-Routledge, 2000.

———. "With Mother/With Child: A True Story." *Qualitative Inquiry* 7, no. 5 (2001): 598–16.

———. *The Ethnographic I: A Methodological Novel About Autoethnography*. Walnut Creek, CA: AltaMira Press, 2004.

———. "Touching Back/Receiving Gifts." *Studies in Symbolic Interaction* 28 (2005): 35–41.

———. "Telling Secrets, Revealing Lives: Relational Ethics in Research with Intimate Others." *Qualitative Inquiry* 13, no. 1 (2007): 3–29.

———. "At Home With 'Real Americans': Communicating Across the Urban/ Rural and Black/White Divides in the 2008 Presidential Election." *Cultural Studies <=> Critical Methodologies* 9, no. 6 (2009): 721–33.

———. *Revision: Autoethnographic Reflections on Life and Work*. Walnut Creek, CA: Left Coast Press, 2009.

———. "Fighting Back or Moving On: An Autoethnographic Response to Critics." *International Review of Qualitative Research* 2, no. 3 (2009): 371–78.

———. "Revisioning an Ethnographic Life: Integrating a Communicative Heart with a Sociological Eye." *Studies in Symbolic Interaction* 38 (2012): 123–51.

———. *Behind the Wall*. Digital video. Directed by Carolyn Ellis, featuring Jerry Rawicki. Warsaw, Poland: Total Film, 2013.

———. "No Longer Hip: Losing My Balance and Adapting to What Ails Me." *Qualitative Research in Sport, Exercise and Health* 6, no. 1 (2014): 1–19.

———. "Seeking My Brother's Voice: Holding onto Long-Term Grief through Photographs, Stories, and Reflections." In *Stories of Complicated Grief: A Critical Anthology*, edited by Eric Miller, 3–21. Washington, DC: National Association of Social Workers Press, 2014.

Ellis, Carolyn, and Leigh Berger. "Their Story/My Story/Our Story." In *Handbook of Interview Research*, edited by Jaber F. Gubrium and James A. Holstein, 849–75. Thousand Oaks, CA: Sage, 2001.

Ellis, Carolyn, and Arthur P. Bochner. "Telling and Performing Personal Stories: The Constraints of Choice in Abortion." In *Investigating Subjectivity: Research on Lived Experience*, edited by Carolyn Ellis and Michael G. Flaherty, 79–101. Newbury Park, CA: Sage, 1992.

Ellis, Carolyn, and Arthur P. Bochner, eds. "Special Issue: Taking Ethnography into the Twenty-first Century." *Journal of Contemporary Ethnography* 25, no. 1 (1996): 3–166.

———. eds. *Composing Ethnography: Alternative Forms of Qualitative Writing*. Walnut Creek, CA: AltaMira Press, 1996.

———. "Autoethnography, Personal Narrative, Reflexivity." In *Handbook of Qualitative Research*. 2nd ed. Edited by Norman K. Denzin and Yvonna S. Lincoln, 733–68. Thousand Oaks, CA: Sage, 2000.

Ellis, Carolyn, Tony E. Adams, and Arthur P. Bochner. "Autoethnography: An Overview." *Forum: Qualitative Social Research* 12, no. 1 (2011).

Ellis, Carolyn, and Michael G. Flaherty, eds. *Investigating Subjectivity: Research on Lived Experience*. Newbury Park, CA: Sage, 1992.

Ellis, Carolyn, Christine E. Kiesinger, and Lisa M. Tillmann-Healy. "Interactive Interviewing: Talking About Emotional Experience." In *Reflexivity and Voice*, edited by Rosanna Hertz, 119–49. Thousand Oaks, CA: Sage, 1997.

Ellis, Carolyn, and Chris J. Patti. "With Heart: Compassionate Interviewing and Storytelling with Holocaust Survivors." *Storytelling, Self, Society* (forthcoming).

Ellis, Carolyn, and Jerry Rawicki, "More than Mazel? Luck and Agency in Surviving the Holocaust." *Journal of Loss and Trauma* 19, no. 2 (2014): 99–120.

———. "Collaborative Witnessing of Survival During the Holocaust: An Exemplar of Relational Autoethnography." *Qualitative Inquiry* 19, no. 5 (2013): 366–80.

———. "Collaborative Witnessing and Sharing Authority in Conversations with Holocaust Survivors." In *Beyond Testimony and Trauma*, edited by Stephen High. Vancouver: University of British Columbia Press, in press.

Elmer, Denise. "Silent Sermons and the Identity Gap: The Communication of Gender Identity in Place and Space." *Iowa Journal of Communication* 40, no. 1 (2008): 45–63.

Erikson, Patricia Pierce. "'Defining Ourselves through Baskets': Museum Autoethnography and the Makah Cultural and Research Center." In *Coming to Shore: Northwest Coast Ethnology, Traditions, and Visions*, edited by Marie Mauzé, Michael E. Harkin and Sergei Kan, 339–61. Lincoln: University of Nebraska Press, 2004.

Eriksson, Thommy. "Being Native: Distance, Closeness and Doing Auto/ Self-ethnography." *ArtMonitor* 8 (2010): 91–100.

Etherington, Kim. "Ethical Research in Reflexive Relationships." *Qualitative Inquiry* 13, no. 5 (2007): 599–16.

Faulkner, Sandra L. *Poetry as Method: Reporting Research Through Verse.* Walnut Creek, CA: Left Coast Press, 2009.

———. "That Baby Will Cost You: An Intended Ambivalent Pregnancy." *Qualitative Inquiry* 18, no. 4 (2012): 333–40.

Fisher, Walter R. "Narration as Human Communication Paradigm: The Case of Public Moral Argument." *Communication Monographs* 51, no. 1 (1984): 1–22.

Foster, Elissa. "Commitment, Communication, and Contending with Heteronormativity: An Invitation to Greater Reflexivity in Interpersonal Research." *Southern Communication Journal* 73, no. 1 (2008): 84–01.

———. "My Eyes Cry without Me: Illusions of Choice in the Transition to Motherhood." In *Contemplating Maternity in an Era of Choice: Explorations into Discourses of Reproduction*, edited by Sara Hayden and D. Lynn O'Brien Hallstein, 139–58. Lanham, MD: Lexington, 2010.

Foster, Kim, Margaret McAllister, and Louise O'Brien. "Extending the Boundaries: Autoethnography as an Emergent Method in Mental Health Nursing Research." *International Journal of Mental Health Nursing* 15, no. 1 (2006): 44–53.

Fox, Ragan. "Re-Membering Daddy: Autoethnographic Reflections of My Father and Alzheimer's Disease." *Text and Performance Quarterly* 30, no. 1 (2010): 3–20.

Fox, Ragan. "Tales of a Fighting Bobcat: An 'Auto-archaeology' of Gay Identity Formation and Maintenance," *Text and Performance Quarterly* 30, no. 2 (2010): 124.

———. "'You Are Not Allowed to Talk About Production': Narratization on (and Off) the Set of CBS's *Big Brother*." *Critical Studies in Media Communication* 30, no. 3 (2013): 189–08.

Frank, Arthur W. *The Wounded Storyteller.* Chicago, IL: University of Chicago Press, 1995.

Freeman, Mark. "Data Are Everywhere: Narrative Criticism in the Literature of Experience." In *Narrative Analysis: Studying the Development of Individuals in Society*, edited by Colette Daiute and Cynthia Lightfoot, 63–81. Thousand Oaks, CA: Sage, 2004.

———. "From Absence to Presence: Finding Mother, Ever Again." In *On (Writing) Families: Autoethnographies of Presence and Absence, Love and Loss*, edited by Jonathan Wyatt and Tony E. Adams, 49–55. Rotterdam, Netherlands: Sense Publishers, 2014.

Frye, Marilyn. *The Politics of Reality: Essays in Feminist Theory*. Trumansburg, NY: Crossing Press, 1983.

Gannon, Susanne. "Sketching Subjectivities." In *Handbook of Autoethnography*, edited by Stacy Holman Jones, Tony E. Adams and Carolyn Ellis, 228–43. Walnut Creek, CA: Left Coast Press, 2013.

Geertz, Clifford. *The Interpretation of Cultures*. New York: Basic Books, 1973.

———. *Local Knowledge*. New York: Basic Books, 1983.

Geist-Martin, Patricia, Lisa Gates, Liesbeth Wiering, Erika Kirby, Renee Houston, Anne Lilly, and Juan Moreno. "Exemplifying Collaborative Autoethnographic Practice via Shared Stories of Mothering." *Journal of Research Practice* 6, no. 1 (2010). Accessed October 3, 2013, http://jrp.icaap. org/index.php/jrp/article/view/209.

Gerber, David A. "The 'Careers' of People Exhibited in Freak Shows: The Problem of Volition and Valorization." In *Freakery: Cultural Spectacles of the Extraordinary Body*, edited by Rosemarie Garland Thomson, 38–54. New York: New York University Press, 1996.

Gingrich-Philbrook, Craig. "Autobiographical Performance Scripts: Refreshment." *Text and Performance Quarterly* 17, no. 4 (1997): 352–60.

———. "Love's Excluded Subjects: Staging Irigaray's Heteronormative Essentialism." *Cultural Studies* 15, no. 2 (2001): 222–28.

———. "Autoethnography's Family Values: Easy Access to Compulsory Experiences." *Text and Performance Quarterly* 25, no. 4 (2005): 297–14.

———. "Evaluating (Evaluations of) Autoethnography." In *Handbook of Autoethnography*, edited by Stacy Holman Jones, Tony E. Adams and Carolyn Ellis, 609–26. Walnut Creek, CA: Left Coast Press, 2013.

Glave, Thomas. *Words to Our Now: Imagination and Dissent*. Minneapolis, MN: University of Minneapolis Press, 2005.

Goodall, H. L. *Casing a Promised Land*. Carbondale: Southern Illinois University Press, 1994.

———. *Writing the New Ethnography*. Walnut Creek, CA: AltaMira Press, 2000.

———. "Narrative Ethnography as Applied Communication Research." *Journal of Applied Communication Research* 32, no. 3 (2004): 185–94.

———. *A Need to Know: The Clandestine History of a CIA Family*. Walnut Creek, CA: Left Coast Press, 2006.

———. *The Daily Narrative* (Blog). http://www.hlgoodall.com/blog.html

Goldschmidt, Walter. "Anthropology and the Coming Crisis: An Autoethnographic Appraisal." *American Anthropologist* 79, no. 2 (1977): 293–08.

Gordon, Avery. *Ghostly Matters: Haunting and the Sociological Imagination.* Minneapolis: University of Minnesota Press, 1988.

Gray, Deborah D. *Attaching in Adoption: Practical Tools for Today's Parents.* Indianapolis, IN: Perspectives Press, 2002.

Griffin, Rachel Alicia. "I AM an Angry Black Woman: Black Feminist Autoethnography, Voice, and Resistance." *Women's Studies in Communication* 35, no. 2 (2012): 138–57.

Halberstam, Judith. *The Queer Art of Failure.* Durham, NC: Duke University Press, 2011.

Hammersley, Martyn. *Methodology: Who Needs It?* Thousand Oaks, CA: Sage, 2011.

Harper, Douglas. "Talking About Pictures: A Case for Photo Elicitations." *Visual Studies* 17, no. 1 (2002): 13–26.

Harris, Anne M. "Ghost-child." In *On (Writing) Families: Autoethnographies of Presence and Absence, Love and Loss,* edited by Jonathan Wyatt and Tony E. Adams, 69–75. Rotterdam, Netherlands: Sense Publishers, 2014.

Harris, Anne, and Rebecca Long. "Smart Bitch: Talking Back in Unity." *Liminalities* 9, no. 3 (2013). Accessed December 2, 2013. http://liminalities. net/9-3/smart.html.

Hayano, David M. "Auto-Ethnography: Paradigms, Problems, and Prospects." *Human Organization* 38, no. 1 (1979): 99–104.

Hayler, Mike. *Autoethnography, Self-narrative and Teacher Education.* Rotterdam, Netherlands: Sense Publishers, 2011.

Hedtke, Lorraine, and John Winslade. *Re-membering Lives: Conversations with the Dying and the Bereaved.* Amityville, NY: Baywood Publishing Company, 2004.

Heider, Karl G. "What Do People Do? Dani Auto-Ethnography." *Journal of Anthropological Research* 31, no. 1 (1975): 3–17.

Hendrix, Katherine Grace. "An Invitation to Dialogue: Do Communication Journal Reviewers Mute the Race-Related Research of Scholars of Color?" *Southern Communication Journal* 70, no. 4 (2005): 329–45.

Hernandez, Kathy-Ann C., and Faith Wambura Ngunjiri. "Relationships and Communities in Autoethnography." In *Handbook of Autoethnography,* edited by Stacy Holman Jones, Tony E. Adams and Carolyn Ellis, 262–80. Walnut Creek, CA: Left Coast Press, 2013.

Herrmann, Andrew F. "My Father's Ghost: Interrogating Family Photos." *Journal of Loss and Trauma* 10, no. 4 (2005): 337–46.

———. "How Did We Get This Far Apart? Disengagement, Relational Dialectics, and Narrative Control." *Qualitative Inquiry* 13, no. 7 (2007): 989–1007.

———. "'Losing Things Was Nothing New': A Family's Stories of Foreclosure." *Journal of Loss and Trauma* 16, no. 6 (2011): 497–10.

Hill, Theon E., and Isaac Clarke Holyoak. "Dialoguing Different in Joint Ethnographic Research: Reflections on Religion, Sexuality, and Race." *Cultural Studies <=> Critical Methodologies* 11, no. 2 (2011): 187–94.

Hill Collins, Patricia. *Black Feminist Thought: Knowledge, Consciousness, and the Politics of Empowerment.* Boston, MA: Unwin Hyman, 1990.

Hinson, Glenn D. "'You've got to Include an Invitation': Engaged Reciprocity and Negotiated Purpose in Collaborative Ethnography." Presentation at the

Annual Meeting of the American Anthropological Association, Chicago, Illinois, April 15–18, 1999.

Holman Jones, Stacy. *Kaleidoscope Notes: Writing Women's Music and Organizational Culture.* Walnut Creek, CA: AltraMira Press, 1998.

———. "The Way We Were, Are, and Might Be: Torch Singing as Autoethnography." In *Ethnographically Speaking: Autoethnography, Literature, and Aesthetics*, edited by Arthur P. Bochner and Carolyn Ellis, 44–56. Walnut Creek, CA: AltaMira Press, 2001.

———. "Emotional Space: Performing the Resistive Possibilities of Torch Singing." *Qualitative Inquiry* 8, no. 6 (2002): 738–59.

———. "(M)othering Loss: Telling Adoption Stories, Telling Performativity." *Text and Performance Quarterly* 25, no. 2 (2005): 113–35.

———. "Autoethnography: Making the Personal Political." In *Handbook of Qualitative Research*, edited by Norman K. Denzin and Yvonna S. Lincoln, 763–91. Thousand Oaks, CA: Sage, 2005.

———. "Autoethnography." In *The Blackwell Encyclopedia of Sociology*, edited by George Ritzer, 230–32. Malden, MA: Blackwell, 2007.

———. *Torch Singing: Performing Resistance and Desire from Billie Holiday to Edith Piaf.* Lanham, MD; AltaMira Press. 2007.

———. "Crimes Against Experience." *Cultural Studies <=> Critical Methodologies* 9, no. 5 (2009): 608–18.

———. "Lost and Found." *Text and Performance Quarterly* 31, no. 4 (2011): 322–41.

———. "Always Strange." In *On (Writing) Families: Autoethnographies of Presence and Absence, Love and Loss*, edited by Jonathan Wyatt and Tony E. Adams, 13–21. Rotterdam, Netherlands: Sense Publishers, 2014.

Holman Jones, Stacy, and Tony E. Adams. "Autoethnography and Queer Theory: Making Possibilities." In *Qualitative Inquiry and Human Rights*, edited by Norman K. Denzin and Michael G. Giardina, 136–57. Walnut Creek, CA: Left Coast Press, 2010.

———. "Autoethnography Is a Queer Method." In *Queer Methods and Methodologies*, edited by Kath Browne and Catherine J. Nash, 195–14. Burlington, VT: Ashgate, 2010.

———. "Undoing the Alphabet: A Queer Fugue on Grief and Forgiveness." *Cultural Studies <=> Critical Methodologies* 14, no. 2 (2014): 102–110.

Holman Jones, Stacy, Tony E. Adams, and Carolyn Ellis, eds. *Handbook of Autoethnography*, Walnut Creek, CA: Left Coast Press, 2013.

———. "Introduction: Coming to Know Autoethnography as More Than a Method." In *Handbook of Autoethnography*, edited by Stacy Holman Jones, Tony E. Adams and Carolyn Ellis, 17–47. Walnut Creek, CA: Left Coast Press, 2013.

hooks, bell. "Theory as Liberatory Practice." *Yale Journal of Law and Feminism* 4, no. 1 (1991/1992): 1–12.

———. "Performance Practice as a Site of Opposition." In *Let's Get It On: The Politics of Black Performance*, edited by Catherine Ugwu, 210–21. Seattle, WA: Bay, 1995.

Hochschild, Arlie. *The Managed Heart: Commercialization of Human Feeling.* Berkeley: University of California Press, 1983.

Hughes, Sherick, Julie L. Pennington, and Sara Makris. "Translating Autoethnography across the AERA Standards: Toward Understanding Autoethnographic Scholarship as Empirical Research." *Educational Researcher* 41, no. 6 (2012): 209–19.

Hunt, Scott A., and Natalia Ruiz Junco, eds. "Two Thematic Issues: Defective Memory and Analytical Autoethnography." *Journal of Contemporary Ethnography* 35, no. 4 (2006): 371–72.

Irwin, Katherine. "Into the Dark Heart of Ethnography: The Lived Ethics and Inequality of Intimate Field Relationships." *Qualitative Sociology* 29 (2006): 155–75.

Jackson, Michael. *At Home in the World*. Durham, NC: Duke University Press, 1995.

Jago, Barbara J. "Chronicling an Academic Depression." *Journal of Contemporary Ethnography* 31, no. 6 (2002): 729–57.

———. "Shacking Up: An Autoethnographic Tale of Cohabitation." *Qualitative Inquiry* 17, no. 2 (2011): 204–19.

Jewkes, Yvonne. "Autoethnography and Emotion as Intellectual Resources: Doing Prison Research Differently." *Qualitative Inquiry* 18, no. 1 (2011): 63–75.

Johnson, Royel M. "Black and Male on Campus: An Autoethnographic Account." *Journal of African American Males in Education* 4, no. 2 (2013): 25–45.

Jorgenson, Jane, and Tracy Sullivan. "Accessing Children's Perspectives through Participatory Photo Interviews." *Forum: Qualitative Social Research*, 11, no. 1 (2009).

Joshi, Sam. "Homo Sutra: Disrobing Desire in the Adult Cinema." *Journal of Creative Work* 1, no. 2 (2007). Accessed October 1, 2012. http://www.scientificjournals.org/journals2007/articles/1188.pdf

Kamboureli, Smaro. "The Politics of the Beyond: 43 Theses on Autoethnography and Complicity." In *Asian Canadian Writing Beyond Autoethnography*, edited by Eleanor Ty and Christl Verduyn, 31–54. Waterloo: Wilfrid Laurier University Press, 2008.

Keller, Evelyn Fox. *Reflections on Gender and Science*. New Haven, CT: Yale University Press, 1985.

Kilgard, Amy K. "Collage: A Paradigm for Performance Studies." *Liminalities: A Journal of Performance Studies* 5 (2009): 1–19. Accessed June 1, 2013. http://liminalities.net/5-3/collage.pdf

King, Stephen. *On Writing: A Memoir of the Craft*. New York: Scribner, 2000.

Kleinman, Sherryl. "Feminist Fieldworker: Connecting Research, Teaching, and Memoir." In *Our Studies, Ourselves: Sociologists' Lives and Work*, edited by Barry Glassner and Rosanna Hertz, 215–32. New York: Oxford University Press, 2003.

Konishi, Shino. "Representing Aboriginal Masculinity in Howard's Australia." In *Global Masculinities and Manhood*, edited by Ronald L. Jackson II and Murali Balaji, 161–85. Urbana: University of Illinois Press, 2011.

Kristeva, Julia. "Stabat Mater." In *The Portable Kristeva*, edited by Kelly Oliver, 308–31. New York: Columbia University Press, 1987.

Kusenbach, Margaret. "Street Phenomenology: The Go-Along as Ethnographic Research Tool." *Ethnography* 4, vol. 3 (2003): 455–85.

La Pastina, Antonio C. "The Implications of an Ethnographer's Sexuality." *Qualitative Inquiry* 12, no. 4 (2006): 724–35.

Laing, R. D. *Knots*. New York: Random House, 1970.

Lamott, Anne. *Bird by Bird: Some Instructions on Writing and Life.* New York: Anchor, 1994.

Langellier, Kristin M. "Personal Narrative, Performance, Performativity: Two or Three Things I Know for Sure." *Text and Performance Quarterly* 19, no. 2 (1999): 125–44.

Langellier Kristin M. and Eric E. Peterson. "Shifting Contexts in Personal Narrative Performance." In *The SAGE Handbook of Performance Studies*, edited by D. Soyini Madison and Judith Hamera, 151–68. Thousand Oaks, CA: Sage, 2005.

Lapan, Stephen D., MaryLynn T. Quartaroli, and Frances J. Riemer, eds. *Qualitative Research: An Introduction to Methods and Designs*. San Francisco, CA: John Wiley & Sons, 2011.

Learmonth, Mark, and Michael Humphreys. "Autoethnography and Academic Identity: Glimpsing Business School Doppelgängers." *Organization* 19, no. 1 (2012): 99–117.

Leavy, Patricia. "Fiction and the Feminist Academic Novel." *Qualitative Inquiry* 18, no. 6 (2012): 516–22.

———. *Fiction as Research Practice: Short Stories, Novellas, and Novels*. Walnut Creek, CA: Left Coast Press, 2013.

———. ed. *Oxford Handbook of Qualitative Research*. Oxford: Oxford University Press, 2014.

LeWitt, Sol. "Paragraphs on Conceptual Art." Accessed July 17, 2013. http://www.tufts.edu/programs/mma/fah188/sol_lewitt/paragraphs%20on%20conceptual%20art.htm

Lindlof, Thomas R., and Bryan C. Taylor. *Qualitative Communication Research Methods*. 3rd ed. Thousand Oaks, CA: Sage, 2010.

Lindquist, Julie. *A Place to Stand: Politics and Persuasion in a Working-Class Bar*. Oxford: Oxford University Press, 2002.

Lionnet, Françoise. "Autoethnography: The An-archic Style of *Dust Tracks on a Road*." In *Autobiographical Voices: Race, Gender, Self-portraiture*, edited by Françoise Lionnet, 97–129. Ithaca, NY: Cornell University Press, 1989.

Lorde, Audre. *Sister Outsider*. Berkeley, CA: The Crossing Press, 1984.

Lozanski, Kristin and Melanie Beres. "Temporary Transience and Qualitative Research: Methodological Lessons from Fieldwork with Independent Travelers and Seasonal Workers." *International Journal of Qualitative Methods* 6, no. 2 (2007): 911–30.

Lundquist, Sara. "The Aesthetics of Enclosure: James Merrill's Inner Rooms." *English Studies in Canada*, 31, no. 1 (2005): 31–53.

Lyotard, Jean-François. *The Postmodern Condition: A Report on Knowledge*. Translated by Geoff Bennington and Brian Massumi. Minneapolis: University of Minnesota Press, 1984.

Madison, D. Soyini. *Critical Ethnography: Method, Ethics, Performance.* 2nd ed. Thousand Oaks, CA: Sage, 2012.

Makagon, Daniel, and Mark Neumann. *Recording Culture: Audio Documentary and the Ethnographic Experience.* Thousand Oaks, CA: Sage, 2009.

Mairs, Nancy. *Remembering the Bone House.* Boston, MA: Beacon, 1995.

Maliszewska, Michalina. "An Autoethnographic Examination of International Student Experiences in the United States." Master's thesis, Northeastern Illinois University, 2009.

Marcus, George E., and Michael M. J. Fischer, *Anthropology as Cultural Critique: An Experimental Moment in the Human Sciences.* Chicago, IL: University of Chicago Press, 1999.

Martin, Emily. "The Egg and the Sperm: How Science Has Constructed a Romance Based on Stereotypical Male-Female Roles." *Signs: Journal of Women in Culture* 16, no. 3 (1991): 485–01.

Marvasti, Amir. "Being Middle Eastern American: Identity Negotiation in the Context of the War on Terror." *Symbolic Interaction* 28, no. 4 (2006): 525–47.

Maso, Ilja. "Phenomenology and Ethnography." In *Handbook of Ethnography*, edited by Paul Atkinson, Amanda Coffey, Sara Delamont, John Lofland and Lyn Lofland, 136–44. Thousand Oaks, CA: Sage, 2001.

Materer, Timothy. "James Merrill's Late Poetry: AIDS and the 'Stripping Process.'" *Arizona Quarterly* 64, no 2 (2006): 123–45.

McIntosh, Peggy. "White Privilege and Male Privilege: A Personal Account of Coming to See Correspondences Through Work in Women's Studies." In *Understanding Diversity: Readings, Cases, and Exercises*, edited by Carol P. Harvey and M. June Allard, 130–139. New York: HarperCollins, 1995.

Medford, Kristina. "Caught with a Fake ID: Ethical Questions About *Slippage* in Autoethnography." *Qualitative Inquiry* 12, no. 5 (2006): 853–64.

Mee, Erin B. "Shattered and Fucked up and Full of Wreckage: The Words and Works of Charles L. Mee." *The Drama Review* 46, no. 3 (2002): 83–104.

Merrill, James. *The Inner Room.* New York: Knopf, 1988.

Metta, Marilyn. *Writing Against, Alongside and Beyond Memory: Lifewriting as Reflexive, Poststructuralist Feminist Research Practice.* New York: Peter Lang, 2010.

———. "Putting the Body on the Line: Embodied Writing and Recovery through Domestic Violence." In *Handbook of Autoethnography*, edited by Stacy Holman Jones, Tony E. Adams and Carolyn Ellis, 486–09. Walnut Creek, CA: Left Coast Press, 2013.

Milgram, Stanley. "Behavioral Study of Obedience." *Journal of Abnormal and Social Psychology* 67, no. 4 (1963): 371–78.

———. "Issues in the Study of Obedience: A Reply to Baumrind," *American Psychologist* 19 (1964): 848–52.

Miller, Lynn. "Saved by Stein: Or the Life You Perform May Become Your Own," *Text and Performance Quarterly* 32, no. 2 (2012): 175–86.

Mingé, Jeanine M. "Mindful Autoethnography, Local Knowledges." In *Handbook of Autoethnography*, edited by Stacy Holman Jones, Tony E. Adams, and Carolyn Ellis. 425–42. Walnut Creek, CA: Left Coast Press, 2013.

———. "The Stained Body: A Fusion of Embodied Art on Rape and Love." *Journal of Contemporary Ethnography* 36, no. 3 (2007): 252–80.

Mingé, Jeanine M., and Amber Lynn Zimmerman. *Concrete and Dust: Mapping the Sexual Terrains of Los Angeles.* New York: Routledge, 2013.

Mingé, Jeanine M., and John Burton Sterner. "The Transitory Radical: Making Place with Cancer." In *Critical Autoethnography: Intersecting Cultural Identities in Everyday Life*, edited by Robin M. Boylorn and Mark P. Orbe, 33–46. Walnut Creek, CA: Left Coast Press, 2014.

Mizzi, Robert. "Unraveling Researcher Subjectivity through Multivocality in Autoethnography." *Journal of Research Practice* 6, no. 1 (2010). Accessed June 1, 2013. http://jrp.icaap.org/index.php/jrp/article/view/201/185.

Myers, W. Benjamin, ed. "Special Issue: Writing Autoethnographic Joy." *Qualitative Communication Research* 1, no. 2 (2012): 157–52.

Muncey, Tessa. *Creating Autoethnographies.* Thousand Oaks, CA: Sage, 2010.

Mykhalovskiy, Eric. "Reconsidering Table Talk: Critical Thoughts on the Relationship between Sociology, Autobiography and Self-Indulgence." *Qualitative Sociology* 19, no. 1 (1996): 131–51.

Neumann, Mark. "Collecting Ourselves at the End of the Century." In *Composing Ethnography: Alternative Forms of Qualitative Writing*, edited by Carolyn Ellis and Arthur P. Bochner, 172–98. Walnut Creek, CA: AltaMira Press, 1996.

Ngunjiri, Faith W., Kathy-Ann Hernandez, and Heewon Chang. "Special Issue: Autoethnography as Research Practice." *Journal of Research Practice* 6, no. 1 (2010). http://jrp.icaap.org/index.php/jrp/issue/view/13

Oakley, Ann. "Interviewing Women: A Contradiction in Terms." In *Doing Feminist Research*, edited by Helen Roberts, 30–61. New York: Routledge, 1981.

Pacanowsky, Michael. "Slouching Towards Chicago." *Quarterly Journal of Speech* 74, no. 4 (1988): 453–67.

Paget, Marianne. "Performing the Text." *Journal of Contemporary Ethnography* 19, no. 1 (1990): 136–55.

Pathak, Archana A. "Opening My Voice, Claiming My Space: Theorizing the Possibilities of Postcolonial Approaches to Autoethnography." *Journal of Research Practice* 6, no. 1 (2010). Accessed June 14, 2012, http://jrp.icaap.org/index.php/jrp/article/view/231.

———. "Musings on Postcolonial Autoethnography." In *Handbook of Autoethnography*, edited by Stacy Holman Jones, Tony E. Adams and Carolyn Ellis, 595–08. Walnut Creek, CA: Left Coast Press, 2013.

Patti, Chris. "Split Shadows: Myths of a Lost Father and Son." *Qualitative Inquiry* 18, no. 2 (2012): 153–61.

Patton, Michael Quinn. *Qualitative Research and Evaluation Methods.* 3rd ed. Thousand Oaks, CA: Sage, 2002.

Paxton, Blake A. "Transforming Minor Bodily Stigmas Through Holding onto Grief: A 'Hair' Raising Possibility." *Qualitative Inquiry* 19, no. 5 (2013): 355–65.

Pelias, Ronald J. "Confessions of Apprehensive Performer." *Text and Performance Quarterly* 17, no. 1 (1997): 25–32.

———. *Writing Performance: Poeticizing the Researcher's Body.* Carbondale: Southern Illinois University Press, 1999.

———. "The Critical Life." *Communication Education* 49, no. 3 (2000): 220–28.

———. *A Methodology of the Heart: Evoking Academic and Daily Life.* Walnut Creek, CA: AltaMira Press, 2004.

———. "Jarheads, Girly Men, and the Pleasures of Violence." *Qualitative Inquiry* 13, no. 7 (2007): 945–59.

———. *Leaning: A Poetics of Personal Relations.* Walnut Creek, CA: Left Coast Press, 2011.

Philaretou, Andreas G., and Katherine R. Allen. "Researching Sensitive Topics through Autoethnographic Means." *The Journal of Men's Studies* 14, no. 1 (2006): 65–78.

Pineau, Elyse. "*Nursing Mother* and Articulating Absence." *Text and Performance Quarterly* 20, no. 1 (2000): 1–19.

———. "The Kindness of [Medical] Strangers: An Ethnopoetic Account of Embodiment, Empathy, and Engagement." In *Writings of Healing and Resistance*, edited by Mary Weems, 63–69. New York: Peter Lang, 2013.

———. "Re-Casting Rehearsal: Making a Case for Production as Research." *Journal of the Illinois Speech and Theatre Association* 46 (1995): 43–52.

Pink, Sarah. *Doing Sensory Ethnography.* Thousand Oaks, CA: Sage, 2009.

Pollock, Della. "Performing Writing." In *The Ends of Performance*, edited by Peggy Phelan and Jill Lane, 73–103. New York: New York University Press, 1998.

———. "Memory, Remembering, and Histories of Change." In *The SAGE Handbook of Performance Studies*, edited by D. Soyini Madison and Judith Hamera, 87–105. Thousand Oaks, CA: Sage, 2006.

Poulos, Christopher N., ed. "Special Issue: Autoethnography." *Iowa Journal of Communication* 40, no. 1 (2008): i-140.

———. *Accidental Ethnography: An Inquiry into Family Secrecy.* Walnut Creek, CA: Left Coast Press, 2009.

———. "Spirited Accidents: An Autoethnography of Possibility." *Qualitative Inquiry* 16, no. 1 (2010): 49–56.

———. "Writing My Way Through: Memory, Autoethnography, Identity, Hope." In *Handbook of Autoethnography*, edited by Stacy Holman Jones, Tony E. Adams and Carolyn Ellis, 465–77. Walnut Creek, CA: Left Coast Press, 2013.

Radley, Alan and Diane Taylor. "Images of Recovery: A Photo Elicitation Study on the Hospital Ward." *Qualitative Health Research* 13, no. 1 (2003): 177–99.

Rambo, Carol. "Impressions of Grandmother: An Autoethnographic Portrait." *Journal of Contemporary Ethnography* 34, no. 5 (2005): 560–85.

———. "Twitch: A Performance of Chronic Liminality." In *Handbook of Autoethnography*, edited by Stacy Holman Jones, Tony E. Adams and Carolyn Ellis, 627–38. Walnut Creek, CA: Left Coast Press, 2013.

Rawicki, Jerry, and Carolyn Ellis. "Lechem Hara (Bad Bread) Lechem Tov (Good Bread): Survival and Sacrifice During the Holocaust." *Qualitative Inquiry* 17, no. 2 (2011): 155–157.

Reed-Danahay, Deborah, ed. *Auto/Ethnography.* New York: Berg, 1997.

———. "Turning Points and Textual Strategies in Ethnographic Writing." *Qualitative Studies in Education* 15, no. 4 (2002): 421–25.

———. "Anthropologists, Education, and Autoethnography." *Reviews in Anthropology* 38, no. 1 (2009): 28–47.

Riedmann, Agnes. *Science That Colonizes: A Critique of Fertility Studies in Africa.* Philadelphia, PA: Temple University Press, 1993.

Reinharz, Shulamit. *On Becoming a Social Scientist.* New Brunswick, NJ: Transaction, 1984.

———. *Feminist Methods in Social Research.* Oxford: Oxford University Press, 1992.

Richardson, Laurel. "Narrative and Sociology." *Journal of Contemporary Ethnography* 19, no. 1 (1990): 116–35.

———. "Writing: A Method of Inquiry." In *Handbook of Qualitative Research,* edited by Norman K. Denzin and Yvonna S. Lincoln, 516–29. Thousand Oaks, CA: Sage, 1994.

———. *Fields of Play: Constructing an Academic Life.* New Brunswick, NJ: Rutgers University Press, 1997.

———. "Evaluating Ethnography." *Qualitative Inquiry* 6, no. 2 (2000): 253–55.

———. "Tales from the Crypt." *International Review of Qualitative Research* 2, no. 3 (2009): 345–50.

———. "Sentimental Journey." In *Handbook of Autoethnography,* edited by Stacy Holman Jones, Tony E. Adams and Carolyn Ellis, 339–56. Walnut Creek, CA: Left Coast Press, 2013.

Riley, Donna. "Hidden in Plain View: Feminists Doing Engineering Ethics, Engineers Doing Feminist Ethics." *Science and Engineering Ethics* 19, no. 1 (2013): 1–18.

Rivera, Dale. "A Mother's Son." *Cultural Studies <=> Critical Methodologies* 13, no. 2 (2013): 88–94.

Robinson, Cynthia Cole, and Pauline Clardy, eds. *Tedious Journeys: Autoethnography by Women of Color in Academe.* New York: Peter Lang, 2010.

Ronai, Carol Rambo. "The Reflexive Self through Narrative: A Night in the Life of an Erotic Dancer/Researcher." In *Investigating Subjectivity: Research on Lived Experience,* edited by Carolyn Ellis and Michael G. Flaherty, 102–24. Newbury Park, CA: Sage, 1992.

———. "Multiple Reflections of Child Sex Abuse." *Journal of Contemporary Ethnography* 23, no. 4 (1995): 395–26.

———. "My Mother Is Mentally Retarded." In *Composing Ethnography: Alternative Forms of Qualitative Writing,* edited by Carolyn Ellis and Arthur P. Bochner, 109–31. Walnut Creek, CA: AltaMira Press, 1996.

Ronai, Carol Rambo, and Carolyn Ellis. "Turn-Ons for Money: Interactional Strategies of the Table Dancer." *Journal of Contemporary Ethnography* 18, no. 3 (1989): 271–98.

Rosaldo, Renato. *Culture and Truth: The Remaking of Social Analysis.* Boston, MA: Beacon Press, 1989.

Saldaña, Johnny, ed. *Ethnodrama: An Anthology of Reality Theatre.* Walnut Creek, CA: AltaMira Press, 2005.

Sandelowski, Margarete. "Writing a Good Read: Strategies for Re-Presenting Qualitative Data." *Research in Nursing & Health* 21 (1998): 375–82.

Schoen, Steven W., and David S. Spangler. "Making Sense under a Midnight Sun: Transdisciplinary Art, Documentary Film, and Cultural Exchange." *Cultural Studies <=> Critical Methodologies* 11, no. 5 (2011): 423–33.

Scott, Julie-Ann. "Problematizing a Researcher's Performance of 'Insider Status': An Autoethnography of 'Designer Disabled' Identity." *Qualitative Inquiry* 19, no. 2 (2013): 101–15.

Sealy, Patricia Ann. "Autoethnography: Reflective Journaling and Meditation to Cope With Life-Threatening Breast Cancer." *Clinical Journal of Oncology Nursing* 16, no. 1 (2012): 38–41.

Sedgwick, Eve Kosofsky. "Teaching 'Experimental Critical Writing.'" In *The Ends of Performance*, edited by Peggy Phelan and Jill Lane, 104–15. New York: New York University Press, 1998.

———. *A Dialogue on Love.* Boston, MA: Beacon Press, 2000.

Siegel, Marcia B. "Virtual Criticism and the Dance of Death." *TDR: The Drama Review* 40, no. 2 (1996): 60–70.

Shields, David. *Reality Hunger: A Manifesto.* New York: Alfred A. Knopf, 2010.

Short, Nigel P., Lydia Turner, and Alec Grant, eds. *Contemporary British Autoethnography.* Rotterdam, Netherlands: Sense Publishers, 2013.

Shostak, Marjorie. *Nisa: The Life and Words of a!Kung Woman.* Cambridge, MA: Harvard University Press, 1981.

Sikes, Pat, ed. *Autoethnography.* Thousand Oaks, CA: Sage, 2013.

Skloot, Rebecca. *The Immortal Live of Henrietta Lacks.* New York: Crown, 2010.

Smith, Linda Tuhiwai. *Decolonizing Methodologies: Research and Indigenous Species.* New York: Zed Books, 1999.

Smith, Phil, ed. *Both Sides of the Table: Autoethnographies of Educators Learning and Teaching With/In [Dis]ability.* New York: Peter Lang, 2013.

Solnit, Rebecca. *A Field Guide to Getting Lost.* New York: Penguin, 2006.

Spivak, Gayatri Chakravorty. "Can the Subaltern Speak?" In *Marxism and the Interpretation of Culture*, edited by Cary Nelson and Lawrence Grossberg, 271–13. Champaign: University of Illinois Press, 1988.

Spradley, James P. *The Ethnographic Interview.* New York: Holt, Rinehart & Winston, 1979.

Spry, Tami. "Performing Autoethnography: An Embodied Methodological Praxis." *Qualitative Inquiry* 7, no. 6 (2001): 706–32.

———. *Body, Paper, Stage: Writing and Performing Autoethnography.* Walnut Creek, CA: Left Coast Press, 2011.

Stein, Arlene. "Sex, Truths, and Audiotape: Anonymity and the Ethics of Exposure in Public Ethnography." *Journal of Contemporary Ethnography* 39, no. 5 (2010): 554–68.

Stewart, Kathleen. *Ordinary Affects.* Durham, NC: Duke University Press, 2007.

Stoller, Paul. *Sensuous Scholarship.* Philadelphia: University of Pennsylvania Press, 1997.

Tamas, Sophie. "Writing and Righting Trauma: Troubling the Autoethnographic Voice." *Forum: Qualitative Social Research*, 10, no. 1 (2009). Accessed June 1, 2013. http://www.qualitative-research.net/index.php/fqs/article/viewArticle/1211

———. *Life after Leaving: The Remains of Spousal Abuse.* Walnut Creek, CA: Left Coast Press, 2011.

———. "Who's There? A Week Subject." In *Handbook of Autoethnography*, edited by Stacy Holman Jones, Tony E. Adams and Carolyn Ellis, 186–01. Walnut Creek, CA: Left Coast Press, 2013.

Taussig, Michael. *I Swear I Saw This: Drawings in Fieldwork Notebooks, Namely My Own.* Chicago, IL: The University of Chicago Press, 2011.

Taylor, Jacqueline. *Waiting for the Call: From Preacher's Daughter to Lesbian Mom.* Ann Arbor: University of Michigan Press, 2007.

Tedlock, Barbara. "Ethnography and Ethnographic Representation." In *Handbook of Qualitative Research*, edited by Norman K. Denzin and Yvonna S. Lincoln, 455–86. Thousand Oaks, CA: Sage, 2000.

Thomas, Jim. *Doing Critical Ethnography.* Newbury Park, CA: Sage, 1993.

Thomas, Stephen B., and Sandra Crouse Quinn. "The Tuskegee Syphilis Study, 1932 to 1972: Implications for HIV Education and Aids Risk Education Programs in the Black Community." *American Journal of Public Health* 81, no. 11 (1991): 1498–505.

Tillmann, Lisa M. "Body and Bulimia Revisited: Reflections on 'a Secret Life.'" *Journal of Applied Communication Research* 37, no. 1 (2009): 98–112.

———. "Don't Ask, Don't Tell: Coming Out in an Alcoholic Family." *Journal of Contemporary Ethnography* 38, no. 6 (2009): 677–12.

———. "Coming Out and Going Home: A Family Ethnography." *Qualitative Inquiry* 16, no. 2 (2010): 116–29.

———. "Wedding Album: An Anti-Heterosexist Performance Text." In *Handbook of Autoethnography*, edited by Stacy Holman Jones, Tony E. Adams and Carolyn Ellis, 478–85. Walnut Creek: Left Coast Press, 2013.

Tillmann-Healy, Lisa M. "A Secret Life in a Culture of Thinness: Reflections on Body, Food, and Bulimia." In *Composing Ethnography: Alternative Forms of Qualitative Writing*, edited by Carolyn Ellis and Arthur P. Bochner, 76–108. Walnut Creek, CA: AltaMira Press, 1996.

———. *Between Gay and Straight: Understanding Friendship across Sexual Orientation.* Walnut Creek, CA: AltaMira Press, 2001.

———. "Friendship as Method." *Qualitative Inquiry* 9, no. 5 (2003): 729–49.

Tolich, Marvin M. "A Critique of Current Practice: Ten Foundational Guidelines for Autoethnographers." *Qualitative Health Research* 20, no. 12 (2010): 1599–610.

Tomaselli, Keyan G. "Stories to Tell, Stories to Sell: Resisting Textualization." *Cultural Studies* 17, no. 6 (2003): 856–75.

———. ed. *Writing in the San/d: Autoethnography Among Indigenous Southern Africans.* Lanham, MD: AltaMira Press, 2007.

———. "Visualizing Different Kinds of Writing: Auto-ethnography, Social Science." *Visual Anthropology* 26, no. 2 (2013): 165–80.

Tomaselli, Keyan G., Lauren Dyll, and Michael Francis. "'Self' and 'Other': Auto-Reflexive and Indigenous Ethnography." In *Handbook of Critical and Indigenous Methodologies*, edited by Norman K. Denzin, Yvonna S. Lincoln and Linda Tuhwai Smith, 347–72. Thousand Oaks, CA: Sage, 2008.

Tomaselli, Keyan G., Lauren Dyll-Myklebust, and Sjoerd van Grootheest. "Personal/Political Interventions Via Autoethnography: Dualisms, Knowledge, Power, and Performativity in Research Relations." In *Handbook of Autoethnography*, edited by Stacy Holman Jones, Tony E. Adams and Carolyn Ellis, 576–94. Walnut Creek, CA: Left Coast Press, 2013.

Toyosaki, Satoshi. "Communication Sensei's Storytelling: Projecting Identity into Critical Pedagogy." *Cultural Studies <=> Critical Methodologies* 7, no. 1 (2007): 48–73.

Toyosaki, Satoshi, and Sandy L. Pensoneau-Conway. "Autoethnography as a Praxis of Social Justice." In *Handbook of Autoethnography*, edited by Stacy Holman Jones, Tony E. Adams and Carolyn Ellis, 557–75. Walnut Creek, CA: Left Coast Press, 2013.

Toyosaki, Satoshi, Sandra L. Pensoneau-Conway, Nathan A. Wendt, and Kyle Leathers. "Community Autoethnography: Compiling the Personal and Resituating Whiteness." *Cultural Studies <=> Critical Methodologies* 9, no. 1 (2009): 56–83.

Tracy, Karen, and Eric Eisenberg. "Giving Criticism: A Multiple Goals Case Study." *Research on Language and Social Interaction* 24 (1990/1991): 37–70.

Tracy, Sarah J. *Qualitative Research Methods: Collecting Evidence, Crafting Analysis, Communicating Impact.* Malden, MA: Blackwell, 2013.

Trenka, Jane Jeong. *The Language of Blood: A Memoir.* St. Paul, MN: Borealis Books, 2003.

———. *Fugitive Visions: An Adoptee's Return to Korea.* St. Paul, MN: Graywolf Press, 2009.

Trenka, Jane Jeong, Julia Chinyere Oparah, and Sun Yung Shin, eds. *Outsiders Within: Writing on Transracial Adoption.* Cambridge, MA: South End Press, 2006.

Trujillo, Nick. *In Search of Naunny's Grave: Age, Class, Gender, and Ethnicity in an American Family.* Lanham, MD: AltaMira Press, 2004.

Tuck, Eve, and C. Ree. "A Glossary of Haunting." In *Handbook of Autoethnography*, edited by Stacy Holman Jones, Tony E. Adams and Carolyn Ellis, 639–58. Walnut Creek, CA: Left Coast Press, 2013.

Tullis, Jillian A. "Self and Others: Ethics in Autoethnographic Research." In *Handbook of Autoethnography*, edited by Stacy Holman Jones, Tony E. Adams and Carolyn Ellis, 244–61. Walnut Creek, CA: Left Coast Press, 2013.

Tullis, Matt. "Journalism Equals Facts While Creative Nonfiction Equals Truth? Maybe It's Not That Simple. A Roundtable Discussion with Chris Jones, Thomas Lake, and Ben Montgomery." *Creative Nonfiction* 47 (2013): 70.

Tullis Owen, Jillian A., Chris McRae, Tony E. Adams, and Alisha Vitale. "truth Troubles." *Qualitative Inquiry* 15, no. 1 (2009): 178–200.

Van Gelder, Lindsy. "Marriage as a Restricted Club." In *Against the Current*, edited by Pamela J. Annas and Robert C. Rosen, 294–97. Upper Saddle River, NJ: Prentice Hall, 1998.

Van Maanen, John. *Tales of the Field: On Writing Ethnography*. Chicago, IL: University of Chicago Press, 1988.

Vande Berg, Leah R., and Nick Trujillo. *Cancer and Death: A Love Story in Two Voices*. Creskill, NJ: Hampton Press, 2008.

Visweswaran, Kamala. *Fictions of Feminist Ethnography*. Minneapolis: University of Minnesota Press, 1997.

Vryan, Kevin D. "Expanding Analytic Autoethnography and Enhancing Its Potential." *Journal of Contemporary Ethnography* 35, no. 4 (2006): 405–09.

Wall, Sarah. "An Autoethnography on Learning About Autoethnography." *International Journal of Qualitative Methods* 5, no. 2 (2006).

———. "Easier Said Than Done: Writing an Autoethnography." *International Journal of Qualitative Methods* 7, no. 1 (2008).

Warren, John T. "Reflexive Teaching: Toward Critical Autoethnographic Practices of/in/on Pedagogy." *Cultural Studies <=> Critical Methodologies* 11, no. 2 (2011): 139–44.

Warren, John T., and Keith Berry, eds. "Special Issue: The Evidence of Experience, Cultural Studies, and Personal(ized) Scholarship." *Cultural Studies <=> Critical Methodologies* 9, no. 5 (2009): 595–95.

Weems, Mary. "Fire: A Year in Poems." In *Handbook of Autoethnography*, edited by Stacy Holman Jones, Tony E. Adams and Carolyn Ellis, 313–20. Walnut Creek, CA: Left Coast Press, 2013.

Weston, Kath. *Families We Choose: Lesbians, Gays, Kinship*. New York: Columbia University Press, 1991.

William-White, Lisa. "Dare I Write about Oppression on Sacred Ground [Emphasis Mine]." *Cultural Studies <=> Critical Methodologies* 11, no. 3 (2011): 236–42.

Wolcott, Harry F. *Ethnography Lessons: A Primer*. Walnut Creek, CA: Left Coast Press, 2010.

Wolf, Margery. *A Thrice Told Tale: Feminism, Postmodernism, and Ethnographic Responsibility*. Palo Alto, CA: Stanford University Press, 1992.

Wolf, Stacy. "Desire in Evidence." *Text and Performance Quarterly* 17 (1997): 343–51.

Wyatt, Jonathan. "Psychic Distance, Consent, and Other Ethical Issues." *Qualitative Inquiry* 12, no. 4 (2006): 813–18.

Wyatt, Jonathan, and Ken Gale. *Between the Two: A Nomadic Inquiry into Collaborative Writing and Subjectivity*. Newcastle upon Tyne: Cambridge Scholars Publishing, 2009.

———. "Getting Out of Selves: An Assemblage/Ethnography?" In *Handbook of Autoethnography*, edited by Stacy Holman Jones, Tony E. Adams and Carolyn Ellis, 300–12. Walnut Creek, CA: Left Coast Press, 2013.

Wyatt, Jonathan, and Tony E. Adams, eds. *On (Writing) Families: Autoethnographies of Presence and Absence, Love and Loss*. Rotterdam, Netherlands: Sense Publishers, 2014.

Wyatt, Jonathan, Ken Gale, Susanne Gannon, and Bronwyn Davies. *Deleuze and Collaborative Writing: An Immanent Plane of Composition.* New York: Peter Lang, 2011.

Julian Yates. "The Briefcase of Walter Benjamin/Benjamin Walter's Briefcase: An Invent/Story." *Rhizomes* 20 (2010). Accessed March 3, 2013. http://www.rhizomes.net/issue20/yates/

Zaķe, Ieva, and Michael DeCesare, eds. *New Directions in Sociology: Essays on Theory and Methodology in the 21st Century.* Jefferson, NC: McFarland & Company, 2011.

Zola, Irving Kenneth. *Missing Pieces: A Chronicle of Living with a Disability.* Philadelphia, PA: Temple University Press, 1982.

INDEX

Note: Page numbers followed by "n" indicates Notes.

Me

Mum

Dad

Brother

Sister

Friend

Teacher

Hospital School teacher

Headteacher.

Clinician.

(Myself as teacher)

18949475R00123

Printed in Poland
by Amazon Fulfillment
Poland Sp. z o.o., Wrocław